# STUDY SKILLS

## Mary Margaret Hosler
### The University of Wisconsin at Whitewater

## GLENCOE
Macmillan/McGraw-Hill

Lake Forest, Illinois
Columbus, Ohio
Mission Hills, California
Peoria, Illinois

Sponsoring Editor: Gail Modlin
Editing Supervisor: Katharine Glynn
Design and Art Supervisor: Caryl Valerie Spinka
Production Supervisor: Albert Rihner

Project Management: Chestnut Hill Enterprises, Inc.
Cover Design: Keithley and Associates, Inc.

**Study Skills**

Send all inquiries to:
Glencoe Division
Macmillan/McGraw-Hill
936 Eastwind Drive
Westerville, Ohio 43081

ISBN 0-07-030503-X

2 3 4 5 6 7 8 9 10 11 12 13 14 15 RRD-C 00 99 98 97 96 95 94 93 92 91

# CONTENTS

# TO THE STUDENT

*Study Skills* offers you all you need to know about good study techniques to be successful in your coursework. These techniques are practical and relevant, regardless of your age, career interests, or your school's location. After you have studied each chapter's information, and practiced your new skills by completing the activities that follow it, you'll gain confidence in your ability to achieve success in all your classes.

The organization of the chapters progresses from setting goals and managing time through to the preparation of reports and speeches. The easy-to-read text is filled with interesting activities that help you assess your personal attitudes and requirements, then focus on the areas that will be most valuable to you.

Each chapter covers a single topic in depth; the chapter's activities add to your understanding of that topic. Chapters are grouped into parts. Each of the seven parts focuses on a group of essential skills for effective studying.

The parts and their contents are as follows:

- *Part 1*: To provide a meaningful framework for your coursework, you'll first learn to examine your personal, educational, and career goals. You'll also learn time management techniques to help you get organized to do your best.

- *Part 2*: Notetaking is the basic study skill used in most school situations. You'll master the techniques involved in taking good notes.

- *Part 3*: You will learn to improve your listening skill and, consequently, your notetaking skill. Notetaking in class depends upon good listening skill.

- *Part 4*: In most courses, you are expected to study a textbook and other written materials. In this part, you'll learn to preview reading assignments such as text chapters and articles.

- *Part 5*: Do you know how to prepare for tests? In this part you will learn how to overcome stress and develop strategies for taking objective and essay tests.

- *Part 6*: This part covers report writing, a valuable skill both for coursework and for many jobs.

■ *Part 7*: On occasion you may be asked to make an oral presentation in class. This part provides the help you need to prepare and deliver a speech with a minimum of stress.

Parts 4, 5, 6, and 7 are each followed by a project that pulls together the information from the chapters into a culminating activity. In this way, you will put all the separate aspects of a major study skill together for effective class achievement.

When you complete *Study Skills*, you will be well on your way to academic success. You'll feel confident because you know you can succeed in school. I wish you each success in the achievements you are aiming for!

*Mary Margaret Hosler*

# TO THE INSTRUCTOR

*Study Skills* is designed to help students learn essential study skills and apply them successfully to college work. The text-workbook also covers essential writing skills, building students' abilities to communicate effectively and correctly. A third theme critical to college success—understanding attitudes toward studying, setting goals, and managing time—is woven throughout the chapters and activities.

## FEATURES OF STUDY SKILLS

*Study Skills* incorporates through readings and application exercises the study skills that most experts agree are essential for success in school. Twelve special features make the program practical and easy to use by the instructor and the student.

**1.** The *Study Skills* program, consisting of the text-workbook, a cassette-based project, and the *Instructor's Manual and Key*, is complete and flexible:

- From its many activities to the inclusion of an entire chapter from a leading textbook, the text-workbook offers a wealth of materials. The *Instructor's Manual and Key* contains additional suggested activities as well as an objective test for each chapter.

- The arrangement of the text-workbook into seven parts and nineteen chapters allows you to organize the program to best suit your students. You may wish to use the program as presented, or to use only certain parts if you have a limited amount of time in which to teach *Study Skills*.

- The many activities provide choices on assignments for students. You can easily individualize your instruction to meet the needs of students by selecting from these activities. Additional materials in the *Instructor's Manual and Key* give even more flexibility to your class when determining the daily class program as well as assignments.

**2.** One specific study skills topic is presented in each chapter. This feature allows the student to gain mastery easily over each important skill involved in a complete study skills program.

**3.** Specific activities are included at the end of each chapter that allow the students to:

- Review the highlights of the chapter through a question-answer format.
- Apply the information from the chapter to a variety of practical school-based activities, including case studies.
- Build skill in using the English language through a presentation/drill format.

**4.** Students are encouraged to take notes in the quickest, most efficient manner. To do this, students are supplied with a comprehensive listing of commonly used longhand abbreviations. Words such as *business, national, with, and* are present to the students as *bus, natl, w,* and *&*. Thus, students do not have to learn a new system of abbreviating while learning appropriate study skills. They, instead, can concentrate on good study skills and use their familiar longhand abbreviations to take notes. A comprehensive appendix alphabetically lists these abbreviations.

**5.** Integrated projects appear at the end of Part 4, *Reading*; Part 5, *Preparing for Tests*; Part 6, *Preparing Reports*; and Part 7, *Making Oral Presentations*. Each project takes the information presented in the part's chapters and combines it into a culminating exercise.

**6.** The text contains numerous illustrations of the written information so students can readily visualize the content of the chapter. These illustrations clarify and reinforce the narrative, making reading each chapter easy and enjoyable.

**7.** An outline of the contents appears at the start of each chapter. This feature allows the student to preview the chapter, which is one of the important activities in learning how to read a textbook successfully. It also permits the student to have a ready-made outline for notetaking purposes.

**8.** A *Summary* concludes each chapter's narrative to provide another method for students to check on their comprehension of the content of that chapter.

**9.** Checklists are included to permit students to analyze their studying habits. These exercises are followed by instructions or comments to the students to help in the interpretation of their responses.

**10.** A unique feature of *Study Skills* is a tape program that permits students to practice their listening and notetaking skills. Ten lectures, on ten different subjects of progressive difficulty, are available for the students after completion of Part 3. At the end of each lecture, students are asked to complete several exercises designed to build their listening ability and their efficiency in taking notes. The lectures are similar to those students might hear in their courses, thus giving them excellent experience in taking good notes from lectures.

**11.** *Study Skills'* perforated pages allow for flexibility in using the materials. For example, students may separate pages and place them into a 3-ring notebook. As activities are completed (from the text or from exercises provided by the instructor), they may be placed with appropriate pages from the textbook.

**12.** A section called *"Improving Your Writing Skills"* appears at the end of each chapter. These exercises will help students become better users of the English language, and thus better communicators. These *Writing Skills* range from identifying subjects, predicates, and sentences to understanding pronouns, conjunctions, numbers, and punctuation.

*Mary Margaret Hosler*

## DEDICATION

*Study Skills* is dedicated to my mentor and husband Russell J. Hosler, who provided the day-to-day motivation and support that made it possible to complete the program. Thank you, Russ.

# THE IMPORTANCE OF STUDY SKILLS

During all the years that you have spent in school, you've undoubtedly done a lot of studying. But have you thought about how studying fits into your life as a whole? If you are like most students, probably not. Part 1 will introduce you to the key study skills and to techniques for improving them. You'll examine your goals in order to provide a meaningful framework for the work you do in school. You will also learn time management techniques to help you get organized to do your best.

In short, Part 1 sets the stage for studying. You will:

- **Understand the key study skills.**
- **Improve your study skills.**
- **Establish realistic goals for yourself.**
- **Develop strategies to meet your goals.**
- **Learn to manage your time.**

# 1 INTRODUCTION TO STUDY SKILLS

You have successfully completed a decade or more of education, probably without studying about studying. Why should you start now?

Learning good study skills is necessary if you are to succeed today. At this point in your education, your instructors expect you to do the course work well, on time, and without prompting. You will be working independently and studying subjects more difficult than the ones you have previously mastered. If you rely on poor study habits from the past, you may find that you have trouble keeping up.

But you can keep up. In fact, you can do well. You can improve your ability to understand and remember material for your courses. With the help of this book, you will learn how to motivate yourself to do well, get organized, and set up a study environment that promotes concentration. You will also learn specific skills that will help you study effectively.

## PREPARING YOURSELF FOR STUDYING

Whether you are taking notes during a class session or studying for a test, there are some basic ways to prepare yourself for studying. First, you must be motivated to do well. Second, you must organize your time. And third, you must be prepared to concentrate on studying.

### Are You Motivated?

If you want to get an *A* in a course, you will apply yourself to studying. Generally, you're motivated to do well when you do something that interests you. However, if you are taking a course because a friend is taking it, or it meets at a convenient time, you may have trouble motivating yourself to study.

Motivation must come from within. Try to determine why you are taking a course, how it relates to your interests, and how it will benefit you. Every course won't benefit you immediately, so think of how the course will fit into your personal or professional goals over time. To do this, be clear about your own short- and long-term goals. Once you have decided on your career or educational goals, you'll be less likely to take a course for the wrong reason, and you'll find that you are naturally motivated to do well.

### Are You Organized?

Do you find yourself cramming the night before a test? Are you late with reading assignments or do you forget them altogether? If this sounds familiar, you need to get organized. With the help of a calendar and other time management techniques, you can start to take control of your time. You can learn to make studying part of your routine, not an emergency task undertaken at the last minute. Once you learn to pace yourself, you'll find that studying is not an overwhelming task. You'll also find that you can plan time for fun.

### Can You Concentrate?

Do you study with the television or stereo on? Do you find yourself daydreaming or making frequent trips to the refrigerator? Are you constantly getting up to find a textbook, notebook, or pen? If so, you are blocking your ability to concentrate on studying, and the time you spend will not be productive.

To study effectively, set up an environment that is as free of distraction as possible. You will need a comfortable (but not *too* comfortable) chair, a desk, and a good reading light. The desk is the ideal place to keep all your study materials within reach. Television, music, and conversation should be out of earshot. If for some reason you can't control noise where you study, you can try to block it out by listening to soft music—and making an effort to concentrate.

## WHAT ARE STUDY SKILLS?

Let's suppose that you are motivated to study, have organized your time, and have set up a good study area. You are now ready to study. The purpose of studying is to learn—to understand and remember what you are hearing or reading. To do this effectively, you need to master the basic study skills: notetaking, listening, reading, studying for tests, preparing reports, and making oral presentations.

### Notetaking

Although volumes of notes are taken, studies have shown that most students record just 20 to 50 percent of what they hear in class. That means that 50 to 80 percent of the content of the lecture goes unrecorded—and is quickly forgotten.

Someone skilled in notetaking can determine what needs to be written down. He or she takes notes in as few words as possible and reviews the notes soon after to fill in missing or garbled information. The benefits of skilled notetaking are twofold. First, good notetaking ensures that you are paying attention to the meaning of the lecture or reading, which will help you understand and remember it. And second, good notetaking gives you a handy study aid. Rather than rereading assignments or struggling to remember lecture material, you can use your notes to study for tests.

### Listening

Listening is the communication skill that is most critical for learning in the classroom. Most people are poor listeners, immediately forgetting much of what they hear. Whether the instructor delivers a lecture without interruption or the class participates in a discussion, your ability to practice effective listening techniques will determine how much you learn while attending class. The ability to listen is a prerequisite for taking good notes in a classroom setting.

## Reading

Reading in order to learn is a process that differs from recreational reading. Reading as a learning process involves previewing material before you read it. It also means reading closely to understand the main ideas and supporting details. And last, it involves notetaking to ensure that the material has been thoroughly understood. This systematic approach to reading increases your ability to comprehend, review, and remember information.

## Studying for Tests

Effective studying for tests depends on the study skills already mentioned. If you have been listening and reading effectively and taking good notes, you have the foundation for studying for an exam. Your notes serve as the basis for your review of the material.

Studying for tests also involves some mental preparation. You will minimize the stress involved in test-taking if you have everything you need in advance and are well rested. While reviewing your notes, try to anticipate what will be asked. Also, learn the specific strategies for answering multiple-choice, true-false, and essay questions.

## Preparing Reports

There are several study skills involved in preparing a report or paper. First, you will learn how to use the library's many resources, including card catalogues, reference books, indexes to periodicals, micrographics equipment, and computerized databases. You will learn how to select a topic, do research systematically, and keep source information organized. You will master the writing skills of outlining, drafting, and revising your paper. Last, you will format the report so that it's neat and appropriately presented.

## Making Oral Presentations

Preparing a report to be delivered orally involves different skills. There are notetaking techniques that are specially designed to help you organize and deliver your speech. You will learn presentation skills, how to prepare visual aids, and how to keep the interest of your audience. You will learn rehearsal methods designed to reduce stress and how to control the appearance of anxiety.

## IMPROVING STUDY SKILLS

With this overview of study skills, you should be able to evaluate your own study skills. Do you continue to use a study habit that you realize is poor? There is a method you can use to improve your study skills. It is called *behavior modification*, and it is designed to change a poor behavior gradually into a good one. Let's see how it works.

Lee is taking a marketing course and needs to read a chapter from his text before each class meeting. He has trouble concentrating and finds excuses to interrupt his reading, so it takes him longer to finish a chapter than it should. Lee wants to modify this behavior so that he can sit down for a period of uninterrupted and productive study time. He approaches this task as follows:

1. As Lee reads today's chapter, he keeps track of the number of minutes he can concentrate before he stops to talk, snack, or daydream. He finds that he can only read for 7 minutes at a time.
2. Lee decides that the next time he has to read a chapter, he will extend his period of concentration to 11 minutes.
3. When he achieves the 11-minute span of concentration, he increases his goal to 15 minutes.
4. Lee continues to monitor his time and to increase his goal by several minutes at a time. His eventual goal is to reach 45 minutes of uninterrupted studying, and it takes 3 weeks to achieve this.

As you can see, behavior modification works by changing a behavior gradually. By setting realistic standards and reaching them immediately, you are able to achieve small improvements that motivate you to try for the next goal.

## SUMMARY

Good study skills are important. They help you function independently in school and master your course work. To prepare for studying, you must be motivated, organized, and able to concentrate.

There are specific techniques and procedures involved in each study skill. Study skills include notetaking, listening, reading, studying for tests, preparing reports, and making oral presentations.

To improve a study skill, use behavior modification, which involves gradually changing behavior over a period of time.

Name _____     Date _____

# CHAPTER 1 ACTIVITIES

## CHECK YOUR UNDERSTANDING

**1.** Why is it important to develop good study skills at this point in your education?

_____

_____

**2.** How can you motivate yourself to do well in your classes?

_____

_____

**3.** How can you improve your ability to concentrate when studying?

_____

_____

_____

**4.** List six basic study skills.

_____

_____

_____

**5.** Describe how you can improve a study skill through behavior modification.

_____

_____

_____

_____

## EVALUATE YOUR STUDY SKILLS

You can use the following checklist to evaluate your present study skills. Be honest when you respond to each item. Remember, your goal is to improve your study skills in order to do well in school. To see how you have improved—and what areas still need work—evaluate your skills again when you finish this text.

|  | NOW | | AFTER TEXT | |
|---|---|---|---|---|
|  | Yes | No | Yes | No |

**Chapter 1:**

1. I have a study area where I keep all my school materials.   ✓

2. I study with the television and stereo off and with conversations out of earshot.   ✓

3. I can concentrate on studying for at least 45 minutes without being distracted.   ✓ (No)

**Chapter 2:**

4. I know what my long-term goals are.

5. I know what my goals are this semester.

6. I know how each of my courses relates to my long- and short-term goals.

7. I am motivated to do well in each of my courses.

**Chapter 3:**

8. I use a calendar to keep track of course deadlines.

9. I have a weekly routine that includes regular study time.

10. I finish assignments on time.

11. I periodically set priorities for studying.

**Chapter 4:**

12. My notes are organized and legible.

|  | NOW | | AFTER TEXT | |
|---|---|---|---|---|
|  | Yes | No | Yes | No |

**13.** I take brief notes in my own words.

**14.** I use a loose-leaf binder for notes.

**15.** I record my notes in an appropriate format.

**16.** I use an outline format whenever possible.

**17.** I use flash cards for course vocabulary.

**Chapter 5:**

**18.** I use phrases rather than full sentences in my notes.

**19.** I use simple abbreviations whenever possible.

**Chapter 6:**

**20.** I prepare for listening in class by reading the text.

**21.** I sit where I can see and hear.

**22.** I pay attention and keep my mind actively processing what I hear.

**23.** I don't let the speaker's voice or appearance distract me.

**24.** I listen for main ideas.

**Chapter 7:**

**25.** I take good notes in class.

**26.** I review my class notes within 24 hours.

**Chapter 8:**

**27.** I preview a book before I start to read.

|  | NOW | | AFTER TEXT | |
|---|---|---|---|---|
|  | Yes | No | Yes | No |
| **28.** I know how to preview a chapter, article, and graphic before reading. | ✓ | ___ | ___ | ___ |

**Chapter 9:**

| **29.** When I read, I mark the material and take notes on one section of a chapter at a time. | ✓ | ___ | ___ | ___ |
| **30.** I know how to read for main ideas. | ✓ | ___ | ___ | ___ |
| **31.** I have a good system for marking a reading. | ___ | ✓ | ___ | ___ |
| **32.** I take good notes on a reading assignment. | ___ | ✓ | ___ | ___ |
| **33.** I review my notes soon after finishing a reading assignment. | ___ | ✓ | ___ | ___ |

**Chapter 10:**

| **34.** I use my notes to study for tests. | ✓ | ___ | ___ | ___ |
| **35.** I am prepared by exam time without cramming. | ✓ | ___ | ___ | ___ |

**Chapter 11:**

| **36.** I can overcome test stress. | ___ | ✓ | ___ | ___ |

**Chapter 12:**

| **37.** I know techniques for taking objective and essay tests. | ✓ | ___ | ___ | ___ |

**Chapter 13:**

| **38.** I use library resources effectively. | ___ | ___ | ___ | ___ |

**Chapter 14:**

| **39.** I know how to select a topic for a paper. | ___ | ___ | ___ | ___ |

| | NOW | | AFTER TEXT | |
|---|---|---|---|---|
| | Yes | No | Yes | No |

**40.** I know how to outline a paper. —  —  —  —

**Chapter 15:**

**41.** I know how to do research for a paper. —  —  —  —

**42.** I know how to record information for bibliographies and footnotes. —  —  —  —

**43.** I can take notes for a paper. —  —  —  —

**Chapter 16:**

**44.** I write a first draft of a paper. —  —  —  —

**45.** I revise the paper until I am satisfied. —  —  —  —

**Chapter 17:**

**46.** I format the paper properly. —  —  —  —

**Chapter 18:**

**47.** I can organize material for an oral presentation. —  —  —  —

**48.** I can adapt a written report for an oral presentation. —  —  —  —

**Chapter 19:**

**49.** I rehearse my oral presentation. —  —  —  —

**50.** I have good techniques for giving a speech. —  —  —  —

## IMPROVE YOUR WRITING SKILLS

Your skill at writing is critical. To communicate effectively, you'll need to build your knowledge of the basics: sentence structure, punctuation such as commas and quotations, and presenting numbers in your reports. These exercises at the end of each chapter will provide the foundation for improving these important skills.

**The Sentence:** A *sentence* is a group of words that expresses a complete thought and makes sense when it stands by itself. When written, a sentence begins with a capital letter and ends with a period, a question mark, or an exclamation point.

Your supervisor will explain the procedure.
Who recommended that you apply for this position?
I don't believe it!

## Practice

For each group of words below that is a sentence, write *S* (indicating "sense—sentence") in the answer space. For each group of words that is not a sentence, write *NS* (indicating "no sense—no sentence").

**1.** All suggestions for improving employee morale. ____

**2.** Do you have a part-time job? ____

**3.** The people waiting patiently to enter the theater. ____

**4.** An appropriate response to the interviewer's questions. ____

**5.** Be sure to include your check or money order. ____

**6.** Reports that a number of the machines were damaged. ____

**7.** Those who may need assistance with the assignment. ____

**8.** Don't bother to ask them! ____

**9.** Anytime you are ready to begin, tell me. ____

**10.** Some department stores at 10 a.m. and close at 6 p.m. ____

# 2 SETTING YOUR GOALS

Have you ever wished that you could change your life in some way? It's natural for people to dream about having more money, better health, exotic vacations, good grades, interesting jobs, and many other things. If wishes were broomsticks, beggars would fly, the old folk saying goes. However, to make a dream come true, you must not only *wish* it, you must *intend* to do something about it. You must make a commitment.

When you make a commitment, you take a dream and say, "I really do want to achieve this goal. I will achieve it, and this is how

I will succeed." A strong commitment will help you focus your actions to achieve your goal. You wil be able to set goals, develop strategies to achieve them, and take pride in reaching them.

## ESTABLISHING GOALS

What you do want to achieve? What do you want to become? How often have you sat down in a quiet place and thought seriously about these questions? If you find it hard to pin down your thoughts, try asking yourself, "What do I want to accomplish in the next three months? within the year? in three to five years?"

You may come up with a range of goals. Some of them may be modest; for example, getting a *B* on a paper. Some may be very ambitious and involve long-term career plans. Whatever the nature of your goals, you can use some techniques to help you define—and accomplish—what you want. These techniques include being positive, being specific, setting deadlines, limiting the number of goals, and writing goal statements.

### Be Positive

Do you feel positive about your life and your ability to change it? Do you feel that you have accomplished something at the end of each day? Or do you drift from day to day without much thought for where you are heading? If you feel that each day is dull and meaningless, it's time for you to examine your life and figure out how to change it for the better. Decide to accomplish something positive, however small.

When setting goals, it is important to believe in your ability to achieve them. If you think at the outset, "I can never do that" or "That's impossible," you are setting the stage for failure. A positive attitude is essential when you are setting goals for yourself. Learn to say "I can" and "I will" as you set goals that will positively influence your education, health, career, family, and community. It may be wise to start with goals that are fairly easily attained. Nothing builds positive feelings quite like success, so take pride in your first achievements, no matter how large—or small—they are.

## Be Specific

When you are thinking about your goals, it helps to be specific. Instead of thinking, "I want to lose weight," for example, decide how much weight you want to lose. Instead of saying, "I will do well in school this term," set a specific grade goal for each course you are taking. By being specific, you are defining precisely what you want to achieve. This will help you focus on what you need to do to accomplish it.

## Set Deadlines

Some goals have natural deadlines. If one of your goals is to get an *A* in a course, you either will or will not accomplish it by the end of the term. For other goals, however, you must set a time limit. If you do not, you will find that time slips by and you have not made any progress in achieving your goal. Postponing things is so natural that you must overcome this tendency by giving yourself deadlines—and then working to beat them.

Goals tend to fall naturally in one of three time categories:

- Short-term goals, from one day to three months.
- Intermediate-term goals, from three months to one year.
- Long-term goals, from one to many years.

Try to set realistic deadlines for yourself. Don't expect to accomplish in one month what really will take a year or more.

## Limit the Number of Goals

How many New Year's resolutions fall by the wayside each year because you vowed to accomplish too many things? When you set goals for yourself, be reasonable about what you can get done. If you set too many goals, you will spread yourself too thin and you will not achieve most of them. Then, instead of feeling good about what you do accomplish, you may feel you have failed simply because you undertook too much.

When you set goals, be realistic about your time and energy. Decide on some short-, intermediate-, and long-term goals to spread your effort over a greater period of time. If you have too many goals, decide which are most important and put the others aside for now. You can undertake them later when you have more time.

## Write Goal Statements

A good way to give yourself a push toward achieving your goals is to write them down. Writing your goals not only helps you define them, it helps you accomplish them. A written statement is a stronger commitment. Each day, you can read what you have said you will achieve. A written statement is a reminder that you should be doing something about your goals.

If you decide to show your goal statements to other people, you can create another source of pressure. Your family and friends will be watching your progress—or lack of progress—in achieving your goals.

Writing goal statements should be done after you have thought about your goals. If you are thinking positively, have a reasonable number of specific goals in mind, and have set deadlines for achieving them, you are ready to write your goals. Here are a few suggestions for writing goal statements.

■ *Set your own goals.* Setting and writing goals is a personal task. When you set your own goals, you are taking control of your actions, hopes, and life. You are responsible for achieving your objectives. If you allow another person to do this for you, you will lose your ownership of your goals and your commitment to achieving them.

■ *Use active, positive words.* State your goals in active, positive language, using the first person pronoun—*I*. Don't say "I will try

---

*Oct. 7*

**Goals**

1. *I will prepare notes for speech to Organizational Behavior class by October 14, and rehearse speech for delivery on October 17.*
2. *I will get a B or better on Business Law test on October 29.*
3. *I will save $500 for airfare and expenses to visit Carol during spring break (April 9).*

A goals statement

to," say "I will." Don't write wordy statements such as "I hope to be able to finish my paper before the due date so that there will be time to find errors to be corrected." Instead, say, "I will finish my paper by April 28 and revise it by May 1."

■ *Indicate the deadline.* Make sure your goal statement includes a time limit. Try to be specific and set actual completion dates such as "July 1" rather than "two or three months."

As you write your goal statements, think about how good you will feel each day as you make progress toward fulfilling the goals.

## DEVELOPING STRATEGIES TO MEET YOUR GOALS

Deciding on and writing down your goals is an important first step. But now the hard work starts: achieving your goals. For each goal, you must decide on an action plan, follow through on it, evaluate your progress, and revise your strategy if necessary—all the while keeping that image of success fresh in your mind.

### Develop an Action Plan

Once you have identified a goal, you need to develop an action plan to achieve it. An action plan is an outline of the tasks that need to be done in a particular sequence, along with deadlines, in order to achieve the goal. For example, if your goal is to get a *B* on a paper, you would plan the steps necessary to select a paper topic and research, outline, write, and revise the paper to the best of your ability.

If your plan involves tasks that are too difficult, you should revise it or you will fail to reach your goal. Think about your past accomplishments, and analyze how you achieved them. Then try to apply these successful strategies to your present action plan. Remember, there is usually more than one way to achieve a goal.

Some goals, especially long-term ones, depend on the accomplishment of many subgoals. It is easier to accomplish a long-term goal if you define and set deadlines for each subgoal. What portion of the long-term goal can be achieved in a month? in two months? in a year? For example, Gail wants to become president of her student association within two years. To get such a top-level job, she realizes that

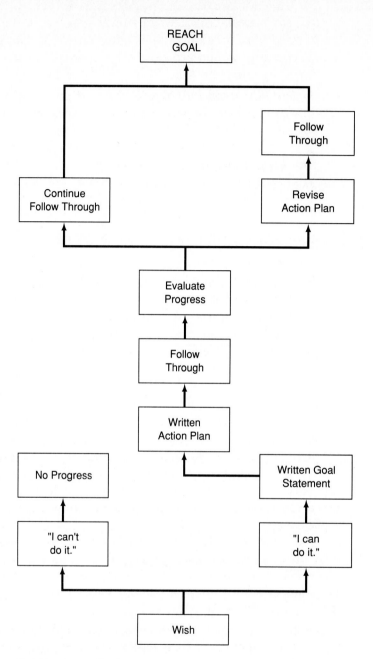

Pathway to reaching a goal

Oct. 7

### Action Plan

**Goal:** *I will save $500 for airfare and expenses to visit Carol during spring break (April 9).*

| Task | Deadline | Date Accomplished |
|---|---|---|
| *Open special savings account* | *Oct. 12* | |
| *Deposit $20 a week* | *Oct. 12* | |
| | *Oct. 19* | |
| | *Oct. 26, etc.* | |
| *Check balance—$60* | *Oct. 26* | |
| *Check balance—$160* | *Nov. 30* | |
| *Check balance—$240* | *Dec. 28* | |
| *Check balance—$320* | *Jan. 25* | |
| *Check balance—$380* | *Feb. 22* | |
| *Check balance—$480* | *Mar. 29* | |
| *Check balance—$500* | *Apr. 5* | |

An action plan

she must make herself known to the student body. She decides first to run for secretary of the student association and work her way up to the higher elected office. Her action plan now includes all the tasks necessary to run for secretary as well as for president later on.

Whether an action plan involves 2 steps toward a goal or 20, you should write the entire plan down. Put your action plans in a place where you will be constantly reminded of them. This will help you keep on target to reach your goals.

## Follow Through on Your Plan

Once your plan is developed, start implementing it. Many good intentions never become reality because goals and plans are forgotten or postponed. Remember, if you don't take the first step, you will never reach the last step—the achievement of your goal. As the American humorist Josh Billings once said, "Consider the postage stamp. It secures success through its ability to stick to one thing until it gets there."[1]

Having a positive mental image of how good you will feel when you have reached your goal helps create the energy you need to start and stick with your action plan. Close your eyes and visualize the positive result you will achieve by carrying out the tasks needed to reach your goal. Motivate yourself to follow the steps in your action plan by keeping this image in mind.

## Evaluate Your Progress

Your goal statement and action plan both include a date for accomplishing the goal as well as deadlines for each step along the way. You can use these dates as checkpoints to evaluate your progress.

If you set a target of Friday to accomplish a short-term goal, with Wednesday to finish the first half of the work, check your progress mid-way. If you're not satisfied, ask yourself, "Why?" Was the action plan unrealistic? Did something over which you had no control interfere with progress on this goal? Did you simply forget to do what you were supposed to do? Don't feel too guilty if the fault was yours, but *do* accept responsibility. Then decide on the best way to get back on track.

Sometimes it's easy to lose sight of the small steps needed to reach a goal when you are thinking ahead to how wonderful it will be to achieve the goal. A football player's objective is to reach the goal line, but to do this he must concentrate on gaining a few yards with each play. If he focuses exclusively on the goal line and not on each play, he may fumble and lose the ball.

## Revise the Action Plan

When you are evaluating your progress, be honest. If your progress has been slow or nonexistent, ask yourself whether you still want to achieve that goal. If the answer is yes, then evaluate your action plan. Is the plan still workable? Can you catch up if you have fallen behind, or should you delay your target date? Is the plan itself faulty? If so, you need to revise it in order to achieve your goal.

Gail, who wanted to become president of the student association, found her progress halted when she lost the election for secretary, something she had not considered when developing her action plan.

She still wants to become president, so she revises her plan. She decides to volunteer to chair one or two student association committees in order to demonstrate her ability to lead and to work with others. In this way she is still preparing to run for president in the next election.

Remember, a plan is just a guide to help you make progress. When it is no longer leading you toward your goal, you must take time out and develop a different approach. What's important is to be flexible and make changes in your action plan when it is necessary.

## REACHING YOUR GOALS

It would be nice if, when you reached an important goal, your achievement would be heralded by those around you. And sometimes this is the case. Friends and family often celebrate special accomplishments such as graduations or new jobs. Sometimes, however, you will find yourself celebrating alone or, worse, feeling let down about your accomplishment.

Can you feel down even though you have reached your goal? Yes, you can. Often when you are working toward an objective, the time you spend seems endless. You imagine that your life will change dramatically or you will be much happier. When you finally reach the goal, you see that life is still going on around you, no one has paid particular attention, and you don't feel any different. You are disappointed that the special day is not more exciting. Now what do you do?

First, praise yourself; tell yourself how wonderful you are for persevering until you accomplished what you wanted to do. Remember why you set out to achieve this goal. Remind yourself that your achievement shows you have the will to control your life and make changes for the better. Then think about some of your other dreams. Start planning to turn another dream into a goal you can achieve.

## REFERENCE

**1.** Josh Billings (Shaw, Henry Wheeler), in Walter Pauk, *How to Study in College*, 3rd ed., Houghton Mifflin Company, Boston, 1984, p. 59.

# SUMMARY

In order to improve your life, it is important to set goals for yourself. When you think about what you want to achieve, you should have a positive attitude, be specific about what you want, and set deadlines. Limit the number of goals you set so that you are not trying to do too much. Writing goal statements is a good way to help motivate yourself to achieve your goals.

Each goal requires a written action plan, an outline of the tasks that need to be done to achieve the goal. Once the plan is developed, you must follow through and take action. As time passes, you should evaluate your progress against the deadlines in your action plan. If necessary, you can revise the plan to improve it.

When you achieve a goal, you should praise yourself for taking control of your life. Then it's time to think about setting more goals for the future.

Name _____                                    Date _____

# CHAPTER 2 ACTIVITIES

## CHECK YOUR UNDERSTANDING

**1.** Why is it important to be specific when you set a goal?

_____

_____

**2.** Characterize each of the following goals as short-term (S), intermediate-term (I), or long-term (L): (a) volunteer to help in a local shelter during the school year, (b) achieve a grade of *B* or higher on an oral presentation, (c) earn $40,000 a year, (d) save money for a vacation next summer.

   **a.** _____        **b.** _____

   **c.** _____        **d.** _____

**3.** What is the purpose of writing a goal statement?

_____

_____

**4.** What is an action plan?

_____

_____

**5.** What should you do if you are not progressing toward a goal as you had planned?

_____

_____

## SET YOUR GOALS AND DEVELOP YOUR STRATEGIES

**1.** What wishes do you have that would change your life? Be honest with yourself and list at least five things you would like to achieve sometime. As you make your list, indicate if your wish can be accomplished in a short (0–3 months), intermediate (3–12 months), or long period of time (over a year). Are there any wishes you think will never become realities? Indicate that on your "wish list."

| | COME TRUE? | | TIME PERIOD | | |
|---|---|---|---|---|---|
| Wish | Yes | No | Short | Intermediate | Long |
| a. _____ | ___ | ___ | ___ | ___ | ___ |
| b. _____ | ___ | ___ | ___ | ___ | ___ |
| c. _____ | ___ | ___ | ___ | ___ | ___ |
| d. _____ | ___ | ___ | ___ | ___ | ___ |
| e. _____ | ___ | ___ | ___ | ___ | ___ |
| f. _____ | ___ | ___ | ___ | ___ | ___ |
| g. _____ | ___ | ___ | ___ | ___ | ___ |

2. Does your wish list represent a good combination of short-, intermediate-, and long-term goals? If not, carefully review and rethink the goals to be sure that each is possible in the time period you have indicated.
3. On a separate sheet of paper, write a goal statement for each wish you checked off as *Yes* (a wish *will* come true).
4. Prepare a written plan of action for each goal statement.
5. If you checked off *No* on any of your wishes (a wish will *not* come true), pause and ask yourself, "Why?" Here is a challenge to you: Write a goal statement and a plan of action for a wish that you think will not come true, assuming for this moment that the wish *can* come true.
6. The following list of goals can be achieved in varying time periods. Check the column for the time period you think it would take to achieve each goal. Personalize the goals—making them *your* goals—as much as you can.

| | TIME PERIOD | | |
|---|---|---|---|
| | Short | Intermediate | Long |
| a. Learn to play a musical instrument. | ___ | ___ | ___ |

**TIME PERIOD**

| | Short | Intermediate | Long |
|---|---|---|---|
| **b.** Own my own business. | ___ | ___ | ___ |
| **c.** Graduate from my school. | ___ | ___ | ___ |
| **d.** Make the Dean's list. | ___ | ___ | ___ |
| **e.** Learn to cook a gourmet meal. | ___ | ___ | ___ |
| **f.** Learn to generate computer graphics. | ___ | ___ | ___ |
| **g.** Learn to speak a foreign language. | ___ | ___ | ___ |
| **h.** Visit residents of a local nursing home. | ___ | ___ | ___ |
| **i.** Read more books. | ___ | ___ | ___ |
| **j.** Learn to fly an airplane. | ___ | ___ | ___ |
| **k.** Learn to cross-country ski or waterski. | ___ | ___ | ___ |
| **l.** Be a millionaire. | ___ | ___ | ___ |
| **m.** Obtain a good job in my chosen field. | ___ | ___ | ___ |

**7.** The following sentences represent someone's awkward attempt to write goal statements. Using what you have learned in this chapter, rewrite each statement.

**a.** I will try to get out of bed each day at 6:30 a.m.

_I will get out of bed each day at 6:30 am._

**b.** Hopefully, on Friday I will have been able to walk ten blocks each day since beginning my walking exercise schedule on Monday.

_I will walk 10 blocks each day_

**c.** Three days this week I will go to the library for a few hours to get data for my paper.

*I will go to the library to get data for my paper*

**d.** I will try to use each Friday morning to evaluate the progress I have made on the goals I have set.

*I will use each Friday morning to evaluate the progress*

**e.** I will take some money out of my paycheck to put into my savings account.

*I will take $ out of my paycheck to put . . .*

**f.** Sometime in the next six months I will pay off my $250 debt.

_____

_____

**g.** I will write a résumé before the end of the semester.

_____

_____

**h.** I should use my free time between 11 and 12 noon on Mondays and Wednesdays to learn the new microcomputer software package.

_____

_____

**i.** By April 11 the banner advertising the play will be finished.

_____

_____

**j.** I will try to call a committee meeting before the Thanksgiving break.

_____

_____

**8.** Right now, your career objective is a long-term goal. Typically, it takes experience doing different tasks and assuming a variety of responsibilities before you reach your ultimate goal for your working life. From your perspective now, what will it take to reach your career goal? You may need more education, an internship or apprenticeship, specific work experience, and so on. What interim subgoals will you need to establish en route to your goal?

**Directions:** Using your career goal, complete each of the following activities on a separate sheet of paper:
   a. Write your specific career goal statement.
   b. Write your interim subgoals.
   c. Prepare a written plan of action inserting target dates to complete the needed steps.
9. Select a short-range goal that will make you feel better physically (for example, starting an exercise program, getting more sleep, or losing or gaining weight).
   a. Write a specific goal statement.
   b. Develop a written action plan to achieve your goal.

## REVISE AN ACTION PLAN

### Case Study

At the start of the school year, Joe decides he wants to compete in the Extemporaneous Speaking event at the national convention of the TJ association next July. He has to succeed at the local and state levels, however, before he is eligible to compete at the national level. Joe writes his specific goal and the subgoals he will have to achieve to make it to the national event. For each subgoal, Joe needs a plan of action so that he has a chance to reach his goal. Joe begins to write:

> Goal Statement: I will compete in the Extemporaneous Speaking contest at the national TJ convention on July 21.
> Subgoal No. 1: I will win the local runoff contest on October 19 and be selected to represent our TJ chapter at the state Extemporaneous Speaking contest.
> Subgoal No. 2: I will win the Extemporaneous Speaking contest at the state-level competition on April 17, which makes me eligible to compete in the national event.

## MY ACTION PLAN:

### Subgoal No. 1

I will study the techniques used by good speakers, which include effective gestures; eye contact; pitch, pace, and volume of voice; and poise. I will read all the books in the library that contain information on these topics by September 30.

I will view all the videotapes in the audiovisual department library that demonstrate speaking techniques before October 10.

I will ask my English teacher to give me topics to use to role-play an extemporaneous speaking situation.

After practicing ten times with ten different topics, I will ask my English teacher to critique my extemporaneous presentation on one topic that she selects.

I will be ready for the local competition on October 19.

I will win the local competition and prepare for the state level.

### Subgoal No. 2

I will read all the newspapers in the library each day from October 20 to April 16 to broaden my knowledge on many subjects.

I will ask another English teacher to help me role-play an extemporaneous speaking situation and critique my performance.

I will compete at the state contest and win on April 17. This will make me eligible to compete at the national level on July 21.

**Directions:** Analyze Joe's action strategies. Is he realistic in what he says he will do? Are his timelines realistic? Does he list all appropriate deadlines? Are his approaches to achieving his subgoals appropriate? On a separate sheet of paper, revise Joe's plan of action if necessary.

## IMPROVE YOUR WRITING SKILLS

**Simple Subjects and Predicates:** To be a *sentence*, the group of words must include a subject and a predicate. The *subject* is the part that names and often describes the person speaking, the person spoken to, or the person or thing spoken about. The *predicate* contains one or more words that express action or a state of being.

If the subject names or names and describes only one person or thing or one group of persons or things, the sentence has a *simple subject.* And if the predicate indicates only one action or state of being, the sentence has a *simple predicate.* For example, each of the following sentences has a simple subject and a simple predicate:

> I have heard the same story from others almost every day. (*I* tells who is speaking; *have heard* expresses the action of the subject; the rest of the predicate tells something about the action.)

> You seem happy with the results of the test. (The subject *You* tells who is spoken to; *seem* indicates state of being, and the rest of the predicate describes the state of being of the subject.)

> Alice McBride uses some other spreadsheet program. (The subject *Alice McBride* tells who is spoken about; *uses* indicates the action of the subject; the rest of the predicate tells something about the action.)

> Diskettes for computers are available in different sizes and with different storage capacities. (*Diskettes* tells what is spoken about; *for computers* tells what kind of diskettes. *Are* expresses state of being; the rest of the predicate tells something about the state of being of the subject.)

In some instances, the subject *you* is understood, not stated. For example:

> Sign both copies and keep one for your records.
> Be sure to confirm your reservations.

**Practice**

In each of the following sentences, identify the simple subject by drawing one line under it or, if appropriate, by writing the word *you* in parentheses in the space provided at the end of each sentence. Draw two lines under the simple predicate.

**1.** We waited for half an hour in the receptionist's office. _____

**2.** A carton of paper was sitting next to the desk. _____

**3.** Our employees will receive their paychecks every other week. _____

**4.** Dick went to Holland for a firsthand look at the dikes. _____

**5.** Please return the book to me before the end of next week. _____

**6.** You should be very proud of your achievement. _____

**7.** Their prices seem quite reasonable to us. _____

**8.** Tuition is a major expense for students and parents. _____

**9.** Those shoes look very comfortable. _____

**10.** I found most of the questions very easy to answer. _____

# 3 MANAGING YOUR TIME

Now that you have thought about your long- and short-term goals, you may be wondering how you will achieve them. The key is to perform the many steps or tasks outlined in your action plan. To do this you must plan and manage your time. You may be used to having someone tell you what to do and when to do it. Now it is up to you to schedule your time.

Some students would rather not make schedules because they want to be "flexible." But people without schedules waste a lot of time and often have no time left for flexibility. As the semester progresses, they discover that time has run out for completing assignments and studying for exams. The result? they feel frustrated, anxious, and defeated.

Managing your time actually enables you to meet your study and work goals *and* have time left for fun. By using a few simple time management tools, you will be able to schedule your activities and become a student who can meet deadlines without rushing. These time management tools include a calendar, a weekly schedule, a daily schedule, and a priorities chart. In addition, there are some other techniques you can use to make the most of your time.

## CALENDAR

The first step in taking control of your time is to get a large calendar, similar to the one below, for your personal use. The calendar should (1) show a month at a time and (2) have enough space to write notes and reminders for each day. Hang the calendar where it is convenient to use.

When an assignment is made in class, place its due date on the calendar. Also write the dates of tests, field trips, and meetings. If your instructor gives you a course syllabus containing assignment

### October

| Sun. | Mon. | Tues. | Wed. | Thurs. | Fri. | Sat. |
|---|---|---|---|---|---|---|
| | 1 | 2 | 3 | 4 | 5 | 6 |
| 7 | 8 Business Law quiz | 9 | 10 | 11 | 12 Computer Lab 2–4 | 13 Paula's Wedding 2 p.m. |
| 14 | 15 | 16 | 17 Speech— Org. Beh. | 18 | 19 Computer Lab 2–4 | 20 |
| 21 | 22 | 23 Marketing field trip 10–12 | 24 | 25 | 26 | 27 Computer Lab 9–11 |
| 28 | 29 Business Law exam | 30 | 31 | | | |

Monthly calendar

```
Log—Tuesday, October 2

7–8:30      Breakfast, dress
8:30–9      Commute
9–10        Microcomputer class
10–11       Marketing class
11–12       Coffee with Brian
12–1        Lunch with Debbie
1–4         Work
4–4:30      Commute
4:30–6      Relax
6–7         Dinner
7–11        Study
11          Bed
```

Daily log

and exam dates, transfer these immediately to your calendar. In other words, use the calendar to write down all school obligations beyond attending class sessions. Don't forget to note important social and family obligations on your calendar as well. These events will affect how you plan your study time.

## WEEKLY SCHEDULE

A monthly calendar will give you the big picture, but you still need to plan your weekly routine. Before you can prepare a weekly schedule, you must know how to spend your time each day. This can be done by logging a day's activities on an hour-by-hour basis and then using the log as the basis for preparing the weekly schedule.

### Daily Log

Keep a log of all your activities for a day or two. Be careful not to underestimate the time spent watching television or talking with friends in person or on the telephone. When the log is complete, study it to see how wisely you have used your time. Would you make changes if you could relive those days? For instance, Cathy Morris's log on the previous page shows she spent a long evening studying. She might have been better off if she had spent some time studying during the day instead of leaving it for a long stretch in the evening, when she was tired.

## Tips for Preparing a Weekly Schedule

You are now ready to prepare a schedule for managing your time each week. Consider the following points as you block out your time:

1. *Schedule definite time commitments first.* Block out the times you will be attending class or working, since these are not generally flexible. Then plan study time. Finally, plan time for eating, sleeping, and recreation.

2. *Make studying part of your routine.* You will need to practice self-discipline in order to stick with a regular time for studying. Since studying is probably not your favorite activity, it's easy to put it off. Remember, however, that you will not achieve your educational goals without studying, so you should make a habit of it.

3. *Allow sufficient study time for each course.* Generally, two hours of study time should be allowed for each hour of class time. For example, if your class meets for three hours each week, you should plan six hours each week for studying, completing assignments, and writing papers. In planning study time, you should consider the difficulty of each course as well as special deadlines that are coming up.

4. *Don't schedule too-short or too-long periods of study time.* Less than an hour is not enough time and more than three hours at a stretch is too much. With less than an hour, by the time you take out books and notes and get organized, you have little time for studying before it is time to pack up. With more than three hours, your studying will become less productive because you will need a break.

5. *Study before and after class.* If you have time between classes, use it to review your classroom notes while they are still fresh in your mind or to read a text assignment before the instructor covers the material in class.

6. *Plan to study when you are most alert.* Are you a "morning person" or a "night person"? Try to schedule your study time at your best time of day.

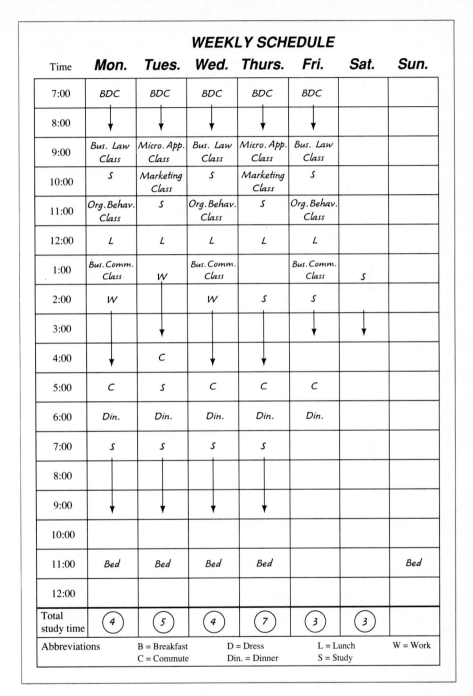

### WEEKLY SCHEDULE

| Time | Mon. | Tues. | Wed. | Thurs. | Fri. | Sat. | Sun. |
|---|---|---|---|---|---|---|---|
| 7:00 | BDC | BDC | BDC | BDC | BDC | | |
| 8:00 | ↓ | ↓ | ↓ | ↓ | ↓ | | |
| 9:00 | Bus. Law Class | Micro. App. Class | Bus. Law Class | Micro. App. Class | Bus. Law Class | | |
| 10:00 | S | Marketing Class | S | Marketing Class | S | | |
| 11:00 | Org. Behav. Class | S | Org. Behav. Class | S | Org. Behav. Class | | |
| 12:00 | L | L | L | L | L | | |
| 1:00 | Bus. Comm. Class | W | Bus. Comm. Class | | Bus. Comm. Class | S | |
| 2:00 | W | ↓ | W | S | S | | |
| 3:00 | | ↓ | | | ↓ | ↓ | |
| 4:00 | ↓ | C | ↓ | ↓ | | | |
| 5:00 | C | S | C | C | C | | |
| 6:00 | Din. | Din. | Din. | Din. | Din. | | |
| 7:00 | S | S | S | S | | | |
| 8:00 | ↓ | ↓ | ↓ | ↓ | | | |
| 9:00 | ↓ | ↓ | ↓ | ↓ | | | |
| 10:00 | | | | | | | |
| 11:00 | Bed | Bed | Bed | Bed | | | Bed |
| 12:00 | | | | | | | |
| Total study time | ④ | ⑤ | ④ | ⑦ | ③ | ③ | |
| Abbreviations | B = Breakfast  C = Commute | | D = Dress  Din. = Dinner | | L = Lunch  S = Study | W = Work | |

Weekly schedule

7. *Be prepared to change your weekly study schedule.* Although you should stick to your schedule as much as possible, you must also be ready to change it when the unexpected occurs.
8. *Be realistic.* Are you scheduling too much? Can you live with your plan and actually carry it out? If you find you are constantly revising your schedule, take another look at it. You may need to make major changes in your schedule.

You can prepare your weekly schedule on a form such as the one Cathy Morris created on the previous page. In addition to a grid showing each day of the week and each hour of the day, she included a space to tally her daily study hours and a key to the abbreviations she used. Notice that she has left extra time on the weekend in case she needs more time to study.

## DAILY SCHEDULE

In addition to a monthly calendar and a weekly schedule, it is often helpful to prepare a daily schedule that you can carry with you. Each evening, record the following day's activities, using your monthly

> **Wednesday 10**
> **October 199—**
>
> | | |
> |---|---|
> | 9:00 | Bus. Law |
> | 10:00 | Study |
> | 11:00 | Org. Behavior |
> | 12:00 | Lunch—Jennifer |
> | 1:00 | Bus. Comm. |
> | 2:00 | Work |
> | 3:30 | Dentist |
> | 4:30 | Commute |
> | 5:00 | Relax, chores |
> | 6:00 | Dinner |
> | 7:00 | Study |
> | 9:00 | Chores; call Sandy |
> | 11:00 | Bed |

Daily schedule

calendar and weekly schedule as a guide. You can use a 3- × 5-inch index card, a small notebook, or a purchased daily diary.

Preparing a plan for each day will give you a psychological boost because you know you are organized. In addition, it gives you an opportunity to revise your routine to accommodate unanticipated events. The page from Cathy Morris's daily schedule shows that she had to change her usual Wednesday routine when she had to go to the dentist unexpectedly.

## PRIORITIES CHART

To be super-organized and in control of your time, you can prepare a chart of your *priorities*, or most important tasks. This can be done on a weekly basis, probably each Sunday night. First, review what will be happening in the coming week, and then decide which are the most important tasks. For example, suppose Cathy Morris has to give an oral presentation in class on Wednesday. Time to prepare and practice would be a high priority on Monday and Tuesday. To accommodate the extra preparation time, other scheduled items will be less important, or will have a lower priority, this week.

Preparing a priorities chart makes you think about and judge the importance of the events of the coming week. Then you can manage your time to achieve the bests results. When establishing priorities, generally look for deadlines, due dates, and tests first. If there are

| | **Priorities Chart** | | | | **Week of** _Oct. 15_ | | |
|---|---|---|---|---|---|---|---|
| | **Mon.** | **Tues.** | **Wed.** | **Thurs.** | **Fri.** | **Sat.** | **Sun.** |
| Priority 1 | Practice speech– finalize note cards | Practice speech | Speech! | Start preparing for computer labs | Finished preparing for computer lab | | |
| Priority 2 | Review notes after each class | | | | Lab–2 p.m. | | |
| Comments | Catch up on studying later in week | Practice speech before bed | | | | Make up study time | |

Priorities chart

none in the near future, then routine studying or beginning a long-term assignment might be priority items that week.

## MAKING THE MOST OF YOUR TIME

There are several other techniques to consider as you establish your time management program:

1. *Be organized.* If you organize your belongings and establish a study area, you will not waste time looking for items you need when it is time to study.
2. *Do two things at the same time.* Carry work with you so that you can study while sitting on the bus, waiting in the doctor's office, or eating lunch alone.
3. *Use spare time to think.* While walking to class or the library, reflect on what you have been learning.
4. *Challenge yourself to complete a task within a certain amount of time.* Estimate the time it will take you to complete an assignment, and then try to complete it within that time. Without a definite deadline, a task will fill up all the time you have. Of course, be careful to allow enough time to complete the assignment thoroughly.

## SUMMARY

In order to achieve your goals, you must learn how to manage your time effectively. There are several time management tools to assist you in making the most of your time. A monthly calendar allows you to see the special events and deadlines coming up several weeks in advance. A weekly schedule enables you to plan your weekly routine and establish regular study times. A portable daily schedule organizes the events of a single day and permits you to incorporate the unexpected in your planning. A priorities chart establishes the importance of the tasks that must be accomplished. Other techniques you can use to make the most effective use of time include studying while doing other things and setting time goals for specific tasks.

Name _____  Date _____

# CHAPTER 3 ACTIVITIES

## CHECK YOUR UNDERSTANDING

**1.** What should a monthly calendar be used for?

_____

_____

**2.** What must you do before you can prepare a weekly schedule?

_____

_____

**3.** What are three suggestions to follow when you are scheduling your weekly studying?

_____

_____

**4.** What should a daily schedule be used for? When should it be prepared?

_____

_____

**5.** What is the purpose of a weekly priorities chart?

_____

_____

## MANAGE YOUR TIME

**1.** Fill in the current month and dates on the calendar on page 40. Then fill in all the events (exams, field trips, social activities, and so on) which have been scheduled. Make new entries on the

**Month** _____

| Sun. | Mon. | Tues. | Wed. | Thurs. | Fri. | Sat. |
|------|------|-------|------|--------|------|------|
|      |      |       |      |        |      |      |
|      |      |       |      |        |      |      |
|      |      |       |      |        |      |      |
|      |      |       |      |        |      |      |
|      |      |       |      |        |      |      |

calendar as they are scheduled. Keep the calendar up to date throughout the month and you will see just how busy you are!

**2.** On a separate sheet of paper or in a notebook, keep a daily log of your activities for one day of the current school week. Start from the time you get up in the morning until the time you go to bed. When the log is completed, answer the following questions:

**a.** How many hours did I attend classes? _____

**b.** How many hours did I study/prepare for classes? _____

**c.** How many hours was I involved in extracurricular activities at school? _____

**d.** How much time did I spend watching television? _____

**e.** How much time did I spend socializing with friends (both over the telephone and in person)? _____

**f.** How much time did my meals take? _____

**g.** How many hours did I work on chores at home and/or at a job away from home? _____

**h.** Any other activities? What? _____

Time? _____

**i.** Any "lost" time—time I cannot account for? _____

Finally, evaluate how wisely you used your time. Would you make any changes if you could "go back in time and live that day over"? What?

_____

_____

3. Using the form on page 42, prepare a weekly schedule that will help you manage your time more effectively. Begin with each class period and other definite commitments of time, such as a part-time job, club meetings, and family gatherings. When will you study? What time do you get up and go to bed each day? Be sure to allow time for recreation so that you avoid an "all work and no play" situation.

4. Maintain a daily schedule of activities that you can carry with you each day. This could be as simple as a 3- × 5-inch card, or it could be a pad of paper or a purchased daily diary. Each night, record your schedule for the next day (using your monthly and weekly calendars as guides). This plan for the day will give you a psychological boost because you'll know you are organized.

5. Create a personal priorities chart like the one on page 37. Maintain the chart for two weeks to determine if this procedure helps you organize your available time better so that you are not rushing to get a job done at the last minute.

## IMPROVE YOUR WRITING SKILLS

**Compound Subjects and Predicates:** If the complete subject names two or more different persons or things (or groups of persons

## WEEKLY SCHEDULE

| Time | Mon. | Tues. | Wed. | Thurs. | Fri. | Sat. | Sun. |
|---|---|---|---|---|---|---|---|
| 7:00 | | | | | | | |
| 8:00 | | | | | | | |
| 9:00 | | | | | | | |
| 10:00 | | | | | | | |
| 11:00 | | | | | | | |
| 12:00 | | | | | | | |
| 1:00 | | | | | | | |
| 2:00 | | | | | | | |
| 3:00 | | | | | | | |
| 4:00 | | | | | | | |
| 5:00 | | | | | | | |
| 6:00 | | | | | | | |
| 7:00 | | | | | | | |
| 8:00 | | | | | | | |
| 9:00 | | | | | | | |
| 10:00 | | | | | | | |
| 11:00 | | | | | | | |
| 12:00 | | | | | | | |
| Total study time | | | | | | | |
| Abbreviations | | | | | | | |

or things), the sentence has a *compound subject.* And if the predicate indicates two or more different actions or states of being, the sentence has a *compound predicate.* Note the following examples:

> Pat Lee and I enrolled in a computer literacy course last semester. (This sentence has a compound subject—*Pat Lee and I.* However, since *enrolled* is the only action indicated, the sentence has a simple predicate.)

> The editors detected and corrected several errors in the manuscript. (This sentence has a simple subject—the naming word *editors.* However, since the words *detected and corrected* indicate two different actions, it has a compound predicate.)

> Ann and Carlos took the test yesterday and passed it with flying colors. (This sentence has both a compound subject—*Ann and Carlos*—and a compound predicate—*took and passed.*)

## Practice

In each of the following sentences, draw one line under the simple or compound subject and two lines under the simple or compound predicate.

1. Tom Stevens proofread and returned the draft of the report to her.

2. Newspapers and newscasts keep us informed and entertained.

3. The lawyers and their clients entered the courtroom and sat near the front.

4. Drug addiction and alcoholism are serious problems.

5. The facts support all the allegations.

6. We need another week or two to complete the project.

7. You and she tied for first place.

8. Harry, Helen, and Hilda did poorly and won nothing in the contest.

9. Try to get some exercise every day.

10. Many restaurants have separate sections for smokers and non-smokers.

# TAKING NOTES

Notetaking is the basic study skill that you will use in most school situations. You will take notes in class, when reading assignments, and when preparing a report or oral presentation. You will use the notes you take for studying for tests. If you can master the techniques involved in taking good notes, you will be well on your way to success in your courses.

In Part 2 you will learn the basics of notetaking, including:

- **The characteristics of good notes.**
- **Notetaking formats for different situations.**
- **Techniques for writing and sketching notes.**
- **Preparing for notetaking.**
- **Shortcuts to improve your speed.**

# 4 NOTETAKING STRATEGIES

WHY TAKE NOTES?

CHARACTERISTICS OF
GOOD NOTES

NOTETAKING FORMATS
AND TECHNIQUES
Notebook
Sectioned Paper Formats
Outline Format
Graphic Notetaking
Summarizing
Vocabulary Cards

SUMMARY

**CHAPTER 4 ACTIVITIES**

CHECK YOUR
UNDERSTANDING

PLAN AND PRACTICE
YOUR NOTETAKING

IMPROVE YOUR WRITING
SKILLS

One of the best ways to learn is to take notes while you are listening in class or reading an assignment. However, many students have not learned how to take notes properly. Some students write down everything, and others write very little. Some students' notes are illegible; other students' notes are scattered throughout their possessions in a disorganized way.

Just taking notes is not enough. Your notes should be taken in an organized, systematic way, so that when you are ready to study for an exam, you will have a good source of information. Your notetaking skills will improve if you understand the importance of notetaking, the characteristics of good notes, and notetaking formats and techniques.

## WHY TAKE NOTES?

You may be asking, Why take notes at all? Why not just tape-record lectures or borrow someone else's notes? Why take notes on what you read when you can just refer to the readings when you study?

When you record a lecture or read a text without notetaking, you haven't really sorted out the important information you need to understand and remember. When you use someone else's notes, you are relying on someone's else's ability to record what is important. In addition, those notes are not tailored to your background and knowledge, so they may not be as helpful to you. What you are doing, in essence, is avoiding the process of learning.

Good notetaking makes the learning process easier. When you take notes, you accomplish many things:

1. *You pay attention.* As you read an assignment or listen to an instructor lecture, it is easy to daydream. The activity involved in notetaking forces you to pay attention. You are keeping your mind engaged in the task at hand—learning.
2. *You sort out the information being presented.* Because you are writing down only what is necessary for you to understand the material, you are thinking about what you are reading or hearing and making it your own.
3. *Your ability to remember improves.* Notetaking helps you remember what you are writing because you are transforming what you hear or read into your own words. This contributes to your ability to remember information on a long-term basis.
4. *You become an active learner.* While you are taking notes, you are associating what you already know with what you are hearing or reading. This makes learning more effective.
5. *You create a study aid.* The notes you take will serve as an external memory device. When you study from your notes, you will absorb the information and store it in your long-term memory.

## CHARACTERISTICS OF GOOD NOTES

To experience all the benefits of taking notes, you should understand what makes notes effective for studying and learning. Here are an example of good notetaking and some pointers:

# 3 APPROACHES TO MANAGEMENT

## Three prevailing schools of thought

It has been clear from the emergence of modern business that effective management will produce higher profits. Accordingly, managers have been highly motivated to understand the nature of their job and to improve their performance. From the last half of the nineteenth century to the present, three theories of management have achieved popularity. These are the classical, the behavioral, and the quantitative approaches to management. Today, management combines features of all of these in a balanced approach.

# CLASSICAL APPROACH

## Features rational analysis

The central belief of the *classical school of management* (sometimes called the traditional school) is that by applying rational analysis to the production and management functions of a business, worker and equipment productivity can be increased, resulting in higher profits. This idea was first introduced around the turn of the century by Frederick W. Taylor in the United States, and Henri Fayol in France, among others. They put forth the view that a logical study of procedures was required in order to improve the efficiency of the increasingly complex businesses that had begun to spring up at that time. Fayol divided the manager's job into specific functions in the belief that this systematic breakdown of responsibilities would promote effectiveness. Taylor was particularly interested in what is now called industrial engineering. His time-and-motion studies, as well as other job studies in the 1880s and 1890s, prepared the way for the mass production and assembly line system of today.

# BEHAVIORAL APPROACH

## Emphasizes human relations

The classical, rational approach to management tended to ignore the human element. Its originators, especially Taylor, believed that higher productivity would permit higher wages and salaries. They made little allowance, however, for other human needs. In the 1930s, there arose a new approach to management stressing the human factors in business. This approach became known as the *behavioral*, or *human relations*, *school*. Its adherents believed that an organization's goals could be met only by first understanding and then consciously dealing with human needs and interactions. Great emphasis was placed on human motivations and on group dynamics. In more extreme expressions of this view, managers were expected to act as psychological counselors for their workers.

*Source:* Lester R. Bittel *et al.*, *Business in Action*, 3rd ed., Macmillan/McGraw-Hill, New York, 1988, p. 103. Reprinted with permission of the Glencoe Division of Macmillan/McGraw-Hill Publishing Company.

Text page (above) and corresponding notes (opposite page).

1. *Notes should be organized.* To be useful, notes must be arranged in some logical system that you can understand and use.
2. *Notes should be legible.* Notes should be written in ink rather than pencil. Enough space should be left so that they are easy to read.
3. *Notes should be complete.* This does not mean that notes should be word for word what you have read or heard. Rather, notes should contain enough important information so that you can recall the complete "story" later.
4. *Notes should be dated and identified.* Each page of notes should indicate the date and source.
5. *Notes should be paraphrased.* Notes should be in your own words whenever possible. When you paraphrase, you are thinking about what you are hearing or reading.

| | |
|---|---|
| 3 Appr. to mngmnt | I. Approaches to Mngmnt. |
| | A. Classical |
| | B. Behavioral |
| | C. Quantitative |
| Classical Approach | II. Class. Appr. |
| | A. Rational analysis of production & mngmnt → increased productivity → higher profits |
| | B. Intro. by |
| Taylor | 1. Frederick W. Taylor—U.S. |
| Fayol | 2. Henri Fayol—France |
| Behavioral Approach | III. Beh. Appr. (Human Relations App.) |
| (human relations | A. Stresses human factors |
| approach) | 1. Motivation |
| | 2. Group dynamics |
| | B. Orig. in 1930s |

**6.** *Notes should be as brief as possible.* This does not mean that notes should contain very little. It means that abbreviations and phrases, rather than full sentences, should be used.

Look carefully at the example of good notetaking on pages 48–9. Compare the textbook excerpt with the notes a student wrote. Notice that the student wrote only the main ideas with some supporting detail. He did not write full sentences, and he used abbreviations. Because the notes are neat and well-organized, they will be useful for studying.

## NOTETAKING FORMATS AND TECHNIQUES

You will need to set up a notetaking system for each course you are taking. The notetaking formats and techniques that are discussed here will help you take good, usable notes. Using an appropriate notebook, sectioned paper formats, outline format, graphic notetaking, summaries, and vocabulary cards will help you get the most out of your notetaking.

### Notebook

A loose-leaf binder with 8½- × 11-inch paper is the most useful type of notebook for notetaking. Pages can be rearranged, removed, and inserted, permitting you to reorganize your notes when you study. The size of the page is ample for taking notes. You can use a separate binder for each course, or you can use one large binder with tabbed dividers. If you use a smaller notebook or a spiral-bound book, you will lose writing space and the flexibility to move pages around.

Also, write only on one side of the page. There are three important reasons for this:

**1.** Your notes will be more legible; sometimes ink bleeds through the paper and is visible on the reverse side of the page.
**2.** When notes are on only one side of the page, you can remove and place several pages side by side to review the sequence of material.
**3.** The blank side can be used to fill in information that is missing from the adjacent written page.

### Sectioned Paper Formats

The purpose of the *sectioned paper format* (dividing the page into various-size columns) is to provide separate columns for different

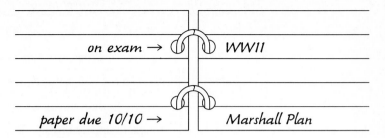

Backside of notebook page with reminders

types of notes. The width and number of columns varies according to the material and the type of course the notes are taken for. Here are three basic ways to section notetaking paper:

**1.** *2½-inch and 6-inch columns.* Draw a vertical line to divide the page into a 2½-inch-wide left-hand column and a 6-inch-wide right-hand column. The wide column is used to take notes. The narrow column is used for key words and phrases, called *recall notes,* and to highlight facts, dates, definitions, assignments, and so on. If you find you do not need 2½ inches for writing supplementary items, you can use the red line already printed on the paper to divide the page. This will give you slightly less than 2 inches for the left-hand column.

The 2½-inch and 6-inch column sectioned format

| Recall Column | Class Notes Column | Text Notes Column |
|---|---|---|
| Downward | Downward communication | Also w/in |
| communication | from higher to lower authority | levels of |
| | ex.—fr. mngmnt. to 1st-level emp. | mngmnt |
| | | |
| 4 prereq. | Prereq. for down. com. | see p. 81 |
| | positive attitude | for ex. |
| | information | |
| | planning | |
| | trust | |

The 2-inch, 5-inch, and 1½-inch column sectioned format

**2.** *2-inch, 5-inch, and 1½-inch columns.* Draw two vertical lines to divide the page into three columns measuring 2, 5, and 1½ inches. The 5-inch column in the middle is used for classroom notes; the 2-inch column for recall words and other highlighting; and the 1½-inch column for textbook information or page numbers that correlate with the classroom notes. This format is handy when an instructor's lecture is the most important material covered and the text supplements the lecture.

**3.** *2-inch, 3½-inch, and 3-inch columns.* Draw two vertical lines to divide the page into three columns measuring 2 inches, 3½ inches, and 3 inches. The 3½-inch column is used for classroom notes; the 3-inch column for textbook notes; and the 2-inch column for recall notes and highlighting. This format is useful when the instructor's lectures appear to follow the textbook. All the course notes on a given topic appear on the same page with this format.

## Outline Format

However you section your notetaking pages, you should try to take notes in outline format whenever possible. In an outline format, you

| Recall Column | Class Notes Column | Text Notes Column |
|---|---|---|
| Landlord-tenant | Landlord-tenant relationship | 5 elements in rel. |
| agreement | Agreement—called lease | 1. consent of landlord |
| lessor | Lessor-landlord | 2. trans. of possession to |
| lessee | Lessee-tenant | tenant in subordination |
|  |  | to rights of landlord |
| reversion | Landlord gives temp. control | 3. Right of reversion— |
|  | of premises | return of prop. to land. |
| consideration | Tenant gives consideration | 4. Leasehold estate— |
| leasehold estate | (usually rent) | creation of ownership |

The 2-inch, 3½-inch, and 3-inch column sectioned format

place the main idea at the left side of the column, with secondary ideas, supporting ideas, and examples indented:

I. Main idea
   A. Secondary idea
   B. Secondary idea
      1. Supporting detail
      2. Supporting detail
         a. Further subordinate material
         b. Further subordinate material

The outline format is easier to use when you are taking notes from a text or article, because there is usually a logical structure to the material and you can take time to figure out what it is. When you are taking notes in class, an outline format is possible only if the instructor presents material in an organized, logical manner and sticks to the lecture outline. You may find it necessary to combine outline and narrative, or paragraph, formats when taking notes in class. In addition, you may not be able to assign numbers and letters to the outlined items. In that case, just use indentions to indicate the relationships between ideas and facts.

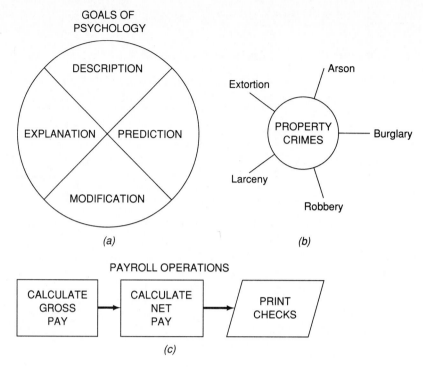

Graphic notetaking: (a) pie chart, (b) "spider," (c) flowchart

## Graphic Notetaking

Some material lends itself naturally to a graphic representation or picture. Instead of using words to describe an object, for instance, you can sketch it in your notebook. Graphic notetaking can also depict ideas and facts and their relationships. This is sometimes called *patterning*, because the graphic is in the form of a pattern such as a timeline, graph (pie chart, line graph, or bar chart), flow chart, diagram, table, or "spider." Some common forms of graphic notetaking are shown above.

## Summarizing

Whatever notetaking formats and techniques you use, you should always allow some space to summarize the material in your own words. By summarizing, you know whether you really comprehend what you heard or read. Place this summary either at the bottom of each page of notes or at the end of your notes for a class session or reading assignment. Two inches of space is enough for a brief summary.

## Vocabulary Cards

In most of your courses, you will be expected to learn special terms used to communicate ideas and facts in that particular field. This special vocabulary, called *jargon,* is easier to learn if you prepare index cards to use as study aids. When you are reading an assignment or listening to a lecture, note the special terms. Then post them, and their definitions, on index cards.

Place the term on one side of an index card and the definition on the other side. You can use the cards as flash cards to test yourself on your growing vocabulary. This technique can also be used to learn other material involving associations, such as historical events and the dates they occurred.

*coalition*

(a)

*coalition*

*a temporary*

*alignment of nations*

*for a specific purpose*

(b)

(a) Front of card (b) Back of card

# SUMMARY

Taking notes helps you pay attention, sort out the information being presented, improve your memory, and become an active learner. It also creates a study aid for tests. Good notes are organized, legible, complete, dated and identified, paraphrased, and brief.

Techniques to improve notetaking skill include using an 8½- by 11-inch loose-leaf binder, writing on one side of the page, sectioning the paper, using outline format, taking notes in graphic form, and summarizing. In addition, index cards can be used to prepare vocabulary flash cards to help you master new terms.

Name                                                                    Date

# CHAPTER 4 ACTIVITIES

## CHECK YOUR UNDERSTANDING

**1.** Briefly describe three important benefits of taking good notes.

_____

_____

**2.** What are four characteristics of good notes?

_____

_____

**3.** What is the purpose of the recall column in the sectioned paper format system of notetaking?

_____

_____

**4.** Why should you generally use the outline format and graphic notetaking rather than take notes in paragraph form?

_____

_____

**5.** How can vocabulary words best be studied?

_____

_____

## PLAN AND PRACTICE YOUR NOTETAKING

**1.** List four courses you are taking this semester. Decide which of the three sectioned paper formats would be most appropriate for each course. On a separate sheet of paper, describe why.

| COURSE | SECTION FORMAT |
|---|---|
| a. _____ | a. _____ |
| b. _____ | b. _____ |
| c. _____ | c. _____ |
| d. _____ | d. _____ |

**2.** Read the paragraphs on "The Purchasing Process" on page 59. Complete the following activities on a separate sheet of paper:

    **a.** Prepare an outline of the paragraphs.

    **b.** Prepare a graphic representation of the steps leading up to the creation of a purchase order.

    **c.** Based on your notetaking, prepare a written summary of what is involved in obtaining goods from a supplier. Your instructor may ask you to present a verbal summary as well.

    **d.** Prepare vocabulary cards for any terms defined in the paragraphs.

## IMPROVE YOUR WRITING SKILLS

**Kinds of Sentences:** A sentence may be classified by its function. If a sentence expresses a statement of fact, opinion, or belief, it is a *declarative sentence.* Such a sentence ends with a period. For example:

> Manhattan is one of the five boroughs of New York City.
> Black shoes are more attractive than brown ones.

An *interrogative sentence* poses a question that requires a spoken or written answer. Such a sentence ends with a question mark:

> What do you plan to do after you graduate?
> Do you have a valid driver's license?

A sentence that expresses a command or a request that requires an action response, not a written or spoken answer, is an *imperative sentence.* This type of sentence also ends with a period:

> Return the top part of this statement with your payment.
> Would you please give a copy of this report to Frank.

# THE PURCHASING PROCESS

## Requisitions, orders, and receipts

The main function of industrial purchasing is to decide how much to buy, at what price, from whom, and when. These decisions are part of a purchasing process that uses a flow of information among the company departments that will use the goods bought, the purchasing department, and outside suppliers.

*INITIATING PURCHASES* The decision to buy goods and services usually originates within the department that is to use them. One of the tasks of production planning is to determine what starting materials must be bought. Other departments determine their need for supplies, equipment, and services in their own planning processes. The initiating department will also decide on the most desirable specifications of the goods or services to be bought. The required specifications are formally communicated to the purchasing department on a *purchase requisition*. This is a written request to obtain the goods or services described.

In practice, the exact specifications of purchases are often negotiable. Similar goods not exactly meeting the requesting department's specifications may serve the intended purpose as well or better. If these can be found at a lower price or from a more reliable supplier, exceptions may be made to the specifications.

*PURCHASING ACTIVITY* When a requisition has been received, actual purchasing activity begins. The main steps are to locate potential suppliers, determine prices, and issue a purchase order. For goods that are bought routinely and frequently, there may be no question about who the supplier will be or even about the price. For many purchases, however, an extensive search may have to be made to find suppliers capable of meeting required specifications. Purchasing agents rely heavily on experience and personal contacts to maintain a current stock of knowledge about the capabilities and reputations of suppliers. Prices may be accepted after a simple quotation, or they may require lengthy negotiation or multiple bids from different suppliers. Prices of some commodities—like vegetable oil, cocoa, or soybeans—change sharply from day to day. Purchasers who buy products like these must stay in constant contact with the trading places when prices are set.

When the supplier and price have been set, the purchasing agent issues a *purchase order*. This is a formal request for an outside supplier to provide goods or services. It is, in effect, a legal document setting forth the terms of the purchase . . .

*Source:* Lester R. Bittel *et al., Business in Action*, 3rd ed., Macmillan/McGraw-Hill, New York, 1988, p. 252. Reprinted with permission of the Glencoe Division of Macmillan/McGraw-Hill Publishing Company.

If a sentence expresses strong emotion or feeling, it is an *exclamatory sentence.* This type of sentence ends with an exclamation point:

Such a price is outrageous!
You're the grand prize winner!

## Practice

Read each sentence and indicate whether it is a declarative sentence (*D*), an interrogative sentence (*I*), an imperative sentence (*IM*), or an exclamatory sentence (*E*). Write your answer in the space provided, and insert the appropriate punctuation mark at the end of the sentence.

**1.** You may bring a guest with you           _____

**2.** We should leave around two o'clock this afternoon    _____

**3.** Does she plan to hire George          _____

**4.** When do we leave          _____

**5.** We need to mount an exciting publicity campaign    _____

**6.** Send in your payment today          _____

**7.** This is terrific          _____

**8.** Remember that all expense accounts must be turned in on Monday          _____

# 5 NOTETAKING SHORTCUTS

Good notetaking involves doing several tasks at once. For example, you must be a good listener and reader to recognize main ideas and to understand the organization of the material. While your brain is working to interpret and remember what you are hearing or reading, you are also hard at work writing. No wonder taking good, usable notes is a challenge!

In this chapter you will learn some techniques for making notetaking easier. These techniques will help you write quickly so that you can pay more attention to what is being said or what you are reading. Some of the techniques involve preparing yourself for notetaking. Other techniques are shortcuts in the writing process.

## PREPARING FOR NOTETAKING

Have you ever arrived at class late, your possessions helter-skelter, to find your instructor already into the lecture? Before you even sat down, you were well on the way to producing an incomplete, disorganized set of notes for the session. Or have you sat down to take notes on a difficult textbook chapter and had trouble because you had missed a couple of class sessions?

In both of these cases, the difficulty in taking good notes was caused by a lack of preparation. Being prepared can make the difference between staying on top of each course through good notetaking and falling behind. Here are some suggestions for making sure you are prepared to take good notes:

- *Attend class regularly.* One of the best ways to ensure that your notes are good is to attend class regularly. If you do this, your understanding of the subject will grow gradually, and your notes will reflect this. Rather than struggling to understand and write down something about which you know little or nothing, you are taking notes on material about which you have background knowledge. This makes it easier to recognize main ideas and write down what is important.

- *Keep up with reading assignments.* Keeping up with reading assignments is another way to make notetaking easier. If you read a related text chapter before attending class, your knowledge of the subject will help you take better classroom notes. Key words will be easier because you have seen them in writing; the sequence and importance of points will be clearer.

- *Keep your notetaking materials organized.* Make sure you have the right notebook, paper, pen, and other tools you need for each notetaking session *before* you start.

- *Prepare your paper ahead of time.* Take some time to rule a supply of notetaking paper with the sectioned paper format you are using for each course. That way you will not waste time ruling the paper before and during a lecture when you should be listening and writing.

- *Be on time.* It is very hard to pick up the organization of lecture material if you come in after the lecture starts. Get to class on time.

## WRITING SHORTCUTS

Being prepared is one way to free your mind so that you can concentrate on what you are hearing or reading while you are taking notes. Another way is to use shortcuts in the actual writing process. The less effort you spend on writing, the more attention you can pay to understanding and remembering.

There are several writing shortcuts that can improve your ability to take good notes. These include using shorthand, writing faster, using phrases, and using abbreviations and symbols.

## Using Shorthand

If you know a symbolic or alphabetic shorthand system such as Gregg shorthand or Speedwriting, you have an excellent skill that will prove very useful. Shorthand systems are designed to speed the writing process so that the notetaker can easily keep up with the pace of the speaker.

If you don't know shorthand, you can, over time, develop your own system for taking abbreviated notes. Using common symbols and abbreviations is one way to develop your own shorthand system.

## Writing Faster

If you don't know shorthand, you can try writing faster. Using a pen rather than a pencil will help you write more quickly. You should also use cursive writing, rather than printing, because the letters are linked and you don't waste time lifting the pen off the page in the middle of a word.

You might improve your writing speed by taking a close look at your handwriting. Do you use a lot of curlicues and fancy lettering? Eliminating nonessential lines will streamline your handwriting and improve your speed.

Practice writing quickly by copying a passage several times, keeping track of the amount of time it takes. You can keep doing this until you are satisfied with the increase in your speed. Remember, however, that writing faster is good *only if you can still read what you have written.*

## Using Phrases

You've been taught since elementary school to write in complete sentences. Well, in notetaking, complete sentences take too long to write. Using phrases when notetaking is not only acceptable, it is preferred.

For example, suppose your instructor said: "The majority of the labor force is now employed in service industries such as retailing, banking, food service, and health." Rather than copying this word for word, you can shorten the sentence to a phrase: "Most workers in service industries—retailing, banking, food service, health." Omit any words that aren't essential to the meaning of the sentence.

## Using Abbreviations and Symbols

There are many common abbreviations and symbols that you can use to shortcut the notetaking process. At first you may be a little hesitant to use abbreviations and symbols because you fear you may not be able to read your notes. You can overcome this by including a key to the abbreviations you use at the bottom of your page of notes. As you become more familiar with common abbreviations and symbols,

| TABLE 5-1 | COMMON SYMBOLS | |
| --- | --- | --- |
| | **Symbol** | **Meaning** |
| | @ | at |
| | &, + | and |
| | + | plus; in addition to; positive |
| | × | by, times (multiplied by) |
| | ÷ | divided by |
| | − | minus; subtracted from; negative |
| | ✔ | check |
| | ∴ | therefore |
| | ∴ | since; because |
| | . . . | and so on |
| | " | seconds; inches; ditto (same as above) |
| | ° | degree |
| | = | equals; is the same as |
| | ≠ | does not equal; is not the same as |
| | ' | feet |
| | < | is less than |
| | > | is greater than |
| | $ | dollars |
| | % | percent |
| | # | number (before a number); pounds (after a number) |
| | ¶ | paragraph |
| | ¢ | cents |

you will develop more confidence in your ability to read what you have written, and the need for a key will decrease. In addition, as time passes, you may even want to develop your own abbreviations to suit the vocabulary of a particular subject.

Among the words and phrases commonly abbreviated are months, days, dates, states, countries, names of organizations, proper names, compass points (north, east, and so on), measurements, and computer terms. Consult Appendix A in the back of this book or any dictionary for a list of common abbreviations.

Symbols can be time-savers as well. There are many common symbols from mathematics and logic that can be used to represent words and in some cases entire phrases, as shown in Table 5-1. Using symbols in place of words can cut down on your notetaking time considerably.

# SUMMARY

Notetaking shortcuts are techniques to help you write quickly so that you can pay more attention to what you are hearing or reading.

Being prepared will help you take more efficient notes, as will attending class regularly, keeping up with reading assignments, keeping your notetaking materials organized, preparing your paper ahead of time, and being punctual.

Writing shortcuts include using symbolic or alphabetic shorthand, writing faster, using phrases, and using abbreviations and symbols.

Name _____     Date _____

# CHAPTER 5 ACTIVITIES

## CHECK YOUR UNDERSTANDING

**1.** Why is it important to keep up with your coursework?

_____

_____

**2.** Briefly list three ways to prepare for taking notes.

_____

_____

_____

**3.** Describe three writing shortcuts that are helpful in notetaking.

_____

_____

**4.** Why is using phrases preferred in notetaking?

_____

**5.** What technique will help you recall abbreviations and symbols you've used in taking notes?

_____

## APPLY YOUR KNOWLEDGE

How ready are you for your classes? Complete the following checklist to evaluate your preparation:

| | Yes | No |
|---|---|---|
| • I attend each one of my classes regularly. | ✓ | |
| • I have chosen the appropriate sectioning format for taking notes for each one of my classes. | | ✓ |

- I section my paper for taking notes *before* going to class.

- I carry a pen and notebook paper to each one of my classes.

- I have a separate notebook for each class or a multi-subject divided notebook to use in taking notes.

- I am regularly on time for each class.

- I keep up with required reading assignments for each class.

- I feel prepared for the start of each class.

- I feel organized before class begins.

- I am motivated to get the most out of each class I attend.

1. For each *No* response you recorded to the checklist questions, ask "Why?" After analyzing the reason on a separate sheet of paper, take steps to alter your behavior to do what is needed to change each *No* answer to *Yes*.

2. For the following sentences, write phrases to take notes on what the instructor has said. Use notetaking shortcuts whenever possible.

| INSTRUCTOR'S WORDS | YOUR WRITTEN PHRASES |
|---|---|
| **a.** Earth Day represents a national effort to make people aware of environmental issues, for example, the destruction of native forests and the draining of wetlands. | _____ |
| **b.** People who start their own businesses are typically energetic, self-directed, creative, and confident. | _____ |
| **c.** To write an effective sales letter, develop each of these four points in your message: (1) attention to your message, (2) interest in the product, (3) desire for the product, and (4) action to take advantage of the offer. | _____ |

| INSTRUCTOR'S WORDS | YOUR WRITTEN PHRASES |
|---|---|

**d.** Countries that export natural oil have been able to make large profits in international trade. Often times this profit comes at the expense of oil importing countries, whose economies have suffered in paying for the oil shipments. _____

**3.** On a separate sheet of paper, write out fully the following passages. Consult Table 5-1 and Appendix A if you need help translating a notetaking abbreviation or symbol.

**a.** The person who says that our country can survive w/o sm bus is lacking in good judgment. Our econ life proves that big bus can't get along w/o sm bus.

**b.** If the total errors are ÷ total words, the % of accuracy is known.

**c.** When writing your report, ¶ whenever the subj chgs. This will help your reader focus attn on specific topics & understand your message. Also keep your ¶s rather short, w approx 8 typed lines in each ¶.

**d.** Fyi, the mdse is mfd by the Russ Co. Inc., which recently moved its hdqrs office from CO to WI. I have personally done bus w Mr. Russ & know him to be a coop, skilled mgr.

**4.** On a separate sheet of paper, rewrite the following passages using notetaking shortcuts. If you need help, consult Appendix A for a listing of abbreviations.

**a.** In 1984 the United States Department of Education ended a national study on the status of persons with disabilities. A large percentage of adults with disabilities were unemployed. However, those who had jobs usually received lower wages and had a less than an average opportunity for upward mobility. Only a very small percentage earned more than the minimum wage.

**b.** Are animals able to communicate with humans? The results of research studies with animals are unclear. Psychologists who have completed research select animals with a high intelligence quotient and social qualities because these are factors necessary to develop language in human beings. Experiments using sign language and word/concept representation by use of objects are presently being conducted to study possible animal communication with human beings.

## IMPROVE YOUR WRITING SKILLS

**Forming Noun Plurals:** A *common noun* is the name of a person, place, or thing:

| Person | Place | Thing |
|---|---|---|
| client | city | aspirin |
| attorney | street | wristwatch |
| neighbor | village | station wagon |

A *proper noun* is the name of a specific person, place, or thing:

| Person | Place | Thing |
|---|---|---|
| Mendez | Memphis | Bufferin |
| Gloria | West Street | Seiko |

To form plurals of nouns, add *es* to singular nouns that end in *s, x, z, ch,* and *sh.* Add *s* to most other singulars.

| ADD *S* | | ADD *ES* | |
|---|---|---|---|
| **Singular** | **Plural** | **Singular** | **Plural** |
| client | clients | Mendez | Mendezes |
| neighbor | neighbors | actress | actresses |
| attorney | attorneys | dish | dishes |
| Gloria | Glorias | wristwatch | wristwatches |
| Seiko | Seikos | lunch | lunches |
| Connelly | Connellys | gas | gases |

**Nouns That End in *Y*:** Nouns ending in *y* need special attention. For common nouns, if the *y* is preceded by a vowel, as in *attorney* above, then simply add *s*. But if the *y* is not preceded by a vowel, change the *y* to *i* and add *es*.

| Y PRECEDED BY A VOWEL | | Y NOT PRECEDED BY A VOWEL | |
|---|---|---|---|
| **Singular** | **Plural** | **Singular** | **Plural** |
| attorney | attorneys | city | cities |
| day | days | territory | territories |
| ploy | ploys | company | companies |
| guy | guys | lady | ladies |

For all proper nouns ending in *y*, simply add *s*, regardless of whether the *y* is preceded by a vowel:

### PROPER NOUNS ENDING IN *Y*

| Singular | Plural |
|----------|--------|
| Connelly | Connellys |
| Dougherty | Doughertys |
| Blaney | Blaneys |
| Devaney | Devaneys |

**Practice**

In the space provided, write the correct plural form of each noun.

1. chimney _____
2. scratch _____
3. agency _____
4. McCoy _____
5. tablecloth _____

6. carton _____
7. box _____
8. disease _____
9. Hillary _____
10. business _____

Now correct any errors in noun plurals in the following sentences.

11. How many orders did the representatives in those territorys receive in the past six months? _____

12. The Kellies and the Foxes rented cabins in the mountains for several summers in a row. _____

13. The secretaries and other employees need to order pencils and various other supplies. _____

14. Some of the carpenters developed callus from using hammers, saws, and other hand tools. _____

15. The trays were filled with radishes, onions, tomatos, peppers, and cucumbers. _____

16. States, counties, cities, villages—all need revenue from taxs to provide services. _____

**17.** Passengers on the flights of most airlines are not permitted to smoke cigares, cigarettes, or pipes.

_____

**18.** Will fake furs save the lives of many mink, beavers, walruses, and other animals?

_____

**19.** Both Patsys offered to pay for the pastrys and chocolates needed for the parties.

_____

**20.** The companies have spent thousands of dollars promoting new products in those territorys.

_____

# LISTENING IN THE CLASSROOM

You may feel you have mastered the basics of good notetaking. But consider: How good will your notes be if, like most of us, you have trouble listening and remembering what you hear? Notetaking in class depends upon good listening skill.

In Part 3 you will improve your listening skill and, consequently, your notetaking skill. You'll learn:

■ **What's involved in good listening.**

■ **Common barriers to good listening.**

■ **Techniques for effective listening.**

■ **Techniques for classroom notetaking.**

■ **How to review your classroom notes.**

# 6 LISTENING SKILLS

Did you know that most people spend more time listening than speaking, reading, or writing? As you communicate daily, research shows that 45 percent of your time is spent listening, while 30 percent is spent speaking, 16 percent reading, and 9 percent writing. Research also shows that most people listen with only 25 to 50 percent efficiency. Over half of what you hear you immediately forget!

Since much of what you learn in your classes comes from listening to instructors and other students, it is important to develop good listening skill. In this chapter, you'll learn what good listening involves and how to transcend the barriers that prevent people from listening. To improve your listening skill, you can learn to use specific techniques and to listen for main ideas during classroom lectures and discussions.

## WHAT IS GOOD LISTENING?

Here are some words that describe the word *listen: hear, observe, focus, pay attention, take notice,* and *lend an ear.* You can begin to see that good listening skill has many components.

Most of us have been blessed with the ability to hear, but hearing is not listening. When you hear, you sense sounds. When you listen, you sense sounds and your brain processes them to give them meaning. Thus listening is both a physical and mental activity. The sense of hearing is not the only sense involved in most listening situations. When you listen, you also see the speaker's expressions, body movements, and gestures. These contribute to your understanding of what you are hearing.

When you read, you can go over the words as many times as necessary in order to understand what you are reading. When you listen, you can't "re-listen" in order to understand what you are hearing. You have to listen efficiently the first time through the presentation. This requires an active commitment on your part. You must *want* to listen to the speaker and believe that the speaker has knowledge that is important to you. You should keep an open mind so that you can understand what the speaker is saying even though you may not always agree with it.

Good listening means you are interacting with the speaker, thinking about what has been said and anticipating what will be said. You are mentally summarizing what you have heard. You are giving the speaker your full attention, ignoring distractions and resisting the temptation to daydream. As you can see, self-discipline is required if you want to become an active, good listener.

## BARRIERS TO GOOD LISTENING

To become a good listener, you must understand the barriers that prevent people from listening efficiently. Then you can overcome these barriers as you encounter them:

**1.** *You know too much.* Some listeners feel that they know enough about a topic, therefore, listening to the speaker is unnecessary. You should keep an open mind and pay attention—there is generally something new to be learned in almost all messages.

**2.** *You know too little.* Some listeners feel their knowledge of the subject is so limited that they can't understand what is being said. You can try to avoid this situation by familiarizing yourself with the topic before the lecture, perhaps by reading related assignments.

**3.** *You pay too much attention to the speaker's appearance or voice.* Some listeners dwell on the dress, weight, hair, accent, voice, or other attributes of the speaker and focus on this, rather than on what is being said. Good listeners concentrate on the information presented by the speaker and not on his or her personal characteristics.

**4.** *The speaker is too controversial.* When a lecture or discussion is on a controversial topic, it is easy to stop listening if you disagree with the speaker. You should not let personal bias interfere with your ability to listen to the message. Perhaps you will understand why others hold opinions that differ from yours.

**5.** *The speaker is too slow. All* speakers are too slow, simply because your brain can process what it hears far faster than people can talk. The average person speaks at the rate of 125 to 150 words a minute, but the average listener can comprehend up to 500 words a minute. A poor listener fills in the extra time with daydreaming; a good listener reviews and anticipates the content of the lecture or discussion.

If you have permitted some of these barriers to influence your listening behavior in the past, you may find that poor listening is affecting your ability to get the most out of class sessions. In addition, if you are accustomed to watching a lot of television, which generally requires little mental effort, you may have difficulty adjusting to the active effort required to listen to a class lecture.

## TECHNIQUES FOR EFFECTIVE LISTENING

As a student, it is important for you to be able to listen and understand what goes on in the classroom so that you have information to use when studying. Practice the following techniques to become an active listener who can hear and understand the spoken word.

**1.** *Prepare.* Many instructors distribute a course syllabus showing the topics to be discussed and the reading assignments that are due each time the class meets. Read the assignments before class so that you know the lecture topic and are familiar with any new or unusual terms. Preparing beforehand will provide you with sufficient information to understand the lecture. It will also allow you to examine any barriers you may have and to deal with them before going to class.

**2.** *Sit near the speaker.* Sit toward the front of the classroom where you can see and hear the person delivering the lecture. You can also see the chalkboard, slides, and transparencies better when you sit close to the front. Sitting near the lecturer also helps you ignore distractions that occur in a class. Movements within the class will be behind you, allowing you to concentrate on what the instructor is saying.

**3.** *Pay attention.* Concentrate. Have the desire to listen to everything the speaker says. Keep your mind active. Learn how to fill in the gaps of time between the rate of the speaker's lecture and the rate at which you can comprehend the speaker's words.

**4.** *Anticipate.* In the gaps of time during the lecture, try to guess what the speaker will say next. This activity helps you listen attentively.

**5.** *Process.* Think about the message and what it means. Can you relate the information to your personal life, your goals, and your experiences? Processing the message in terms of your own interests will help you pay attention.

**6.** *Ask questions.* Formulate questions as the instructor is presenting the information. The answers to your questions may come as the lecture moves along, or there may be time later to ask your questions. Developing questions keeps your mind active and improves your concentration.

**7.** *Summarize.* Periodically during the lecture, use any free time to summarize what has been said. Summarizing helps you understand the message and to anticipate ideas and information to come.

**8.** *Give feedback.* During the lecture, you can demonstrate your ability to listen by giving the instructor feedback. This can be done by nodding your head to show agreement or understanding, by maintaining appropriate eye contact and leaning toward the speaker to show interest, and by showing understanding or lack of understanding through your facial expressions. This two-way communication between the speaker and the listener gives important feedback to the speaker and helps the listener practice good listening skills.

## LISTENING FOR MAIN IDEAS

In a lecture situation, you can't backtrack through what has been said in order to determine the main ideas of the presentation. You need to recognize main ideas as they are presented so that you can listen for supporting details and examples and understand the framework of the lecture topic.

Many cues or signals can help you recognize the main points of a lecture. Most of these involve understanding your instructor's approach to a lecture and the words and phrases he or she will use to introduce important topics.

**1.** *Previewing.* Your instructor may begin the class period by previewing the lecture and highlighting the main topics for discussion. In this preview you are given a spoken outline of the lecture, including the main topics and subtopics.

**2.** *Repetition.* An instructor may emphasize the main ideas of the lecture by making statements and then repeating them in a different manner.

**3.** *Writing.* Sometimes main ideas are written on the chalkboard or presented on transparencies or slides. On occasion the outline of the lecture may even be written on the chalkboard.

**4.** *Introductory phrases.* Certain phrases may signal the introduction of a main point. Examples of these phrases are "Today I will cover the following topics . . . ," "Next, let's take a look at . . . ," "Don't forget that . . . ," "It is important to note that . . . ."

**5.** *Gestures.* The instructor may use gestures to indicate main topics. The person may raise fingers to indicate the first, second, and third points. He or she may emphasize the importance of a topic by hitting a desk or the chalkboard. A pause may be used to indicate that here is an important point to be discussed. After listening to your instructor two or three times, you will be able to detect the announcement of the main points.

**6.** *Volume.* The instructor's voice, whether loud or soft, can be a clue to the significance of what is being said.

**7.** *Definitions and enumerations.* Definitions and enumerations (lists) usually signal main ideas and should be written down.

Whether the lecturer adds stories to keep the class interested, or strays off the topics, these clues to listen for the main points will help you to be a better listener.

## SUMMARY

Listening is the most frequently used communication skill, but most people listen with only 25 to 50 percent efficiency. Good listening is an active mental process that can involve both hearing and sight. Becoming a good listener means overcoming the barriers to good listening. These barriers include feeling that you know too much or too little about the topic; focusing on the personal characteristics of the speaker; tuning out controversial subjects; and filling in the time lag between speaking and listening by daydreaming.

Some techniques for effective listening include preparing for the lecture, sitting near the speaker, paying attention, anticipating what will be said, processing what you hear, asking or formulating questions, summarizing, and giving feedback. To listen effectively to a lecture, you must recognize main ideas. Main ideas are often signaled by previewing, repetition, writing, introductory phrases, gestures, volume of voice, definitions, and enumerations.

Name _____  Date _____

# CHAPTER 6 ACTIVITIES

## CHECK YOUR UNDERSTANDING

**1.** What is the difference between hearing and listening?

_____

_____

**2.** Briefly describe three barriers to good listening.

_____

_____

_____

**3.** Before the instructor starts lecturing, what should you have done to ensure that you will be a good listener?

_____

_____

**4.** What can you do to be an active listener during a lecture?

_____

_____

**5.** List five cues, or signals, that indicate a main idea during a lecture or speech.

_____

_____

_____

## EVALUATE YOUR LISTENING SKILLS

**1.** How do you measure up as a listener? Whether you are part of a one-on-one conversation or a student attending a lecture, listening is important.

**Directions:** Read the questions listed below, and rate yourself on each one of the listening characteristics, by circling the appropriate number. Use the scale to test your listening effectiveness: 4 = Always; 3 = Almost Always; 2 = Sometimes; 1 = Never

| Listening Characteristic | Response |
|---|---|
| **a.** Do I allow the speaker to express his or her thoughts without interrupting? | 1  2  3  4 |
| **b.** Do I have the desire to listen to everything that is said? | 1  2  3  4 |
| **c.** Do I actively try to develop the ability to remember important facts? | 1  2  3  4 |
| **d.** Do I write down the most important details of a message? | 1  2  3  4 |
| **e.** Do I listen to the speaker even though the message may seem dull? | 1  2  3  4 |
| **f.** Do I listen to the speaker although I don't personally like the speaker? | 1  2  3  4 |
| **g.** Do I ignore distractions when listening? | 1  2  3  4 |
| **h.** Do I display a genuine desire to listen to others speak? | 1  2  3  4 |
| **i.** Do I keep listening to what someone is saying although I may not agree with it? | 1  2  3  4 |
| **j.** Do I avoid daydreaming by anticipating what the speaker will say next? | 1  2  3  4 |

*Scoreboard:* Give yourself 4 points for every "4" you circled, 3 points for every "3," etc. Then total your points:

30–40 points  You listen effectively. Congratulations!
20–29 points  You are a good listener, but can work on further improvement.
10–19 points  You need help! Review the good listening techniques in Chapter 6, and resolve to improve your listening skills.

## PRACTICE YOUR LISTENING SKILLS

**1.** Read the selection on page 83 in preparation for the lecture your instructor will give on "The Role of Management in Business."

# 1 MANAGEMENT DEFINED

## Attaining results with the help of others

The managers of all businesses, small as well as large, must perform the same functions as the managers of CIGNA. As compared with the millions of employees everywhere who perform the actual day-to-day work of a business—working at machines and desks and sales counters—managers make a uniquely different contribution to the business. They are charged with planning, overseeing, and coordinating the work activities of other people. To succeed in business, it is essential for you to understand the difference between the work of managers and the work of nonmanagers.

The process of planning, organizing, directing, and controlling the use of a firm's resources to effectively and economically attain its objectives is called *management*. A business can be viewed as a system: a group of related parts organized to work together for some purpose. Management is the function that integrates the parts of this system and makes sure that they work together toward a desired purpose. *Administration* is another term with nearly the same meaning, though it is more often used to refer to the management of institutions, such as schools or hospitals. It may, however, also be applied to business firms, particularly to the functions of higher-level management.

# MANAGERS

## Perform common duties although exact roles differ

*MANAGER* A person who performs the unique work of management is called a manager. That is, a *manager* plans, organizes, directs, and controls a company's business.

An important characteristic of managers is that they do their jobs by working with and through *other people*. If the manager of a furniture plant wishes to manufacture a thousand coffee tables, he or she does not go to the plant and start producing them. The manager directs other employees to do the work. When directly creating products, a manager is not performing the management function.

In many small businesses, managers work only part-time at management. They then devote the rest of their time to selling, production, or some other business function. A carpenter who heads a crew of workers for a construction company has a similar role. Half of the carpenter's time may be spent actually using the tools of the trade, while the remainder of the time may be spent telling others what to do and checking the quality of their work. The latter exemplify the true management functions.

*Source:* Lester R. Bittel *et al.*, *Business in Action*, 3rd ed., Macmillan/McGraw-Hill, New York, 1988, p. 101. Reprinted with permission of the Glencoe Division of Macmillan/McGraw-Hill Publishing Company.

2. As your instructor presents the lecture, jot down the points you think are important.

3. After "listening" to the lecture and using your notes, answer the following questions:

   a. What are some of the reasons people want to be managers?

   _____

   _____

   b. What is the definition of *management*? _____

   _____

   _____

   c. How many categories can the roles of managers be divided into? _____ Name them. _____

   _____

   _____

   d. What are the main points to remember about each type of management role? _____

   _____

   _____

4. Your instructor has two additional lectures that may be given in class. If the lectures are given, take notes and be prepared to answer similar questions about them. The more you practice, the better your listening skill will become!

## IMPROVE YOUR WRITING SKILLS

**Possessive Nouns:**   The *possessive form* of a noun shows ownership. To form the possessive of a plural noun that ends in *s*, add only an apostrophe ( ' ).

| Plural Noun ending in *s* | Possessive Form |
| --- | --- |
| managers | managers' |
| states | states' |
| actresses | actresses' |
| employees | employees' |
| babies | babies' |

For plural nouns that do not end in *s*, add *'s* to form the possessive.

| Plural Noun Form | Possessive Form |
|---|---|
| women | women's |
| children | children's |
| alumni | alumni's |
| oxen | oxen's |

For all singular nouns, add *'s* to form the possessive:

| Singular Noun Form | Possessive Form |
|---|---|
| employee | employee's |
| boss | boss's |
| actress | actress's |
| Marx | Marx's |
| Wilson | Wilson's |
| James | James's |
| Dr. Jones | Dr. Jones's |

*Note this exception:* In some possessive constructions, the additional "s" sound of the *'s* is not pronounced because it sounds rather awkward. In such cases, use only the apostrophe, without the *s*, to form the possessive.

Mendez    Mendez' ("Mendezes" would sound awkward.)

## Practice

Write the possessive form of the following nouns.

**1.** secretary    _____

**2.** waitress    _____

**3.** Fritz    _____

**4.** Ms. Devoe    _____

**5.** the Lutzes    _____

**6.** ladies    _____

**7.** Parrish    _____

**8.** programmer    _____

**9.** plaintiff    _____

**10.** parent _____

**11.** attendants _____

**12.** attorney _____

**13.** judge _____

**14.** Tex _____

**15.** grandchildren _____

Now correct any errors in the use of possessive forms in the following sentences.

**16.** According to Jane's letter, the Jones'es house on Willis Avenue is for sale. _____

**17.** This publisher's specialty is childrens' books. _____

**18.** The store sells ladies's and men's clothing. _____

**19.** Bess' recommendation is that we accept Felix's proposal. _____

**20.** Both customer's complaints deal with the manufacturer's limited warranty. _____

**21.** Patsy's opinion is that the project will be at least two day's work. _____

**22.** The patient's car was in the doctors' parking space. _____

**23.** Does the mayor's statement conflict with the governor? _____

**24.** The sale's price published in the store's ad was incorrect. _____

**25.** Don's ability to gain employee's support enables him to meet some of the firm's goals. _____

# 7 TAKING CLASSROOM NOTES

**TIPS FOR CLASSROOM NOTETAKING**

**REVIEWING CLASSROOM NOTES**
Editing Notes
Using the Recall Notes
Summarizing

**SUMMARY**

**CHAPTER 7 ACTIVITIES**

**CHECK YOUR UNDERSTANDING**

**REVIEW TEN STEPS TO GOOD NOTETAKING**

**PRACTICE YOUR EDITING SKILLS**

**WRITE, EDIT, REVIEW, AND SUMMARIZE YOUR LECTURE NOTES**

**IMPROVE YOUR WRITING SKILLS**

Even good listening skill is not enough to ensure that you will remember most of what you have heard in a classroom. Studies have shown that you probably will forget 80 percent or more of what you have heard within two weeks. In order to remember more of what you hear, you must take notes during lectures.

You have already learned basic notetaking techniques in Chapters 4 and 5. In this chapter you will learn specific strategies for taking notes while listening to classroom lectures and discussions. You will also learn how to review and study the notes you have taken during class.

## TIPS FOR CLASSROOM NOTETAKING

Taking notes in class involves listening and writing at the same time, so you should record only what is necessary in order to keep from falling behind. Necessary information, generally, includes main ideas, supporting details, defined terms, and examples. Here are some suggestions to help you take notes efficiently:

**1.** *Section your paper.* Use the most appropriate notetaking format (see Chapter 4), and section the paper before you go to class. Remember to use only one side of the paper.

**2.** *Label each page.* Record the course name, instructor, date, lecture subject, and page number at the top of each day's page(s) of notes. If your pages get out of order when you study, it will be easy to rearrange them.

**3.** *Use a pen.* Notes written with a pen are faster to take, easier to read, and more permanent than notes written with a pencil. Be sure to have a spare pen handy in case you run out of ink!

**4.** *Be ready.* Be prepared to take notes the moment the instructor starts the class. At the end of class, make sure the instructor has finished before you pack up your notetaking supplies.

**5.** *Use outline format if possible.* If the lecturer has provided an outline of the lecture, either on the board or in a preview, follow the outline in your notetaking. When you are not furnished an outline in advance, you will have to organize your notes as you go. Use these techniques:

- Listen for main ideas and record them in the left column of your paper.
- Indent supporting details and examples.
- Place definitions at the left side of the main section.
- Identify headings that introduce enumerations, or lists, at the left side of the main column. Indent each item in the list.
- Write down all words or illustrations written on the board or shown on visuals. Label this material with a circled letter *V*.
- Leave a line of space blank to show a change in subject matter.

**6.** *Label opinions.* If you record opinions expressed by the instructor, label them in your notes with a circled letter *O* or with brackets (*[ ]*) around the statement.

**7.** *Be prepared to take notes during discussions.* The instructor may provide important details during discussions that are not included in the formal lecture.

You may be wondering how many notes to take. There is no definite amount. The appropriate amount of notetaking will vary with the subject and the instructor.

You will develop a feel for what needs to be recorded after sitting through two or three classes. If you aren't sure whether something is worth recording, record it. Remember, you will not have a second chance to take notes on a lecture. When you review your notes after class, you can decide what is important and ignore the rest.

## REVIEWING CLASSROOM NOTES

During the class session, you are busy listening for information and recording significant ideas and facts. To help fix the information in your memory, review your notes and edit them into usable form for studying. Spend a few minutes reviewing the lecture while it is still fresh in your mind. Then write a brief summary of the lecture at the end of the notes.

### Editing Notes

As soon as possible after class—always within 24 hours—review and recite your notes. Read through them to determine if they make sense. Are there gaps in places where you missed a linking idea? Are headings, especially for lists, missing? Is anything unclear? If the information is still fresh in your mind, you may be able to fill in the missing parts. Otherwise, see if your textbook or a classmate can clarify the information. If this doesn't work, talk with your instructor.

Edit or revise your notes by filling in any missing information and clarifying anything that is unclear. Don't rewrite; this is a waste of

| | |
|---|---|
| | *Microcomputer Applications, DeStefano* |
| | *Computer Graphics, Oct. 25* |
| | |
| *Uses* | *Comp. graph. used in* |
| | *entertainment—video games* |
| | *media—TV commercials, ads, etc.* |
| | *bus.—graphs, diagrams, visuals* |
| | |
| *Types of bus. graphics* | *Two types of graphics software for bus.* |
| *software* | *1. analytic graphics pkgs—take* |
| | *numeric data & display them graphically* |
| | *2. presentation graphics packages—* |
| | *design visuals* |
| | |
| *Features of analytic* | *Analytic graphics pkgs* |
| *graphics pkgs* | *offer different types of graphs* |
| | *add labels to graph* |
| | *plot graphs from numeric data* |
| *Types of graphs* | *Types of graphs* |
| | *line* |
| | *bar* |
| | *pie chart* |
| | |
| *Labels* | *Labels* |
| | *parts of graph* |
| | *title* |

Classroom notes with editing

time. When the notes are complete, use a highlighter or a pen to underscore the main ideas. Write recall notes in the left-hand column reserved for this purpose.

## Using the Recall Notes

During the 24-hour period after the class session, review the lecture by using the recall notes. Turn each recall note into a question and recite the answer. For example, one of the recall notes in the illustration on page 90 says "Types of graphs." You can turn this into "What types of graphs can analytic graphics software prepare?" After you answer the question, check your notes to see if you recalled the information. Turning each recall note into a question to be answered can help you (1) understand the information presented in class, (2) fix the information firmly in your memory, and (3) prepare for the next class session.

## Summarizing

Finally, write a brief summary of the lecture at the end of your notes to ensure you understand the material. You can use this summary to review right before the next class session. You can do a quick review of the entire course by reading all these summaries in sequence.

## SUMMARY

Taking notes during classroom lectures and discussions helps you understand and remember what you have heard. Suggestions for classroom notetaking include sectioning and labeling each page, using a pen, taking notes from start to finish during a class, using an outline format when possible, labeling opinions, and taking notes during discussions.

Classroom notes should be reviewed within 24 hours to improve retention of information. When reviewing classroom notes, edit them by filling in missing or unclear information. Highlight or underscore main ideas, and add recall notes. The lecture can be reviewed by turning each recall note into a question and answering it. Last, a brief summary of the lecture should be written at the end of the notes.

Name                                                    Date

# CHAPTER 7 ACTIVITIES

## CHECK YOUR UNDERSTANDING

**1.** List three notetaking tips that can improve your classroom note-taking.

_____

_____

**2.** What should you look for when you first review your classroom notes?

_____

_____

**3.** What should you add to your notes during this review?

_____

_____

**4.** How can recall notes be used while studying?

_____

_____

**5.** What is the purpose of summarizing the notes?

_____

_____

## TEN STEPS TO GOOD NOTETAKING

Copy the following "Notetaking Checklist" in a place where it will always be handy—on a 3- × 5-inch index card or on the first page of your notebook. Take a few minutes to review the ten steps before each class lecture for the next week or two until you've "got them down pat."

**Notetaking Checklist**

1. Section the paper.
2. Label the paper.
3. Outline the lecture.
4. Record main points, supporting details, and examples.
5. Record and identify information from visuals.
6. Record examples and important ideas.
7. Edit notes within 24 hours of each lecture.
8. Write recall notes.
9. Create questions from recall notes.
10. Summarize notes.

## PRACTICE YOUR EDITING SKILLS

The lecture notes below are from a psychology lecture on "How Humans Learn." The lecturer started by asking, "What is learning?"

Instincts—biologically determined/
   imp to survival Ex spider & web
Reflexes—inborn, unlearned
   Ex blink at bright light
Learning—permanent change in behavior
   1. Habituation—simplest, get used
      to something
   2. Associative—form assoc
      between 2 events
      a. classical conditioning
         Ex Pavlov & his dogs
      b. operant conditioning
         consequences of behavior
         determine whether it
         will be repeated
   3. Cognitive—mental activity
      between stimulus & response

and then proceeded to describe the types of learning. The notes are incomplete; some editing is needed to make the notes usable for study. Edit the notes by:

**1.** Inserting a heading.
**2.** Adding recall notes.
**3.** Writing questions based on the recall notes.

_____

_____

_____

_____

_____

_____

**4.** Writing the answers to the questions.

_____

_____

_____

**5.** Summarizing the notes.

_____

_____

_____

_____

## WRITE, EDIT, REVIEW, AND SUMMARIZE YOUR LECTURE NOTES

Your instructor will be presenting a brief lecture that might be given in a business communications class. The title of the lecture is "The Bad News Letter."

**1.** As you "listen" to the lecture, take notes.

**2.** When the lecture is over, edit your notes.

**3.** Using your recall notes, write three or four questions to ask yourself.

a. _____

b. _____

c. _____

d. _____

**4.** Summarize your notes.

_____

_____

## IMPROVE YOUR WRITING SKILLS

**Verbs:** The parts of most verbs are formed in a highly regular manner, for example:

| Present Tense | Third-Person Singular | Past Tense | Past Participle | Present Participle |
|---|---|---|---|---|
| work | works | worked | worked | working |
| deny | denies | denied | denied | denying |
| play | plays | played | played | playing |
| raise | raises | raised | raised | raising |
| spot | spots | spotted | spotted | spotting |

A number of commonly used verbs, however, are very irregular. Of these, the verb *to be* is the most irregular of all: it has eight parts instead of the normal five.

| To Be | Examples |
|---|---|
| am | I am in my office. |
| is | He is in a position to assist you. |
| are | They (or we) are almost certain to get the ontract. |
| was | I was at work, but he was at his home. |
| were | Their prices were much lower last year. |

| To Be | Examples |
|-------|----------|
| been | A new model should have been available last onth. |
| | Pat has been our manager for three years. |
| being | She is being unusually cooperative. |
| be | He will be our next sales manager. |
| | Sue suggested that he be more enthusiastic. |
| | Be careful when you unpack those boxes. |

The verbs *to do* and *to have* are also commonly used irregular verbs, as illustrated here:

| To Do, To Have | Examples |
|----------------|----------|
| do | We do our share of the work. |
| does | It does little good to call them. |
| did | He did as much as he could. |
| done | The work was done by her. |
| doing | Dick is doing a good job. |
| | |
| have | I have a copy of the program. |
| has | Beth has excellent academic credentials. |
| had | He had an opportunity to work for them. |
| had | All of them have had the usual childhood diseases. |
| having | They are having a farewell party for her. |

As these examples illustrate, each part of *to be, to do, to have,* and other verbs may be used as the main verb in a sentence or clause. Unlike other verbs, however, the various parts of *to be, to do,* and *to have* are frequently also used as helping verbs. For example:

| | | | |
|---|---|---|---|
| am going | is allowed | are tested | was delivered |
| were signed | has made | had tried | does permit |

If a sentence expresses a condition that is not true, is not possible, or is very doubtful, use *were* instead of *was.* Such a condition may be indicated by *if, as if, as though,* or *wish.*

If I were in charge of the project, I would handle it differently.

He wishes that he were able to spend more time out of the office.

## Practice

Decide which form of the verb shown in parentheses is correct; then underline it.

**1.** I (*am, be, is*) certain that he (*has, have*) made other plans.

**2.** We (*had, have*) an opportunity to meet with him while he (*was, were*) here yesterday.

**3.** Bill (*am, are, is*) sure that Nancy (*has, have*) (*did, done*) everything possible to help them.

**4.** While you (*was, were*) out of the office, Paul (*did, done*) most of your work.

**5.** (*Was, Were*) the projected work completed last week, or (*are, is*) some of the work still in progress?

**6.** Both firms (*was, were*) reported to be interested in the property, but neither (*has, have*) made an offer to purchase it.

**7.** Such an assignment (*do, does*) seem strange, (*doesn't, don't*) it?

**8.** If Grace (*was, were*) in the office yesterday, I (*did, do*) not see her.

**9.** Mike acts as if he (*was, were*) the project leader, but he (*is, was, were*) not involved with the project in any way.

**10.** She (*don't, doesn't*) know when the price increase (*was, were*) put into effect.

Name                                                    Date

# PART 3 PROJECT

## YOUR OBJECTIVES

When you complete this project, you will have demonstrated your ability to:

- Listen effectively.
- Identify main ideas.
- Take effective notes while listening to lectures.
- Review and edit your notes.

**Directions:** In Chapters 6 and 7, you learned that good listening alone is not enough to ensure that you will remember what you have heard in the classroom. In order to remember more of what you hear, you must take good notes.

This project is designed to improve your listening skill and your notetaking skill. A series of ten lectures is recorded on the cassette tape. The lectures vary in subject, length, and difficulty. In completing this project, you should follow the steps listed here in your text. These steps will tell you when to turn on the tape recorder and listen to a lecture. After you listen to a lecture, you should turn back to these instructions and complete the activities that are listed. As you complete the project, be sure to follow the instructions carefully and answer the questions completely.

This project will provide you with all the practice you need to listen and take notes effectively in all of your courses.

**Listening to the Tapes:** In Part 3 you learned the techniques for effective listening and classroom notetaking. Now practice your skills by following these steps in sequence.

## Lecture #1: Painting

### Step 1. *Gather materials for notetaking.*

Make sure you have plenty of paper and pens or pencils before you begin listening to the lecture.

**Step 2.** *Turn on your tape recorder and listen to the introduction.*

**Step 3.** *Listen to Lecture #1 and take notes on the lecture.*

Lecture #1 is three minutes in length. Listen to the lecture, and when you are instructed to turn off the tape recorder, do so and then turn to this page in your text.

**Step 4.** *Review your notes.*

- Are they organized?
- Are the listings orderly and are they labeled 1, 2, 3, etc.?
- Do your notes appear to contain complete information on the important points made in the lecture?

**Step 5.** *Write a brief summary of the lecture.*

**Step 6.** *Check the organization of your notes.*

- The main subject of the lecture was the nine kinds of subjects that a painter may choose to use for a painting. Do you have numbers 1 through 9 listed in your notes? Do you have a subject written next to each number? Here are the nine subjects that should appear in your notes: landscape, portraits, figures, still lifes, animals, history, religion and mythology, everyday life, and dreams.
- Under each of the nine headings, you should have a few details to explain the subject in more detail.
- Are your notes missing any of these points? If so, listen to the lecture again so your notes will be complete before answering the questions that follow.

**Step 7.** *Answer questions based on the notes you took while listening to the lecture.*

Write your answers in the space provided.

**1.** How many different subjects may be used by a painter for making a picture?

_____

_____

**2.** What is the subject of this lecture?

_____

_____

**3.** What is the oldest type of subject that has been used by painters?

_____

_____

**4.** In what two types of paintings is the painter left to use his or her imagination?

_____

_____

### Step 8. *Check your answers.*

See if you have answered these questions correctly by checking your answers with those provided on page 117.

### Step 9. *Review.*

Were you able to answer all the questions correctly? If you did, congratulations, you are on your way toward becoming a good notetaker. If you had problems answering any of the questions, listen to the lecture again and fill in any missing information in your notes.

## Lecture #2: Résumé Preparation

### Step 1. *Gather materials for notetaking.*

Make sure you have plenty of paper and pens or pencils before you begin listening to the lecture.

### Step 2. *Turn on your tape recorder.*

### Step 3. *Listen to Lecture #2 and take notes on the lecture.*

Lecture #2 is three minutes in length. Listen to the lecture, and when you are instructed to turn off the tape recorder, do so and then turn to this page in your text.

**Step 4. *Review your notes.***

Answer the following questions about your notes:

■ Are they organized?

■ Are the listings orderly and are they labeled 1, 2, 3, etc.?

■ Do your notes appear to contain complete information on the important points made in the lecture?

**Step 5. *Write a brief summary of the lecture.***

**Step 6. *Check the organization of your notes.***

■ The main subject of the lecture was the preparation of the one-page résumé. There were seven items discussed as part of the résumé. You should have numbers 1 through 7 appearing in your notes and a subject head for each number. The seven subject heads are:

1. Name, address, telephone number
2. Education
3. Work experience
4. Skills
5. Awards, scholarships, special achievements
6. Hobbies and interests
7. References

■ After each of the seven headings, you should have explanatory information.

■ Are your notes missing any of these points? If so, listen to the lecture again so your notes will be complete before answering the questions that follow.

**Step 7. *Answer questions based on the notes you took while listening to the lecture.***

Write your answers in the space provided.

**1.** How many pages should be used for writing your résumé?

_____

_____

**2.** How many items that may appear on a résumé were discussed in the lecture?

_____

**3.** What is the last item to appear on the résumé?

_____

**4.** What is the first item to appear on the résumé?

_____

**5.** Identify some words that show action and are good to use to describe experiences you have had.

_____

**6.** Which item on the résumé has no direct link to the job you are applying for, but yet an employer likes to see it on a résumé?

_____

**7.** Why does the employer want to know your hobbies and interests?

_____

**8.** What two parts of the résumé are listed in chronological order?

_____

**Step 8.** *Check your answers.*

See if you have answered these questions correctly by checking your answers with those provided on page 117.

**Step 9.** *Review.*

Were you able to answer all the questions correctly? If you did, congratulations, you are on your way toward becoming a good notetaker. If you had problems answering any of the questions, listen to the lecture again and fill in any missing information in your notes.

## Lecture #3: Hummingbird

**Step 1.** *Gather materials for notetaking.*

Make sure you have plenty of paper and pens or pencils before you begin listening to the lecture.

**Step 2.** *Turn on your tape recorder.*

**Step 3.** *Listen to Lecture #3 and take notes on the lecture.*

Lecture #3 is three minutes in length. Listen to the lecture, and when you are instructed to turn off the tape recorder, do so and then turn to this page in your text.

**Step 4.** *Review your notes.*

Answer the following questions about your notes:

■ Are they organized?
■ Are the listings orderly and are they labeled 1, 2, 3, etc.?
■ Do your notes appear to contain complete information on the important points made in the lecture?

**Step 5.** *Write a brief summary of the lecture.*

**Step 6.** *Answer questions based on the notes you took while listening to the lecture.*

Write your answers in the space provided.

**1.** How many different types of birds are there in the world?

_____

**2.** What four things do all birds have in common?

_____

_____

**3.** What are the four items that make the hummingbird unique?

_____

_____

_____

**4.** Four facts were provided about hummingbirds—what are these four facts?

_____

_____

_____

**5.** What do you know about the bee hummingbird?

_____

**6.** What is the name of the largest hummingbird?

_____

**Step 7.** *Check your answers.*

See if you have answered these questions correctly by checking your answers with those provided on page 118.

**Step 8.** *Review.*

Were you able to answer all the questions correctly? If you did, congratulations, you are on your way toward becoming a good notetaker. If you had problems answering any of the questions, listen to the lecture again and fill in any missing information in your notes.

## Lecture #4: Northern Lights

**Step 1.** *Gather materials for notetaking.*

Make sure you have plenty of paper and pens or pencils before you begin listening to the lecture.

**Step 2.** *Turn on your tape recorder.*

**Step 3.** *Listen to Lecture #4 and take notes on the lecture.*

Lecture #4 is three minutes in length. Listen to the lecture, and when you are instructed to turn off the tape recorder, do so and then turn to this page in your text.

**Step 4.** *Review your notes.*

Answer the following questions about your notes:

- Are they organized?
- Are the listings orderly and are they labeled 1, 2, 3, etc.?
- Do your notes appear to contain complete information on the important points made in the lecture?

**Step 5.** *Write a brief summary of the lecture.*

**Step 6.** *Check the organization of your notes.*

- The first section of your notes should contain introductory material in which you recorded the terms sunspot, sunstorm, and solar flares.

■ The next section of your notes should provide information on the Northern Lights or the Aurora Borealis and how this glow was named. You should also have information about the three different forms or appearances this glow can take on. Colors of the lights should be listed with green as the most common color seen.

**Step 7.** *Answer questions based on the notes you took while listening to the lecture.*

Write your answers in the space provided.

**1.** What does Aurora Borealis mean?

_____

**2.** What are the three forms the lights may take on in the sky?

_____

_____

**3.** What colors are most commonly seen in the Northern Lights?

_____

**4.** What person was among the first to link the Aurora Borealis to electricity?

_____

**5.** When is the best time to view the Northern Lights?

_____

**Step 8.** *Check your answers.*

See if you have answered these questions correctly by checking your answers with those provided on page 118.

**Step 9.** *Review.*

Were you able to answer all the questions correctly? If you did, congratulations, you are on your way toward becoming a good notetaker. If you had problems answering any of the questions, listen to the lecture again and fill in any missing information in your notes.

## Lecture #5: The Changing American Family

**Step 1. *Gather materials for notetaking.***

Make sure you have plenty of paper and pens or pencils before you begin listening to the lecture.

**Step 2. *Turn on your tape recorder.***

**Step 3. *Listen to Lecture #5 and take notes on the lecture.***

Lecture #5 is five minutes in length. Listen to the lecture, and when you are instructed to turn off the tape recorder, do so and then turn to this page in your text.

**Step 4. *Review your notes.***

Answer the following questions about your notes:

- Are they organized?
- Are the listings orderly and are they labeled 1, 2, 3, etc.?
- Do your notes appear to contain complete information on the important points made in the lecture?

**Step 5. *Write a brief summary of the lecture.***

**Step 6. *Answer questions based on the notes you took while listening to the lecture.***

Write your answers in the space provided.

**1.** What are the statistics regarding the increasing number of women in the workforce?

_____

_____

_____

**2.** With mother and father working, what changes have occurred in family living?

_____

_____

**3.** What are the three major institutions that will change procedures or policies to accommodate the working parent?

_____

**4.** Cite two examples of how education will change to accommodate the working parent.

_____

_____

**5.** What legislation might take place to help the working parent?

_____

**6.** Identify three changes that are occurring in business to accommodate the working parent.

_____

**7.** Define a telecommuter.

_____

**Step 7. _Check your answers._**

See if you have answered these questions correctly by checking your answers with those provided on pages 118–19.

**Step 8. _Review._**

Were you able to answer all the questions correctly? If you did, congratulations, you are on your way toward becoming a good notetaker. If you had problems answering any of the questions, listen to the lecture again and fill in any missing information in your notes.

## Lecture #6: Trees

**Step 1. _Gather materials for notetaking._**

Make sure you have plenty of paper and pens or pencils before you begin listening to the lecture.

**Step 2. _Turn on your tape recorder._**

**Step 3. *Listen to Lecture #6 and take notes on the lecture.***

Lecture #6 is five minutes in length. Listen to the lecture, and when you are instructed to turn off the tape recorder, do so and then turn to this page in your text.

**Step 4. *Review your notes.***

Answer the following questions about your notes:

- Are they organized?
- Are the listings orderly and are they labeled 1, 2, 3, etc.?
- Do your notes appear to contain complete information on the important points made in the lecture?

**Step 5. *Write a brief summary of the lecture.***

**Step 6. *Check the organization of your notes.***

- Your notes probably show five main headings to represent the material in the lecture.
- Heading #1 should be the general introduction to the topic of trees. The introduction should include notes on the number of species of plants, photosynthesis to manufacture food for the tree, and how trees differ from other plants in that they continue to grow until they die.
- The second major heading should be the "Needle-Leaf Tree," and details should follow. These details contain information on the seeds, the location of these trees, the fact that the needle-leaf tree is a softwood and an evergreen. Examples of the types of trees considered softwood should be listed. The term *evergreen* should be defined.
- The third heading should be the "Broad-Leaf Tree." Your notes should follow the same outline as they did for the needle-leaf tree; namely, supplying information that would describe this tree. The term *deciduous* should be defined.
- The fourth heading should be "Other Trees," in which you should note the palm trees of the South and the bamboo trees of the Orient.
- The final major heading should list the contributions of trees to our lives. Several ways in which trees benefit people and the environment should be included in your notes.

**Step 7.** *Review.*

If any of the major parts are missing in your notes, or if the details are missing from the major discussion points, play the tape again to complete your notes.

## Lecture #7: Entrepreneurship

**Step 1.** *Gather materials for notetaking.*

Make sure you have plenty of paper and pens or pencils before you begin listening to the lecture.

**Step 2.** *Turn on your tape recorder.*

**Step 3.** *Listen to Lecture #7 and take notes on the lecture.*

Lecture #7 is five minutes in length. Listen to the lecture, and when you are instructed to turn off the tape recorder, do so and then turn to this page in your text.

**Step 4.** *Review your notes.*

Answer the following questions about your notes:

- Are they organized?
- Are the listings orderly and are they labeled 1, 2, 3, etc.?
- Do your notes appear to contain complete information on the important points made in the lecture?

**Step 5.** *Write a brief summary of the lecture.*

**Step 6.** *Answer questions based on the notes you took while listening to the lecture.*

Write your answers in the space provided.

**1.** Define an *entrepreneur*.

_____

**2.** Cite statistics about small businesses.

_____

**3.** Name the seven characteristics of an entrepreneur.

_____

_____

**4.** What are the expenses that need to be considered before realizing a profit after a year in business?

_____

_____

### Step 7. *Check your answers.*

See if you have answered these questions correctly by checking your answers with those provided on page 119.

### Step 8. *Review.*

Were you able to answer all the questions correctly? If you did, congratulations, you are on your way toward becoming a good notetaker. If you had problems answering any of the questions, listen to the lecture again and fill in any missing information in your notes.

## Lecture #8: Lakes

### Step 1. *Gather materials for notetaking.*

Make sure you have plenty of paper and pens or pencils before you begin listening to the lecture.

### Step 2. *Turn on your tape recorder.*

### Step 3. *Listen to Lecture #8 and take notes on the lecture.*

Lecture #8 is five minutes in length. Listen to the lecture, and when you are instructed to turn off the tape recorder, do so and then turn to this page in your text.

### Step 4. *Review your notes.*

Answer the following questions about your notes:

- Are they organized?
- Are the listings orderly and are they labeled 1, 2, 3, etc.?
- Do your notes appear to contain complete information on the important points made in the lecture?

### Step 5. *Write a brief summary of the lecture.*

**Step 6.** *Check the organization of your notes.*

■ You should have each one of the five lakes written as a heading in your notes. Under the name of each lake you should have information on its size and the states or provinces that border it.

**Step 7.** *Answer questions based on the notes you took while listening to the lecture.*

Write your answers in the space provided.

**1.** Which lake is the largest body of fresh water in the United States?

_____

**2.** Which lake lies entirely within the border of the United States?

_____

**3.** Which lake is the shallowest of all the Great Lakes?

_____

**4.** Which lake is the highest above sea level?

_____

**5.** Which lake is the smallest of the Great Lakes?

_____

**6.** By taking the first letter of each lake in the system, what word is spelled?

_____

**Step 8.** *Check your answers.*

See if you have answered these questions correctly by checking your answers with those provided on page 119.

**Step 9.** *Review.*

Were you able to answer all the questions correctly? If you did, congratulations, you are on your way toward becoming a good notetaker. If you had problems answering any of the questions, listen to the lecture again and fill in any missing information in your notes.

## Lecture #9: Nonverbal Communication

**Step 1.** *Gather materials for notetaking.*

Make sure you have plenty of paper and pens or pencils before you begin listening to the lecture.

**Step 2.** *Turn on your tape recorder.*

**Step 3.** *Listen to Lecture #9 and take notes on the lecture.*

Lecture #9 is ten minutes in length. Listen to the lecture, and when you are instructed to turn off the tape recorder, do so and then turn to this page in your text.

**Step 4.** *Review your notes.*

Answer the following questions about your notes:

- Are they organized?
- Are the listings orderly and are they labeled 1, 2, 3, etc.?
- Do your notes appear to contain complete information on the important points made in the lecture?

**Step 5.** *Check the organization of your notes.*

- This is a fairly complicated lecture to take organized notes on. You must listen very carefully to construct notes that do follow a pattern.
- Your first notes should consist of an introduction to the topic of nonverbal communication. You probably noted that nonverbal communication can convey attitudes, feelings, status, and other things. Nonverbal communication can contradict what was expressed verbally.
- The lecturer told you that there would be six categories of nonverbal communication. You should have notes on these six— facial expression, gestures, body posture, body movement, territory, and physical appearance. You now have an outline established to follow with each of the six categories used as a main topic and information and examples as subsets.
- Under the heading "facial expressions," you should have recorded the types of smiles; namely, simple, upper, broad, and oblong. A short description of each should be included.

■ Under the heading "Hand Gestures," you should have noted the closed fist. An example of the umpire could be in your notes. The experiment of crossed arms could also be included. You should have noted the open hand as a giving, appealing, receiving, or lifting expression.

■ Posture is next. You listed each of the seven types discussed along with a descriptive statement for each of the seven. Under "Posture" you also used a subhead of "Walking" and noted five types of walk and what each type means.

■ The fourth category should be "Body Movement." You noted jerky, slow, flowing, and toward the listener along with a brief explanation of each movement.

■ The next category should be "Territory." The examples of an elevator, bus, library, or classroom could be noted to show how people claim personal space. Your notes should show the types of space people claim: intimate, friendly, or formal. You may have included a note on the hoopskirts under formal distance.

■ The last category should be "Physical Appearance." You should have included clothes, hair, and jewelry as part of this appearance. You should also have noted that people may select to belong or not belong to a group based on appearance.

**Step 6. *Review.***

How did your notes compare with this model? Were you able to record complete notes in an organized form? If you had trouble, listen to this lecture again and try to take notes that are complete and useful for you.

**Step 7. *Write recall notes.***

When your notes are complete and organized, write recall notes in the margin as you would if you were using these notes to study for a test.

**Step 8. *Write a brief summary.***

Write a brief summary at the bottom of your notes on the lecture on nonverbal communication.

## Lecture #10: Sleep

**Step 1. *Gather materials for notetaking.***

Make sure you have plenty of paper and pens or pencils before you begin listening to the lecture.

**Step 2.** *Turn on your tape recorder.*

**Step 3.** *Listen to Lecture #10 and take notes on the lecture.*

Lecture #10 is ten minutes in length. Listen to the lecture, and when you are instructed to turn off the tape recorder, do so and then turn to this page in your text.

**Step 4.** *Review your notes.*

Answer the following questions about your notes:

- Are they organized?
- Are the listings orderly and are they labeled 1, 2, 3, etc.?
- Do your notes appear to contain complete information on the important points made in the lecture?

**Step 5.** *Check the organization of your notes.*

- Did you notice that this lecture challenged you to listen carefully to record organized notes? Several clues by the speaker that would normally help you take good notes were missing from this lecture. It did not provide you with identified enumerations such as a one, two, or three. During the lecture, enumerations were given, but they were not sequenced for you. Instead, you had to listen to hear words like, "in the next stage," or "then we move to the last stage." At the end of the lecture six reasons for sleep were given, but only one of these carried an identification of "a third." You had to listen for the beginning and ending of items to note each one of the six reasons.
- Some extraneous material was contained in the lecture. The reference to the poodle was not essential information and should not have been recorded in your notes.
- No transition statement was given after the discussion on circadian rhythms to the start of the discussion on why we need sleep. You had to recognize that the discussion topic had changed, and your notes should reflect the introduction of a new subject.

**Step 6.** *Review your notes for orderliness and completeness.*

- Were you able to adjust to this more difficult material and take notes that are useful and complete?
- Do you feel confident that you have recorded the important information?

- Are your notes easy to read?
- Have you signalled enumerations from the lecture?
- Have you noted examples and definitions?
- If you answer *No* or *Maybe* to any of these questions, play the tape again and work on your notetaking skill. Then return to the next step to complete another activity based on your notes.

**Step 7.** *Write a brief summary statement of the lecture.*

**Step 8.** *Answer questions based on the notes you took while listening to the lecture.*

Write your answers in the space provided.

**1.** What do the initials EEG represent?

_____

**2.** What is the purpose of the EEG?

_____

**3.** What are the two types of sleep in which brain wave patterns, breathing, heart rates, and dream patterns are different?

_____

**4.** What are the four stages of non-REM sleep?

_____

_____

**5.** How long does it take to go through the four-stage sleep cycle?

_____

**6.** REM sleep is also called what kind of sleep?

_____

**7.** What contradictions are found in REM sleep?

_____

_____

**8.** If humans had no signals of time, how many hours would be in a day?

_____

**9.** What are "circadian rhythms"?

_____

**10.** Why do we sleep? List the six reasons given in the lecture.

_____

_____

_____

### Step 9. *Check your answers.*

See if you have answered these questions correctly by checking your answers with those provided on page 120.

### Step 10. *Review.*

Were you able to answer all the questions correctly? If you did, congratulations, you are on your way toward becoming a good notetaker. If you had problems answering any of the questions, listen to the lecture again and fill in any missing information in your notes.

## Answers to Questions

### Lecture #1: Painting

**1.** at least nine
**2.** the kinds of paintings created by painters
**3.** animals
**4.** history, dreams

### Lecture #2: Résumé Preparation

**1.** one
**2.** seven
**3.** references
**4.** your name, address, and phone number
**5.** accurate, dependable, flexible, prompt, loyal, poised, tactful, courteous, greeted, prepared, initiated, maintained
**6.** hobbies and interests
**7.** Your personal interests can be the opening question in an interview. By talking about something familiar to you, the interviewer can evaluate your ability to communicate.
**8.** education and work experience

### Lecture #3: Hummingbird

**1.** about 9,000

**2.** hatch from an egg, have a bill or beak, have two legs, and have wings

**3. a)** within the family is found the smallest bird in the world
   **b)** some members of the family are among the most brightly colored birds in the world
   **c)** highest metabolic rate per unit of body weight of all birds
   **d)** live only in the Western Hemisphere

**4. a)** size: the male hummingbird is the smallest bird in the world—only 2 inches long; the female is ¼ inch longer; weighs less than the weight of a penny; the giant hummer is 9 inches long
   **b)** wings: moves at 60 to 80 beats per second; so fast the human eye cannot see the wings move; allows birds to suspend in air
   **c)** food: bills and tongue are constructed to obtain nectar and insects
   **d)** location: 400 types live in the Western Hemisphere; 18 types live in the United States in the western and southwestern states; one type, the ruby-throated hummingbird, lives east of the Mississippi River

**5.** male is the smallest bird in the world at 2 inches; the female is 2¼ inches long; located in Cuba; may be on the endangered list; wings move at 80 beats per second

**6.** giant hummer, 9 inches long

### Lecture #4: Northern Lights

**1.** northern dawn

**2. a)** bands like a thick curtain
   **b)** patches like glowing clouds
   **c)** rays in a very large star burst

**3.** green is the most common; then red, pink, and purplish-blue

**4.** Benjamin Franklin

**5.** March and September, around midnight, skies are dark, and the moon is new

### Lecture #5: The Changing American Family

**1.** 1900: 2 of every 10 married women work away from home
   1975: 40% of all women above the age of 16 are in labor force
   1989: 57% of all women above the age of 16 are in labor force

**2.** 50% of marriages end in divorce; single-parent households are increasing; roles of men, women, and children are changing

**3.** education, legislation (politics), and business
**4. a)** the word *family* used in place of mother or father
   **b)** letters addressed to parent or guardian
   **c)** staffs adjusting workday to meet needs of working parent
   **d)** instituting a friend's day
**5.** national funding to increase salaries of child-care workers
**6. a)** job sharing
   **b)** flextime scheduling
   **c)** telecommuting
**7.** a person working from home connected to the office by a computer

## Lecture #6: No Answers Required

## Lecture #7: Entrepreneurship

**1.** An entrepreneur creates new consumer demand and takes the risk of making a profit in organizing and managing an enterprise.
**2. a)** More than 16 million small businesses are operating in the United States.
   **b)** Ninety percent of the small businesses employ fewer than 10 persons.
   **c)** Small businesses are responsible for 47 percent of the total production of the United States.
   **d)** Single-employee businesses will increase from 7 million to about 12 million by the next century.
**3. a)** the first-born child
   **b)** held three or more jobs before age 15
   **c)** started first business before age 20
   **d)** hard-working
   **e)** demanding boss
   **f)** self-confident
   **g)** sense of direction and goals
**4.** supplies, materials, rent, heat, light, telephone, insurance, taxes, labor, transportation, advertising, and commissions

## Lecture #8: Lakes

**1.** Lake Superior
**2.** Lake Michigan
**3.** Lake Erie at 210 feet
**4.** Lake Superior
**5.** Lake Ontario
**6.** HOMES

### Lecture #9: No Answers Required

### Lecture #10: Sleep

**1.** electroencephalograph
**2.** the EEG measures brain wave activity
**3.** **a)** rapid-eye-movement sleep (REM)
  **b)** non-rapid-eye-movement sleep (NREM)
**4.** **a)** light sleep, transition from wakefulness to sleep
  **b)** drifting into a deeper sleep; two brain wave patterns show up on the EEG
  **c)** transition step between stage 2 and stage 4; a delta rhythm appears
  **d)** deepest sleep; delta wave prominent
**5.** about 90 minutes for humans
**6.** paradoxical
**7.** There are two paradoxes or contradictions at this state: (1) the brain waves are very similar to the waking state but the person is asleep, and (2) the brain is active but the muscles will not move.
**8.** about 25 hours
**9.** a process that governs the amount of sleep needed during the day
**10.** **a)** restore bodies and brains from fatigue of daily activity
  **b)** prevent exhaustion
  **c)** ancient adaptive patterns for survival passed down through the generations
  **d)** state of tissue growth and repair
  **e)** life-preserving purpose
  **f)** overcome sleepiness

# READING

Attending classes and taking notes on lectures and discussions will help you do well in your courses. However, in most courses you are expected to study a textbook and other written material as well.

In Part 4 you will use a study method that will help you understand and remember what you read. You'll learn to:

■ **Preview a book before starting to read it.**

■ **Preview chapters, articles, and graphics.**

■ **Read material in a way that will improve your comprehension.**

■ **Take notes on what you read.**

■ **Review your notes.**

# 8 PREVIEWING READING ASSIGNMENTS

## PREVIEWING A BOOK
1. Read the Title
2. Skim the Preface or Introduction
3. Read the Table of Contents
4. Skim the Back of the Book
5. Skim the Chapter Pages

## PREVIEWING A CHAPTER
1. Read the Chapter Title
2. Skim the First and Last Paragraphs
3. Find Relationships Between Heads and Subheads
4. Write Questions
5. Look for Key Words and Graphics

## PREVIEWING AN ARTICLE
1. Read the Title
2. Read the Byline and About the Author
3. Skim the First and Last Paragraphs
4. Find Relationships Between Heads and Subheads
5. Look for Key Words and Graphics

## PREVIEWING A GRAPHIC
1. Read the Title, Subtitle, and Caption
2. Read the Source of the Information
3. Read the Copy at the Top, Side, and Bottom

## SUMMARY

## CHAPTER 8 ACTIVITIES

### CHECK YOUR UNDERSTANDING

### PRACTICE YOUR PREVIEWING SKILLS

### IMPROVE YOUR WRITING SKILLS

You have no doubt gone to the movies and seen the "coming attraction," or a preview of some movie to come. Sometimes instructors tell you at the beginning of class what they plan to cover that day. Why does the theater show a preview? Why does an instructor provide an overview of the day's material? In both cases, the preview is meant to engage your interest in the material and give you a framework for understanding it.

Previewing should be a basic part of the reading process as well. Reading a book or article without previewing it first is like setting off on a long car trip without first consulting a map. You may reach your destination, but the trip will take longer and you may get lost on the way. In this chapter you will learn how to preview a book, chapter, article, and graphic in order to get the most out of your reading assignment.

## PREVIEWING A BOOK

When you first get a textbook for a course (or any other book you must read), you should find out as much about it as you can in 15 or 20 minutes. You do this by *skimming*, or glancing through, the book to get a feeling for what it is about.

How can you preview an entire book in just 15 to 20 minutes? You can do it by looking at the parts of the book that you may have skipped over before. You briefly (1) read the title, (2) skim the preface or introduction, (3) read the table of contents, (4) skim the back of the book, and (5) skim the chapter pages. By following these steps, you will gain an overview of the book in a short time.

### 1. Read the Title

Start your preview with the title, and guess what the book is about. Some titles distinctly express the subject matter of the book. For example, a title like *Chronicles of Time—A World History* clearly tells you that this is a book about world history over a long period of time. Other titles may not be as clear. A title such as *The Spoken Word* may leave you wondering if it is about giving speeches, oral history, or oral communication in general.

As you reflect on the title and what it means, ask yourself if you

# FASHION MERCHANDISING

## An Introduction

### Fifth Edition

**Elaine Stone**

Professor, Merchandising and
Marketing, Coordinator of the
Small Business Center, and
Director of the Export
Advisory Service,
Fashion Institute of Technology
New York, New York

Contributor
**Jean A. Samples**

Instructor
Texas Southern University
Houston, Texas

Gregg Division
McGraw-Hill Publishing Company
New York   Atlanta   Dallas   St. Louis   San Francisco
Auckland   Bogotá   Caracas   Hamburg   Lisbon
London   Madrid   Mexico   Milan   Montreal   New Delhi
Paris   San Juan   São Paulo   Singapore
Sydney   Tokyo   Toronto

*Note:* This and the subsequent illustrations on pages 126, 127, 128, and 130 are reprinted with permission from Elaine Stone and Jean A. Samples, *Fashion Merchandising: An Introduction,* 5th ed., Macmillan/McGraw-Hill, 1990.

Title page

have had experience with the subject matter. Whenever you can connect personal experience with a new encounter, you will feel more comfortable working with the new item. And so it is with a book. If you can relate to the subject matter, you are more likely to concentrate on reading.

## 2. Skim the Preface or Introduction

The introductory section may be only one paragraph or it may be much longer. Quickly skim it to find out more about the book. You may find information on the book's organization, why it was written, and even hints on how to study it. If the book is a second or third edition, the preface may tell you what is new in this printing. Sometimes the preface reveals personal information about the author(s), including qualifications for writing the book.

## 3. Read the Table of Contents

The table of contents shows all the major topics in a book. The contents may also provide subtopics to indicate the direction or focus of the book. The subject material may be in chronological order or in topical arrangement. If it is in chronological order, notice the breaks in time as well as the time periods covered. If it is in topical arrangement, ask yourself why this particular organization of subject matter was used. Does one chapter develop out of previous chapters, or are the chapters independent of one another? Must the chapters be read sequentially?

## 4. Skim the Back of the Book

The last few pages of a book can be very helpful and interesting because they may contain an array of miscellaneous information. Some books provide a glossary (a list of words and definitions used in the book), additional sets of drills (each set correlated with a chapter), sources for specific information and further reading, or a basic review of what should be prior knowledge. A book on business communications, for example, may have a section on the principles of grammar and word use. Most books also contain an index, which is an alphabetic list of topics and their page numbers.

By including the back pages in your preview, you become aware of special aids the author is giving you. Take advantage of these as you work through the textbook and the course.

# PREFACE

The fashion business is exciting, stimulating, fascinating! Because it is also ever-changing, we have developed *Fashion Merchandising: An Introduction,* Fifth Edition, to provide a structured learning process to help students discover the innovation and challenges of today's fashion business.

*Fashion Merchandising: An Introduction,* Fifth Edition, reflects the survey nature of an introductory course by covering all the interdependent levels of the fashion business so that students can be made aware of the many careers in fashion. The concepts and practices developed are equally applicable to the merchandising of all fashion-influenced goods, although the text treats them largely in terms of men's, women's, children's apparel and accessories. To keep our readers current in the most recent happenings in the fashion business, each chapter concludes with a discussion of the latest developments and upcoming trends.

This fifth edition provides hundreds of new up-to-date examples and illustrations. In addition, the text has been substantially rewritten to sharpen its focus on fashion and to allow space for expanded material on: (1) the business of fashion, (2) domestic and foreign markets, (3) the impact of technology on each level of fashion, and (4) the global sourcing that is so important to the internationalization of fashion.

## ORGANIZATION OF THE TEXT

The fifth edition of *Fashion Merchandising: An Introduction* uses the successful classroom-tested organization of the previous editions. It is structured in the following sequential learning order: Unit 1, The Dynamics of Fashion; Unit 2, The Producers of Fashion; Unit 3, The Markets for Fashion; Unit 4, The Merchandising of Fashion.

## Unit 1: The Dynamics of Fashion

The first five chapters acquaint the student with the fundamentals of fashion and the basic principles that govern all fashion movement and change. This unit also teaches the fundamentals of the business of fashion. Many new examples and illustrations have been provided.

Chapter 1, "The Nature of Fashion," introduces fashion terminology, examines the components of fashion, and explains why fashion is always subject to change. Chapter 2 explores the manner in which economic, sociological, and psychological factors influence fashion demand. Chapter 3 discusses the rhythmic changes in silhouette, the cyclical movement of fashion, and how to predict fashion trends with relative accuracy. Chapter 4 explains how fashions start; the roles and responsibilities of designers, manufacturers, and retailers; the major theories relating to fashion adoption and dissemination; and why most people follow rather than lead fashion change. Chapter 5 explores the scope of the fashion business, explains the different types of business organizations, and allows the student to investigate the different forms of business structure.

## Unit 2: The Producers of Fashion

The next seven chapters trace the history and development, organization and operation, merchandising and marketing activities, and trends in industries engaged in producing fashion. Chapter 6 discusses textile fibers and fabrics. Chapter 7 explains the fur industry and the leather apparel and accessories industry. Chapter 8 explores the women's apparel business with emphasis on current changes and future trends. Chapter 9 covers children's apparel, both boys and girls. Chapter 10 details the operations of

iii

# CONTENTS

vi

Contents—first page

# Glossary

**Absolute quota** A limit to the quantity of goods entering the United States.

**Active sportswear** The sector of sportswear that includes casual attire worn for sports such as running, jogging, tennis, and racketball.

**Adaptations** Designs that have all the dominant features of the style that inspired them, but do not claim to be exact copies.

**Advertising** The paid use of space or time in any medium. This includes newspapers, magazines, direct-mail pieces, shopping news bulletins, theater programs, catalogs, bus cards, billboards, radio, and television.

**Ambiance** The atmosphere encountered when entering a store.

**Apparel contractor** A firm whose sole function is to supply sewing services to the apparel industry.

**Bilateral agreement** Two countries reaching a separate agreement regarding their trade arrangements.

**Board of directors** Chief governing body of a corporation.

**Boarding** (hosiery) A heat-setting process through which hosiery acquires permanent shape.

**Bodywear** Coordinated leotards, tights, and wrap skirts.

**Boutique** A shop associated with few-of-a-kind merchandise, generally of very new or extreme styling, with an imaginative presentation of goods. French word for "shop."

**Branch store division** A separate function or division within a large retail firm's organizational structure that is responsible for seeing that the firm's policies are carried out

# Index

Back-of-book items—glossary and index

### 5. Skim the Chapter Pages

After skimming the front and back of the book, flip through the pages. Are there introductions at the beginnings of the chapters? The introduction may be a paragraph or a list of main points in the chapter. It may be a statement of objectives or competencies to be learned in the chapter.

Some books like *Study Skills* contain summaries or concluding statements at the end of each chapter to pull together the details presented. Occasionally textbooks have a summary statement at the beginning of each chapter; the rest of the chapter then fills in the details.

As you continue to flip through the pages of the book, do you see questions or exercises to help you apply the information from the chapter? Are tables, charts, graphs, diagrams, or pictures used? These graphics aren't used simply to fill up a page; they are there to clarify information for you.

## PREVIEWING A CHAPTER

Just as you gained an overview of a book by previewing it, you should preview a chapter before reading it. Perhaps you think that previewing a chapter is a waste of time. "I should be able to pick up a book," you say, "turn to the beginning of a chapter, and read." If that is how you approach your reading assignments, you may find that previewing seems to slow you down. However, you will discover that the time spent previewing will help you read more quickly and improve your comprehension.

Previewing a chapter involves five steps: (1) reading the title, (2) skimming the first and last paragraphs, (3) finding relationships between the heads and subheads, (4) writing questions using the heads and subheads, and (5) looking for key words and graphics.

### 1. Read the Chapter Title

Every chapter has a title. What does that title mean? What does it tell you will be discussed in the chapter? Do you know anything about this subject? Perhaps a short statement or a quotation will be given to explain further what is covered in the chapter.

are cellulose-based, they can be produced with a minimum of chemical treatment. The cellulose used to make these fibers comes mostly from soft woods such as spruce.

**Noncellulosic Fibers** Petroleum, natural gas, air, and water are used to make **noncellulosic fibers.** They are produced from various combinations of carbon, hydrogen, nitrogen, and oxygen. Fiber chemists working in laboratories link the molecules into long chains called **polymers.**

The Federal Trade Commission has assigned **generic names** or nontrademarked names, to eighteen noncellulosic fibers. These are:[2]

| | | |
|---|---|---|
| acrylic | metallic | polyester |
| anidex | modacrylic | rubber |
| aramid | novoloid | saran |
| azlon | nylon | spandex |
| glass | nytril | vinal |
| lastrile | olefin | vinyon |

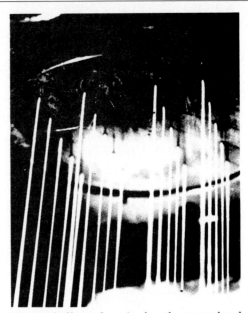

Man-made fibers of varying lengths are produced by forcing thick liquids through the tiny holes of a device known as a spinnerette.

Of these, anidex, azlon, lastrile, and vinal are not currently produced in the United States.

The properties of these fibers greatly influences the behavior of the finished fabric made from them. Polyester, for example, is strong and wrinkle-resistant, which contributes to its durability and washability.

## Organization and Operation

Because of the differences in the origin and characteristics of fibers, each industry—the natural fiber industry and the man-made fiber industry—is organized along different lines.

### The Natural Fiber Industry

Cotton is produced in four major areas of the United States: the Southeast; the Mississippi Delta; the Texas–Oklahoma Panhandle; and New Mexico, Arizona, and California.

Nearly all cotton growers sell their product in local markets, either to mill representatives or, more typically, to wholesalers. The cotton wholesalers bargain at central markets in Memphis, New Orleans, Dallas, Houston, New York, and Chicago.

The wool produced in the United States comes from relatively small sheep ranches in the Western states. Boston is the central marketplace for wool, both domestic and imported.

Linen, silk, and ramie are not produced in any great quantities in the United States, and are imported from foreign sources.

The natural fiber industry in the United States has been greatly affected by the advent of man-made fibers. Man-

Typical chapter page

# CHAPTER 21
# Real Property

**OUTLINE**

21-1  The Nature of Real Property
    Trees and Vegetation
    Air Rights
    Subterranean Rights
    Water Rights
    Fixtures

21-2  Easements

21-3  Estates in Real Property
    Estates in Fee Simple
    Life Estates

21-4  Co-Ownership of Real Property
    Tenancy in Common
    Joint Tenancy
    Tenancy by the Entirety
    Tenancy in Partnership

21-5  Methods of Acquiring Title to Real Property
    Title by Sale or Gift
    Title by Will or Descent
    Title by Occupancy

21-6  Zoning Laws

21-7  Eminent Domain

**COMMENTARY**

Walter and Melonie Kahn were excited! They were about to make the largest purchase of their lives—their first home. It was a pretty house, beautifully landscaped with newly planted trees. Inside, the floors were covered with wall-to-wall carpeting, and the windows had new curtains. One side of the property formed the bank of a stream. Another side was bordered by a fence covered with roses. Many questions came to mind as they entered into this important transaction. Did the curtains and wall-to-wall carpeting go with the house? Were the rose bushes and newly planted trees included in the purchase? What rights would the Kahns have to the stream and the water flowing through it, and at what point in the stream was the property line. What kind of deed would they receive? Who would own the property if one of them died? This chapter examines these and other important questions that arise when people acquire title to real property.

**OBJECTIVES**

1. Explain what constitutes real property.
2. Identify three ways of creating an easement.
3. Differentiate between freehold and leasehold estates.
4. Describe the different types of co-ownership of real property.
5. Identify three methods of acquiring title to real property.
6. Give an example of a nonconforming use of real property, and discuss the granting of a variance.
7. Explain eminent domain.

283

*Source:* Brown *et al.*, *Business Law*, 7th ed., Macmillan/McGraw-Hill, New York, 1989, page 283. Reprinted with permission of the Glencoe Division of Macmillan/McGraw-Hill Publishing Company.

First page of chapter with outline of heads, introductory paragraph, and learning objectives

## 2. Skim the First and Last Paragraphs

Next, skim the first and last paragraphs of the chapter. Often the first paragraph states a central purpose or theme. At times you may also have to skim the second paragraph before you are able to identify the purpose. The concluding paragraph sometimes provides a concise review of the entire chapter. The last paragraph may even be labeled "Summary." Later, the details you will read between the first and last paragraphs will be easier to understand because you have previewed the chapter.

When looking at the end of the chapter, be sure to check any exercises that appear. The applications or questions reflect the major points that were made in the chapter.

## 3. Find Relationships Between Heads and Subheads

Take a look at the heads and subheads in the chapter. How do the subheads relate to the heads? What does each head mean? Usually key ideas are found under the subheads, since a subhead is a breakdown of the main topic.

Most textbooks use two or three levels of heads: the main head, the subhead, and the sub-subhead. You can distinguish the levels of heads because they are set into type differently: the main head is the most prominent, the subhead a little less prominent, and the sub-subhead the least prominent. In this book, for example, main heads are set in all-capital letters in large colored type, subheads appear in capital and lowercase colored letters, and both stand on a separate line. Sub-subheads are set in smaller type on the same line as the text that follows.

## 4. Write Questions

To increase your comprehension of the material, turn each head into a question. You can do this by using words such as *who, what, when, which, why, how,* and *how significant.* Make a brief note of the questions that come to mind as you look at the heads; you will look for answers to these questions later when you read the paragraphs closely. This questioning activity keeps your mind alert, active, and ready to concentrate on reading the material. You are engaged in a thinking process that is necessary for learning to take place.

Questioning the heads is a simple procedure. Notice how the following heads can be made into questions by using some of the question words mentioned above:

| Head | Question |
|------|----------|
| Increase in Single-Parent Families | Why have single-parent families increased? |
| Revolution in Women's Employment | How is women's employment changing? What caused the revolution? |
| More Dual-Career Families Today | Why are dual-career families common today? |
| Changing Status of Divorce | In what way is divorce changing? What is the status of divorce now? |

## 5. Look for Key Words and Graphics

Last, look over the narrative to find words in quotation marks or boldface print, underscored or italicized. Also look for any illustrations or graphics. These key items will be important later when you read closely and take notes.

## PREVIEWING AN ARTICLE

Sometimes you must read an article from a newspaper, popular magazine, trade journal, or academic journal to supplement class information or to prepare a report. In general, the approach to previewing an article is the same as previewing a chapter, but there are some differences. These differences arise from the less formal structure of most articles. Articles in academic journals are often as highly structured as textbook chapters, but those in trade journals, magazines, and newspapers are less structured. You may find when using these types of periodicals that your previewing is gaining you less information than usual. In that case, just skim the entire article to get an idea of what it is about.

When you preview an article, (1) read the title, (2) read the byline and about the author, (3) skim the first and last paragraphs, (4) find relationships between heads and subheads, (5) look for key words and graphics.

# WHAT NOT DOING WINDOWS COSTS LOTUS

It's enough to drive Lotus Development Corp. to whining. Lotus spent three frustrating years and millions of dollars to bring out two versions of its 1-2-3 spreadsheet program that can work with Microsoft Corp.'s OS/2 Presentation Manager, the basic software, or operating system, that was supposed to turn every PC into a Macintosh. But OS/2 isn't selling well. And Microsoft, unexpectedly is selling loads of an alternative called Windows, an earlier program that has lots of Presentation Manager's easy-to-use graphics.

Microsoft wins no matter which program takes off. Its own spreadsheet, called Excel, works with both. But Lotus isn't so lucky. Its advanced new 1-2-3, called Release 3.0, won't work with Windows. As Excel makes inroads, "Lotus has found that there's this large installed base of Windows users that it decided to ignore," says analyst David Readerman at Shearson Lehman Hutton Inc.

**LATEST WOE** That has led to some public griping. For software companies, "choosing an operating system" to write programs for "should not be equivalent to betting on a horse race," Lotus CEO Jim P. Manzi told some of his peers in a recent speech. "Windows is like a horse that was about to be put to pasture but was then revitalized."

**SPREADSHEET WARS**

LOTUS 1-2-3*

MICROSOFT EXCEL

'88  '89  EST.

▲ THOUSANDS OF COPIES SHIPPED
*INCLUDES ALL VERSIONS OF 1-2-3
DATA: GOLDMAN, SACHS & CO.

Indeed, corporate buyers such as Eastman Kodak Co. and BankAmerica Corp., which want to upgrade programs like 1-2-3 and use Windows as well, are confused. Less powerful versions of 1-2-3 work with Windows, but they can't take advantage of many of its graphical features. Lotus probably will solve that problem: "We're not naive," says Frank A. Ingari, vice-president of its PC spreadsheet division. But analysts say the revised program could take a year to produce.

The Windows flap is just the latest woe for seven-year-old Lotus. True, customers are buying more of 1-2-3 than competing products, giving Lotus 65% of the $600 million world market for PC spreadsheets. But so far, Release 3.0 may not be doing as well as its other new version, called Release 2.2, which runs on less powerful PCs. Some customers even are sticking with Release 2.01, now more than three years old. At Softsel Inc., a software distributor, Release 2.2 is outselling 3.0 by 3 to 2. Corporate Software Inc. says its ratio is more than 2 to 1. Lotus disputes such numbers, claiming that 2.2 and 3.0 are selling about the same.

The split means a lot to Lotus, which gets two-thirds of its profits from spreadsheets. Next year, it will lift 3.0's list price to $595, some $100 higher than other versions. That might add $20 million or more to Lotus' overall revenues in 1990. But it might not: "The question is, does Lotus see a fall-off after this initial upgrade bubble?" says Richard G. Shurlund, an analyst at Goldman Sachs & Co.

Profits dipped while Lotus struggled to get 3.0 out the door. But it now expects to finish this year with strong earnings. Its spreadsheet sales have returned to historical levels of about 110,000 units a month. And sales of 2.2 and 3.0 will boost revenues by $30 million this year. Now, all Lotus needs is one more product—so it can bet on two Microsoft horses at once.

*By Keith H. Hammonds in Boston*

Article

## 1. Read the Title

The title of an article may contain a clear statement of the topic, especially if it appears in a trade or academic journal. However, a title, or headline, that appears in a newspaper or popular magazine may be designed more to capture your attention than to give information.

## 2. Read the Byline and About the Author

The title of an article is generally accompanied by a byline, which states the author's name. Sometimes you will also find, generally at the bottom of the first page or at the end of the article, a sentence or two describing the author's background and credentials. This will help you judge the point of view of the article, and the importance and reliability of the information.

## 3. Skim the First and Last Paragraphs

Articles are generally less formally structured than textbook chapters, so skimming the first and last paragraphs may give you information ranging from a complete overview to just a few clues about the topic. To capture a reader's interest, many writers start with an anecdote, or story, the point of which may not be entirely clear until you read further. In addition, articles often lack summaries and almost always lack activities and questions at the end.

## 4. Find Relationships Between Heads and Subheads

Again, because of the range of articles and periodicals, the information you gain from reading the heads and subheads may be either the entire structure of an article or a few random ideas. There may be only one level of head, and it may be designed only to break up long blocks of text, rather than to give information.

## 5. Look for Key Words and Graphics

Finally, look for words emphasized by quotation marks, boldface or italic type, or underscoring. Look also for graphics and illustrations. These key items often contain clues as to what you will need to concentrate on as you read. If steps 1 through 4 have not yielded much information, this step should provide you with a general sense of what the article is about.

## PREVIEWING A GRAPHIC

As you learned in Chapter 4, taking notes graphically is a good way to clarify the relationships between facts and ideas. Often you will find that the author of your text or article has provided graphic material to help you understand the subject more easily. The graphic

### SOME PRIMITIVE REFLEXES IN HUMANS

| Name of Reflex | Stimulation | Behavior | Approximate Age of Dropping Out |
|---|---|---|---|
| Rooting | Cheek stroked with finger or nipple | Head turns; mouth opens, sucking movements begin | 9 months |
| Moro (startle) | Sudden stimulus such as a loud noise or being dropped | Extends legs, arms, and fingers; arches back, draws back head | 3 months |
| Darwinian (grasping) | Palm of hand stroked | Makes such a strong fist that baby can be raised to standing position if both fists are closed around a stick | 2 months |
| Swimming | Put in water face down | Well-coordinated swimming movements | 6 months |
| Tonic neck | Laid down on back | Head turns to one side; assumes "fencer" position; extends arms and legs on preferred side, flexes opposite limbs | 2 months |
| Babinski | Sole of foot stroked | Toes fan out, foot twists in | 6–9 months |
| Walking | Held under arm, with bare feet touching flat surface | Makes steplike motions that look like well-coordinated walking | 2 months |
| Placing | Backs of feet drawn against edge of flat surface | Withdraws foot | 1 month |

*Source:* Diane E. Papalia and Sally Wendkos Olds, *Psychology,* 2nd ed., McGraw-Hill, New York, 1988, p. 316. Reprinted with permission of McGraw-Hill, Inc.

Table with previewing items highlighted

Source: Julie Bailey, "Jobs for Women in the Nineties," *Ms.*, July 1988, p. 75.

Graph with previewing items highlighted

may take the form of a table, diagram, or graph. When space has been given to present information graphically, you can be sure it is important to preview the material.

The following steps are used to preview graphic material: (1) read the title, subtitle, and caption, (2) read the source of the information, and (3) read the copy at the top, side, and bottom of the graphic.

## 1. Read the Title, Subtitle, and Caption

Reading the title, subtitle, and caption (if any) will help you understand what information the graphic is trying to convey. If you can understand the purpose of the graphic, you will have an easier time understanding the details. A caption often serves to point out specific aspects of the graphic to which you should pay particular attention.

## 2. Read the Source of the Information

Some graphics, although by no means all, are prepared by or based on information from sources other than the author of the book or article. For example, many authors use data from the U.S. Bureau of the Census to illustrate trends in population movements, marketing, ethnic groups, family composition, and so on. Knowing the source of the information in the graphic helps you judge its importance or reliability.

## 3. Read the Copy at the Top, Side, and Bottom

In a table, information is arranged by type in columns and rows that are usually labeled at the top and left side. In a graph, the copy along the side indicates what is being measured vertically and the copy along the bottom indicates what is being measured horizontally. Diagrams often have descriptive labels with arrows pointing to parts of the diagram. Reading these items will help you understand how information is organized in the graphic.

# SUMMARY

Previewing a book, chapter, article, or graphic before you read will give you a framework for understanding it.

To preview a book, you should (1) read the title, (2) skim the preface or introduction, (3) read the table of contents, (4) skim the back of the book, and (5) skim the chapter pages.

The steps in previewing a chapter are to (1) read the chapter title, (2) skim the first and last paragraphs, (3) find relationships between heads and subheads, (4) write questions, and (5) look for key words and graphics.

To preview an article, you should (1) read the title, (2) read the byline and about the author, (3) skim the first and last paragraphs, (4) find relationships between heads and subheads, and (5) look for key words and graphics.

Previewing a graphic means you should (1) read the title, subtitle, and caption, (2) read the source of the information, (3) read the copy at the top, side, and bottom.

Name                                                        Date

# CHAPTER 8 ACTIVITIES

## CHECK YOUR UNDERSTANDING

**1.** How will previewing help you when you read an assignment?

_____

_____

**2.** List the steps in previewing a book.

_____

_____

_____

**3.** What steps are involved in previewing a chapter?

_____

_____

_____

**4.** Why does previewing an article sometimes yield less information than previewing a text chapter?

_____

_____

**5.** How should a table or graph be previewed?

_____

_____

_____

## PRACTICE YOUR PREVIEWING SKILLS

**1.** Preview this book. When you are finished, your instructor will ask you and the other members of the class to answer questions about *Study Skills*.

**2.** Preview the next chapter in *Study Skills* (Chapter 9). Once again, be prepared to respond to your instructor's questions.

**3.** Preview the article on page 136, and answer your instructor's questions about it.

**4.** Preview the two graphics on pages 136 and 137; your instructor will ask questions about both graphics.

## IMPROVE YOUR WRITING SKILLS

**Other Irregular Verbs:** As indicated in the following chart, the past tense and past participle of a number of verbs besides *to be, to do,* and *to have* are formed in an irregular manner.

| Present | Past | Past Participle |
|---------|------|-----------------|
| become | became | become |
| begin | began | begun |
| blow | blew | blown |
| break | broke | broken |
| bring | brought | brought |
| buy | bought | bought |
| catch | caught | caught |
| choose | chose | chosen |
| come | came | come |
| draw | drew | drawn |
| drink | drank | drunk |
| drive | drove | driven |
| eat | ate | eaten |
| fall | fell | fallen |
| fight | fought | fought |
| fly | flew | flown |
| forget | forgot | forgotten |
| freeze | froze | frozen |
| get | got | got |
| give | gave | given |
| go | went | gone |
| grow | grew | grown |
| hide | hid | hidden |
| know | knew | known |
| lay | laid | laid |
| leave | left | left |

| Present | Past | Past Participle |
| --- | --- | --- |
| lie ("to recline") | lay | lain |
| lose | lost | lost |
| make | made | made |
| pay | paid | paid |
| ride | rode | ridden |
| ring | rang | rung |
| rise | rose | risen |
| run | ran | run |
| see | saw | seen |
| set | set | set |
| shake | shook | shaken |
| shrink | shrank | shrunk |
| sing | sang | sung |
| sit | sat | sat |
| speak | spoke | spoken |
| steal | stole | stolen |
| strike | struck | struck |
| take | took | taken |
| throw | threw | thrown |
| wear | wore | worn |
| write | wrote | written |

## Practice

For each of the following sentences, decide which of the verb forms shown in parentheses is correct and underline it.

1. If he had (*spoke, spoken*) to her about it, it would not have (*took, taken*) so long to resolve the matter.

2. I (*begin, began, begun*) working for them in 1988 and left as soon as I (*see, saw, seen*) there was no opportunity for advancement.

3. She must have (*forgot, forgotten*) who (*give, gave, given*) it to her.

4. If we had (*knew, knowed, known*) we would have to walk, we would have (*wore, worn*) more comfortable shoes.

5. After we (*fly, flew, flown*) to Dallas, we rented a car and (*drive, drove, driven*) to Houston.

6. The letter was (*write, wrote, written*) and mailed two weeks ago, but it apparently was (*loose, lose, lost*) in the mail.

7. We now (*know, knew, known*) exactly how much their prices have (*rise, rose, risen*) during the past six months.

8. Two of the people who have (*set, sit, sat*) near me (*bring, brought*) a lot of camera equipment with them.

9. We should have (*choose, chose, chosen*) plants that would (*grow, grew, grown*) well in the shade.

10. The wind has (*blew, blowed, blown*) so hard that the limbs of several trees have already (*break, broke, broken*) and (*fall, fell, fallen*) to the ground.

# 9 READING AND NOTETAKING

In the previous chapter, you learned the importance of previewing a reading assignment to gain a perspective on what an author is trying to communicate. You are now ready for the next step in the reading process: reading the assignment in order to understand and remember it.

Have you ever memorized information for a test but later realized that you didn't really comprehend what you had memorized? Or have you ever understood what you have read but then couldn't remember it? Both comprehension and retention are important goals when you read for your courses. To achieve these goals, you need to adopt an approach to reading that involves previewing, reading, taking notes, and reviewing your notes. In this chapter you will learn how to read an assignment, take notes from written material, and review your notes.

## READING

Before we discuss what is involved in developing good reading skills, let's briefly examine what you should *not* be doing. First, you should not try to read when you are tired. Second, you should not try to read if you have something very important on your mind. Both fatigue and preoccupation interfere with your ability to concentrate. If you read under these circumstances, you will find yourself rereading the same few sentences with no idea of the content.

Thus, the first two prerequisites for productive reading are that you be rested and relaxed. The third is that you be prepared. In addition to having your book or article, make sure you have a pen, several sheets of paper, and a dictionary. With these things taken care of, you are ready to decide which basic reading approach to use to read for main ideas and to mark the reading.

### Basic Approaches to Reading

Before you start reading your assignment, you must decide, based on the material, which of two basic approaches to reading will be better for you. Your choices are to:

**1.** *Read twice—the first time quickly and the second time slowly.* The first reading is to answer the questions raised by the preview; the second reading is to comprehend the material fully and take notes. This method works well for complicated or very long assignments.

**2.** *Read once slowly.* In this method you take notes as you read. This works well for easy or short reading assignments.

Both methods have advantages and disadvantages. Reading an assignment twice generally gives you better comprehension and retention of the material, but it takes longer. On the other hand, reading material once may save you time, but you may sacrifice some understanding. Since you are taking notes as you read the first time, you may be struggling to understand a point that, unknown to you, is clarified later in the chapter or article.

Whichever method you select, when you read for comprehension—the "slow" read—remember the axiom, "A whole is the sum of its parts." To understand the whole reading, you must understand each part. This means that you read one paragraph or section at a time, look for main ideas, mark the passage, take notes, and *then* move on to read the next paragraph or section.

What happens when you read something very complicated and are still confused? You may have to go back to step 1, previewing, and start again. A second preview may help you gain a clearer understanding of the organization of the material and prepare you for rereading.

## Reading for Main Ideas

When you read an assignment, you look for the main idea of each paragraph as well as other important ideas that indicate definitions or relationships.

**Main Idea of Paragraph.**   As you know, a paragraph is a group of related sentences about a topic. Your task, when reading, is to identify the main idea of each paragraph along with supporting information. The main idea is often in the first sentence of the paragraph. However, the main idea can appear elsewhere in the paragraph, even at the end. Whatever its location, the main idea covers all the points made in the paragraph.

Writers use a variety of methods to reinforce the message of each paragraph. Some of the more common methods are:

■ Providing a specific example to illustrate the main idea.

■ Paraphrasing the main idea later in the paragraph.

■ Providing reasons, proofs, or details that support the main idea.

■ Illustrating the main idea graphically.

Read this short paragraph. Which sentence expresses the main idea?

Harmful substances that get into food as it is grown, processed, sorted, or packaged are called *contaminants.* High doses of some contaminants have been linked to serious health problems such as cancer, birth defects, and allergies. Some of the contaminants which may be present in food are pesticides, industrial chemical wastes, and chemicals used in raising farm animals.[1]

You were correct if you said the first sentence expresses the main idea. Notice that the sentence is broad enough to cover all the points made later in the paragraph, but it does not go beyond the information presented. Now, what methods has the author used to support the main idea? She has used two: she has provided reasons for considering contaminants harmful (they have been linked to specific health problems); she has given examples of contaminants (pesticides, chemical industrial wastes, and so on).

**Signals for Important Ideas.**   In addition to reading for the main idea of each paragraph, you must look for other important ideas in your reading. Again, writers provide signals to show what is important in the message they are trying to convey. These signals include defined terms, enumerations, repetition, and words indicating importance or transition. The passage on page 148 shows how the signals are used to help communicate the meaning.

■ *Defined terms.* Words and phrases that are critical to an understanding of the subject matter are usually defined when they are first mentioned. The defined term is often highlighted by the use of quotation marks, italics, or boldface type. Sometimes examples are provided as well.

■ *Enumerations.* Enumerations, or lists, usually give supporting information to the main idea of the paragraph that introduces them. They are often introduced by a sentence or phrase describing the contents of the list. Enumerated items are generally set off on separate lines and numbered. Sometimes each item of an enumeration is a paragraph with its own main idea.

■ *Repetition.* A repeated statement or phrase is generally an important one. Sometimes, the repetition is a paraphrase, intended to clarify. At other times, repetition is used to link paragraphs, indicating the same subject matter but changing main ideas.

■ *Words indicating importance.* When an author wants to call

| TABLE 9-1 | COMMON TRANSITIONAL WORDS AND PHRASES | | | |
|---|---|---|---|---|
| | Cause and Effect | Continuation and Emphasis | Thought Reversal | Example |
| | therefore<br>thus<br>consequently<br>then<br>so<br>hence | furthermore<br>besides<br>in addition<br>moreover<br>likewise<br>also | however<br>on the contrary<br>but<br>yet<br>nevertheless<br>instead<br>otherwise | for example<br>that is<br>namely<br>for instance<br>like<br>such as |

attention to a particularly important fact, statement, or idea, he or she may introduce it with words such as *the main factor is, a significant issue is, especially important is, the basic idea is.* The ideas or statements following such introductory phrases are worth noting.

■ *Words indicating transition.* Relationships between facts, ideas, paragraphs, and sections can be signaled by the use of words that indicate transition, or change. If you can spot these words, you will better understand the organization of the ideas in the reading.

There are many transitional words and phrases, some of which are shown in Table 9-1. When a discussion is resuming or continuing, for example, the author may signal this by using words such as *in addition, the next point, the third reason,* or *also.* The continued discussion can lead to another example or additional statements supporting the main theme of the paragraph or section:

Employee turnover can have several negative consequences, especially if the turnover rate is high. Often it is difficult to replace the departed employees, and the direct and indirect costs to the organization of replacing workers are expensive. The remaining employees may be demoralized from the loss of valued coworkers and both work and social patterns may be disrupted until replacements are found. *Also,* the organization's reputation in the community may suffer.[2]

Words indicating thought reversal show that a point has been made but now the writer is modifying it, perhaps to show exceptions or contrary opinions. Examples of words that signal a reversal are *on the other hand, however, but, yet,* and *instead.* This sentence follows the quotation above, indicating that the results of employee turnover may not be entirely negative:

> *However,* some benefits may arise from turnover . . .[3]

Other transitional words show cause and effect and introduce examples. Completing the paragraph quoted above is the following phrase introducing examples:

> . . . *such as* more opportunities for internal promotion and the infusion of expertise from newly hired employees.[4]

Read the following passage from start to finish to see how many of the signals—defined terms, enumerations, repetition, words indicating importance, and transitional words—are used to help communicate the meaning.

> Have you ever read the ingredients on a food label and then had second thoughts about eating? Over 2800 additives are used today and many have tongue-twisting names. Actually, sugar, salt, and corn syrup are the most widely used. Additives fill several (basic) (purposes):  *Words indicating importance*
>
> *Enumeration* ■ (They) add nutrients. Some substances added to food make it more nutritious. Vitamins and minerals, (for example), are fre- *Transition* quently added to improve the nutritional value of foods. . . .
>
> ■ (They) give flavor. Some fresh foods, (for instance), vary in flavor *Transition* from one growing season to the next. Flavorings make sure that *Repetition* a product such as canned cherry pie filling always has the same flavor.
>
> ■ (They) preserve food. Foods are often processed months before they are eaten. Many of these foods would spoil in a short time without the additives. (Thus) additives increase the shelf life of *Transition* the food. The (shelf life) is the length of time food holds its *Defined term* original flavor and quality in a store or your home. Calcium propionate, (for instance), keeps bread from getting moldy. *Transition*
>
> ■ *They maintain texture.* Every food has a certain texture—such as smooth, chewy, or crunchy—that people are used to. Some foods can lose their texture easily when processed. With the use of additives, pickles stay crisp and whipped mixtures such as dessert toppings remain light and fluffy. . . .

■ *They give color.* Processed foods often lose their natural color or have a color that most people would not like. To make the food look appetizing, artificial coloring is added. For example, *Transition* the cheese sauce in a package of frozen vegetables includes ingredients to give it a yellow color.

■ *They control acidity.* Some additives control the acidity of food. Many foods keep their flavor, color, and nutrients longer when they have the proper level of acidity. Acids are also used to *Transition* give a tart flavor to fruit drinks.

■ *They help age foods.* Some foods, such as flour or cheese, may *Transition* be aged before they are sold. Additives can speed up the aging process.[5]

What devices do the authors use to communicate the main idea, that additives have many uses?

■ First, they use enumeration to present each use of food additives.

■ They use the signal word *basic* when introducing the list to indicate that these are important broad purposes of food additives.

■ They use repetition of the word *they* to reinforce the idea that all the items in the list are related.

■ They show a defined term in boldface type for emphasis.

■ Last, they use transitional words to show cause and effect and introduce examples.

If you recognized all or most of these signals, you are well on your way to better comprehension of what you read.

## Highlighting the Material

Now that you have read a passage and recognized the main idea of each paragraph and other signals for important material, you are ready to *highlight*, or mark, the material. First, you decide what to mark; then, you decide how to mark it.

**What to Highlight.** If you understand how to look for main ideas, you have a good idea of what to highlight in your reading. Remember, you are selecting key information and supporting data that are important for your understanding of the material. Highlight main ideas, defined terms, enumerations, and other important material that shows the development of the subject matter.

Beware of falling into the "highlight everything syndrome." Students sometimes get carried away and mark nearly everything, which is as helpful as marking nothing. Keep in mind, you are trying to mark *only* the information you must understand and the important ideas you must remember. Be selective.

**How to Mark.**   Some students mark their books using a combination of highlighting, underlining, stars, brackets, and so on, to flag ideas

---

### Temperament

One baby seems to smile and laugh almost all the time, hardly ever crying, while another reverses the pattern. Such differences often show up right from birth, demonstrating distinct differences in temperament—a person's characteristic style of approaching people and situations. After following 133 babies from birth, researchers identified 9 different aspects of temperament that appear inborn (Thomas, Chess, & Birch, 1968): (1) activity level; (2) regularity in biological functioning (sleeping, eating, eliminating); (3) readiness to accept new people and situations; (4) adaptability to change; (5) sensitivity to noise, light, and other sensory stimuli; (6) mood (cheerfulness or unhappiness); (7) intensity of responses; (8) distractibility; and (9) persistence. Biological differences may be at the root of such temperamental diversity. Newborns with lower levels of the enzyme monoamine oxidase (MAO) are more active, more excitable, and crankier than those with higher MAO levels (Sostek & Wyatt, 1981). Previous research has established a probable genetic basis for such variations.

Certain combinations of these nine temperamental traits produce three distinctive personalities. *1* About 40 percent of the children studied can be described as *easy* children: they're happy most of the time; adjust easily to new situations; and sleep, eat, and eliminate on a fairly predictable schedule. *2* About 10 percent are *difficult:* they cry easily, are irregular in body functions, and take a long time to adjust to a new routine. *3* And about 15 percent are *slow to warm up:* mild in their responses, with a need to take time adjusting to new experiences and people (Thomas & Chess, 1977). Of course, many children do not fit neatly into any of these categories.

*Source:* Diane E. Papalia and Sally Wendkos Olds, *Psychology,* 2nd ed., McGraw-Hill, New York, 1988, p. 327. Reprinted with permission of McGraw-Hill, Inc.

Marked reading assignment

| TABLE 9-2 | MARKING A READING | | |
|---|---|---|---|
| | **What to Mark** | **How to Mark It** | **Symbol** |
| | Main idea of paragraph | Underline it | _____ |
| | Defined term | In margin, write *df* | *df* |
| | Important idea | Underline, asterisk in margin | _____* |
| | Long important material | Bracket it in margin | ] |
| | Difficult material | Question mark in margin | ? |
| | Enumerations | Number them if they are not already numbered | 1  2  3 |
| | Notebook material | Check mark in margin | ✔ |

they will later note on a separate sheet of paper. If you don't wish to write in your book (or can't because it doesn't belong to you), you can still mark the reading by writing on removable self-adhesive slips of paper, which you can stick on each page and remove after you have finished notetaking.

You can use a highlighting pen, a pencil, or a pen to show the important points you want to note for studying later. Don't try to get fancy by mixing a variety of colors and ending up with a rainbow effect. Remember, you are marking to learn. Keep your marking simple. Table 9-2 shows some easy symbols for marking a reading, and the illustration on page 150 shows a marked passage.

## TAKING NOTES

As you learned in Part 2, taking notes makes you an active learner. When you take notes on a reading assignment, you are forced to be an active reader. Your understanding of the material will improve, and you will remember more of what you read. In addition, the notes you take will serve as a study aid and reduce studying time before exams. Instead of rereading your text, you can study from your notes.

Here are some suggestions to help you make the most out of taking notes on what you read:

```
Papalia, Ch. 9, "Early Development," (cont.)

Temperament    | Temperament
               |   Def.—characteristic way of dealing with
               |   people and events
               |
9 aspects      |   9 aspects of temperament:
               |     1. activity level
               |     2. biological regularity
               |     3. acceptance of new people & situations
               |     4. adaptability to change
               |     5. sensitivity to stimuli
               |     6. mood
               |     7. intensity
               |     8. distractibility
               |     9. persistence
               |
3 personality  |   3 personality types produced by 9 aspects
   types       |   of temperament.
               |     1. easy
               |     2. difficult
               |     3. slow to warm up
```

Sample of notes on a reading assignment

1. Use the most appropriate sectioned paper format, as described in Chapter 4.
2. Write legibly in ink.
3. Identify the textbook reading by indicating the author, chapter number, and chapter title on the top of the page. If you are taking notes on an article or other book, identify the author, title, publisher or journal, page number, and so on.

4. Take notes section by section so that you can focus on small portions of information.
5. Record heads, subheads, enumerations, and other important ideas.
6. Use the outline format where possible.
7. Use phrases and words, not full sentences, and paraphrase where possible.
8. When you finish a section, read and mark the next section and then take notes.
9. When you have finished the article or chapter, summarize it briefly in your own words.

## REVIEWING YOUR NOTES

When you have finished taking notes on a chapter or article and have written a summary, you should immediately review your notes. First, fill in any incomplete material and correct garbled information by referring to the reading. Then add recall words to the left-hand column you have reserved for this purpose.

When you study your notes for a test, use the recall notes to give yourself a quiz on the material. Cover the main column(s) of notes, leaving only the recall notes visible. Then change each recall note into a question, and answer the question orally or in writing without referring to your notes. Check your answers. Have you responded correctly? Mark any material you are having trouble with, and go back over it again until you are satisfied with your understanding and retention.

## REFERENCES

1. Helen Kowtaluk and Alice O. Kopan, *Food for Today*, Glencoe Publishing Company, Mission Hills, Calif., 1986, p. 25. Reprinted with permission.
2. Keith Davis and John W. Newstrom, *Human Behavior at Work*, 8th ed., McGraw-Hill Book Company, New York, 1989, pp. 181–182. Reprinted with permission.
3. Ibid., p. 182. Reprinted with permission.
4. Ibid. Reprinted with permission.
5. Kowtaluk, op. cit., pp. 22–23. Reprinted with permission.

# SUMMARY

Both comprehension and retention are necessary results of reading for your courses. To achieve these goals, you must learn how to read an assignment, take notes, and review your notes.

There are two basic approaches to reading: (1) reading twice, the first time quickly and the second time slowly, or (2) reading once slowly, for comprehension. Whichever approach you use, you must read, mark, and take notes on one section at a time.

Reading for main ideas involves identifying the main idea of each paragraph and recognizing other important ideas. Signals writers use to identify main ideas are defined terms, enumerations, repetition, words indicating importance, and words indicating transition. To help you understand the material, mark main ideas, defined terms, enumerations, and other important items.

Taking notes on a reading assignment, one section at a time, will help you understand and remember the material. Your notes will serve as a study aid. Instead of rereading the text, you can review your notes when you study for an exam.

Name                                                                                    Date

# CHAPTER 9 ACTIVITIES

## CHECK YOUR UNDERSTANDING

**1.** Briefly describe the two basic approaches to reading an assignment.

_____

_____

**2.** What four methods are commonly used by writers to help the reader understand the message of a paragraph?

_____

_____

_____

**3.** List five methods writers use to signal important ideas.

_____

_____

_____

**4.** What items should you highlight in your reading?

_____

_____

**5.** Why does taking notes on reading assignments save you time when you are studying for a test?

_____

_____

## APPLY YOUR READING AND NOTETAKING SKILLS

**1.** Referring to the selection entitled "Civil Liberties and Civil Rights" on pages 156–158, answer the following questions.

## Civil Liberties and Civil Rights

The term "civil liberty" is frequently used interchangeably with the term "civil right." One can speak of free speech as either a civil liberty or a civil right. But the term "civil liberty" emphasizes the freedom one has to do something, while the term "civil right" emphasizes one's just and equal claim to something. Freedom of speech in strict usage is a civil liberty; the entitlement to equal access to the courts is a civil right. . . .

## HOW ARE RIGHTS PROTECTED?

Protection of civil rights and liberties involves some of the most difficult kinds of judgments Americans are called upon to make. This is because protection of rights in particular circumstances often involves issues affecting fundamental constitutional questions. Will increased freedom for works thought obscene by some lead to a more robust and open society or to a sordid society without the self-restraint needed for a people who are to govern themselves? Where does privacy begin and the reach of government stop? Should competing views of the importance of various rights be resolved by the courts or by legislatures?

## Issues in Determining Rights

In general, there are four important questions citizens and political leaders must face in trying to secure the equal rights of all citizens.

First: *Who has rights?* This is one of the most fundamental questions. Right-to-life advocates, for example, argue that an unborn child has the same right to life as a person who has been born. Freedom-of-choice proponents argue (and the Supreme Court agrees) that a fetus has no civil rights. The Supreme Court recently ruled that the state of California could discriminate against noncitizens in hiring peace officers (*Cabell v. Chavez-Salido*, 1982). Before the Civil War, some people argued that blacks possessed no rights under the Constitution. These kinds of disagreements have involved questions of the most profound kind: Who is human? What is a citizen? (Brant, 1965).

Second: *What is a right?* People sometimes disagree whether an alleged right is indeed a right. In *Griswold v. Connecticut* (1965) the Supreme Court held that there is a Constitutional right of privacy which protects the right to use or to advise others in the use of contraceptives. This same right was later held to limit the state's power to regulate abortions (*Roe v. Wade*, 1973) and marriage (*Zoblocki v. Redhail*, 1978). The Court argued that this right, although not explicitly mentioned in the Constitution, was implied by various provisions of the Bill of Rights (*Griswold*

Reading assignment: "Civil Liberties and Civil Rights"

*v. Connecticut,* 1965). Others have thought that the judges invented this right in order to achieve the policy result they desired.

Interpretation of particular rights frequently involves defining more exactly what the right in question is. When motion pictures were first invented, the question arose as to whether they were protected by the First Amendment, which safeguards freedom of the press but which makes no mention, of course, of freedom of motion pictures. At first the Court held that motion pictures were not protected because movies were not a medium for informing citizens as the press was, but instead were an entertainment medium akin to amusement parks or horse racing. As such, they could be regulated. Later the Court reversed itself, giving freedom of the press a broader meaning that accorded protection to movies.

Third: *How are rights reconciled with other rights and duties?* The protection of the rights of one person may conflict with the protection of the rights of another person or with the security of the country or orderly civil life. When Dr. Samuel Sheppard, a wealthy Cleveland doctor, was tried for murdering his wife, newspapers and radio covered the story and Dr. Sheppard's love life in lurid detail. Journalists flooded the courtroom, frequently disrupting the proceedings. The Supreme Court ruled that such freedom for the news media had undermined Dr. Sheppard's right to a fair trial (*Sheppard v. Maxwell,* 1966).

In time of war, unrestricted rights to publish whatever one wants may conflict with the government's duty to secure the lives of its citizens and the victory of its armies. When Charles Schenck mailed circulars to young men urging resistance to the draft during World War I, the Supreme Court ruled that the threat of disruption of the war effort was such an evil that Schenck's freedom to publish could be restricted (*Schenck v. United States,* 1919).

Fourth: *Who secures rights?* Just as people disagree over what rights should be secured, or which rights are more important than others, they also disagree about who should make such decisions. In the complex system of government found in the United States there are often several choices. Should rights be protected by the national government or by state and local governments? Liberals generally have argued that national protection is needed to guard against local prejudices, while conservatives have argued that local and state officials understand better the particular problems of an area in attempting to reconcile the conflicting claims characteristic of civil rights enforcement.

Within the national government, where should protection originate? All the branches of government have assumed some responsibility in protecting rights. In recent years Congress has passed important civil rights acts, the president has supplemented these with executive orders and has used presidential powers to enforce laws and court orders, and the courts have made many landmark rulings. But where should the primary responsibility lie—with elected representatives who have their fingers on the pulse of the country or with judges protected from popular prejudices? Who should decide, if there are disagreements among the branches, how civil rights ought to be enforced? This issue has led to conflict among the three branches over such issues as school prayer, busing for the purpose of school integration, and protection of the rights of those accused or convicted of crimes.

Source: Ceasar et al., *American Government*, McGraw-Hill, New York, 1984, pp. 575–577. Reprinted with permission of McGraw-Hill, Inc.

**a.** What is the most appropriate reading method? Why?

_____

_____

_____

**b.** What are the main ideas of the selection?

_____

_____

_____

**c.** What are the supporting ideas of the selection?

_____

_____

_____

**d.** What transitional signals are used in the selection?

_____

_____

**e.** What enumeration signals are used in the selection?

_____

_____

**2.** Mark, or highlight, the selection above (pages 156–158). Then complete the following activities on a separate sheet of paper.
   **a.** Using the marked selection, take notes about what you have read.
   **b.** Using your notes, create recall notes.

    **c.** Using your recall notes, create questions for a self-quiz.

    **d.** Prepare a brief summary of what you have read.

**3.** Referring to the article entitled "At Today's Supermarket, The Computer Is Doing It All" on pages 160–162, answer the following questions.

    **a.** What is the most appropriate reading method? Why?

        _____

        _____

        _____

    **b.** What are the main ideas of the selection?

        _____

        _____

        _____

        _____

    **c.** What defined terms are included in the article?

        _____

        _____

        _____

        _____

    **d.** What are some enumeration signals used in the article?

        _____

        _____

    **e.** What are some transitional words used in the article?

        _____

        _____

**4.** Mark, or highlight, the article (pages 160–162). Then complete the following activities on a separate sheet of paper.

    **a.** Using the marked article, take notes about what you have read.

    **b.** Using your notes, create recall notes.

    **c.** Using your recall notes, create questions for a self-quiz.

    **d.** Prepare a brief summary of what you have read.

# AT TODAY'S SUPERMARKET, THE COMPUTER IS DOING IT ALL

## IT HAS MOVED BEYOND THE CHECKOUT TO TRACK EVERYTHING FROM PILFERAGE TO PROFIT

Ronald K. Springer isn't one to get nostalgic. When he started in the grocery business 25 years ago, one of his chores was to take home piles of invoices and figure his store's gross profit on truckloads of food. Today, as manager of the Super Shop 'n Save in South Portland, Me., Springer oversees a market that beeps and whirs as computers do everything from figuring those dreaded invoices to setting up work schedules for checkout clerks. "I don't think the old days were simpler," he says. "They were more difficult."

More than half of the nation's supermarkets are equipped with scanners, those computerized checkout machines that read the bar code on a box of Wheaties. At least one in four uses a central computer to help run the business. But now, food stores such as Springer's are going beyond that, becoming what might be called "electronic supermarkets" permeated by computers. Says Timothy M. Hammond, senior vice-president of the Food Marketing Institute, a grocers' trade group: "Within the last couple of years, the industry has moved to phase two—using the mound of scanning data to influence management."

"Phase two" is rewriting the rules of the trade, both for small outfits such as Gromer Super Markets Inc. in Elgin, Ill., and for giants such as Safeway Stores Inc. Data of unprecedented precision, on everything from pilferage to profit per item, are giving the best supermarket managers a competitive advantage that some analysts say could double profit margins, which today average only 1.2%. It's even having a major impact on foodmakers such as Campbell Soup Co. The numbers, for instance, can help tell a manufacturer that better packaging will sell more of his products.

The new system is working well at Hannaford Brothers, the Scarborough (Me.) owner of Shop 'n Save stores. In 1980, Hannaford posted a respectable 1% profit margin, then the industry average. Since that time, by using computers in all phases of its business, Hannaford has boosted margins steadily, to 1.8% in the first quarter of this year. "I would characterize what's happening as a revolution," says Hugh C. Smith, a product management specialist at Hannaford.

With data flowing from stores and warehouses to an *IBM* 4381 mainframe at headquarters, Hannaford calculates virtually every cost involved in getting its goods from manufacturer to consumer—including shipping expenses, warehouse handling requirements, bulkiness of display, energy needs at the store, and the time canned corn spends on the shelf

Reading assignment: "At Today's Supermarket, The Computer Is Doing It All" before it's bought. Hannaford crunches these data for each of its more than 17,000 products and each of its 65 stores.

**'EYE-OPENER.'** The resulting richness of detail is staggering. "We can call up a report on the direct profit contribution of pickle Brand X at store Z during some seven-week period," says James J. Jermann, Hannaford's vice-president for merchandising. Armed with such information, retail buyers and marketers can for the first time make truly informed decisions on, say, which brands of gherkins to carry and how to price them. That's a far cry from the not-so-distant days when a grocer's only guide to profit contribution was the markup percentage on a given item, which often ignored variable costs such as transportation.

"Computerized profit calculations have been a real eye-opener for the retailer," says John R. Phipps of Touche Ross & Co. As the accounting firm's director for food industry consulting, Phipps is the guru of what the industry calls direct product profitability (*DPP*) analysis (table). The concept was born in the early 1960s, but it wasn't until the cost of mainframe computing power fell in the 1980s that *DPP* caught on.

Retailers have always known that certain items must be priced as "loss leaders," carried primarily to bring shoppers into the store. But Phipps says that "*DPP* is showing that about 20% of the items in a typical grocery store actually lose money, which means that the more of those you sell, the more you lose." In these cases, *DPP* analysis serves two novel functions. It identifies exactly which products hemorrhage profit, and it offers clues about how to stop the bleeding.

**UNEXPECTED WINNER.** The results are often surprising. House brands, once considered big money-makers because of their low initial cost, turn out to be skimpy performers compared with better-advertised name brands that move faster. Paper products are also a drag on profit, given their bulk and small price. Stores must sell toilet paper, but *DPP* numbers suggest limiting variety and avoiding costly promotions.

One of the supermarket's unexpected winners, according to *DPP*, is the freezer section. It has traditionally been perceived as too energy-intensive to reap big returns. But frozen meals actually outperform the average grocery item almost two to one because of their large markups. Once enough frozen items have been sold to cover energy costs, profits soar. Soft drinks, dairy goods, snack foods, magazines, and other products delivered directly to stores by manufacturers also make more money than previously thought, because store employees aren't used to stock them.

The wealth of detail compiled by *DPP* often helps retailers and manufacturers streamline their operations. At Hannaford and other chains, *DPP* is translated into "Plan-a-Grams"—printouts that show store managers, shelf by shelf, exactly where to place their stock to maximize profit. A decision on whether to display three rows of Skippy peanut butter rather than two has never been trivial from a profit standpoint. But with Plan-a-Grams, that decision can be based on more than instinct.

**NEW SOPHISTICATION.** *DPP* information also helps Procter & Gamble

Co., Campbell Soup, and other manufacturers design more efficient containers and shipping methods. *DPP* studies have shown that stores prefer to stock lighter-weight packages of detergent, so manufacturers have set out to limit the air and water content in their packages. "We get calls every week from manufacturers interested in our *DPP* findings," says Hannaford's Smith. Hannaford and an increasing number of other chains sell access to their scanning data and cooperate with manufacturers running *DPP* experiments. Some, such as Safeway, staff a separate office to design and run such tests for manufacturers they deal with.

Hoping to build on the industry's new sophistication, automation consultants, market researchers, and hardware and software producers are promoting an expanding array of scanning spinoffs. Set to debut later this year in some markets is the "electronic shelf," which will offer shoppers cost and nutrition information at the touch of an electronic display—and let retailers constantly revise prices at the touch of their own buttons. Assuming that consumers don't mind having their privacy invaded, new identification cards tied to scanners will let stores track individual families' purchases and target them with coupons and ads. In the long run, scanning and *DPP* analysis will not be limited to supermarkets. Drug chains, convenience stores, and even department stores already are planning their own versions of the system.

The move toward *DPP* analysis could also transform the staff back at the headquarters of the new electronic supermarket. Managers who know computers are already in increasing demand. "Retailing has always had an image problem with *MBAs*," says Walter J. Salmon, an expert in the field at Harvard business school. "If in fact *DPP* leads to reorganizations in favor of sophisticated product managers, *MBAs* will be more attracted to the food industry."

Even so, store managers don't seem to see automation as a threat to their authority or their intuition. Ron Springer says he needs help to manage his 250 employees and 17,000 products: "Bring it on. Bring it on."

*By Gary Geipel in Scarborough, Me.*

## IMPROVE YOUR WRITING SKILLS

**Subject-Verb Agreement:**   The basic principle of subject-verb agreement is that a verb must agree with its subject in person and number. If you remember these points, subject-verb agreement should not be a problem:

**1.** The verb *to be* is the only verb that has a special first-person form: the present-tense form *am*, which is used with the first-person subject pronoun *I*.

## USING INFORMATION TO MAKE SUPERMARKETS MORE EFFICIENT

**STEP 1:** Raw data flow from stores and warehouses to a mainframe computer, usually at chain headquarters. Included are sales records from checkout stands, data on product delivery schedules, employee work schedules, energy use, and the amount of time products spend in chain warehouses before they're shipped to stores.

**STEP 2:** The numbers are crunched to help make better decisions about what products to sell, how to display them, and how to make their storage and delivery more efficient. Headquarters can determine which brands of soap make the most money, for example, and cut back on the least profitable ones. Or it can use computer-projected cost estimates to gauge how profitable a new brand of soap might be. The numbers might also suggest whether products should be delivered directly to stores or go to a central warehouse first.

**STEP 3:** Headquarters sends its recommendations back to the store and to warehouse managers and their assistants. Sometimes called "Plan-a-Grams," these instructions include detailed schematics of every shelf, showing the store manager where to display each of the up to 17,000 products sold in large supermarkets. The plan may even recommend prices for these goods.

**STEP 4:** Headquarters also gives or sells the numbers generated in Step 1 to manufacturers, which may subsequently modify their products. For instance, the numbers may tell a soap maker that its products would sell better if they were packaged differently.

2. All verbs have a special present tense form for use with a singular noun or pronoun other than the pronoun *I*. For verbs other than *to be*, this special form ends in *s*, for example, *plays, denies*, and *makes*.

3. All verbs except *to be* have one past-tense form that is used with all subjects regardless of person or number: *played, denied, made*, and so on. The verb *to be* has the singular past-tense form *was* and the plural past-tense form *were*.

4. Except in very formal writing, *will* plus a main verb is used to indicate future tense with all subjects. In very formal writing, *shall* is used with the subject *I* or *we* and *will* is used with all other subjects.

## Practice

Applying the preceding general principle of subject-verb agreement, underline which of the verbs shown in parentheses is correct in each of the sentences below.

**1.** I (*am, are, be*) very happy to learn of your promotion.

**2.** We (*am, are, be*) fortunate to have him on our team.

**3.** You (*know, knows*) more about the subject than she (*do, does*).

**4.** He (*are, be, is*) the leading candidate for the position.

**5.** The members (*pay, pays*) annual dues of $60.

**6.** The store (*sell, sells*) appliances at discount prices.

**7.** She (*manage, manages*) a large real estate firm.

**8.** Two applicants (*was, were*) interviewed and hired today.

Name                                                               Date

# PART 4 PROJECT

## YOUR OBJECTIVES

When you complete this project, you will have demonstrated your ability to:

- Preview a textbook efficiently.
- Preview a chapter efficiently.
- Preview graphics.
- Read for the main ideas in a chapter.
- Identify signals for important ideas.
- Mark the reading material for notetaking.
- Take good notes.
- Use your notes as study aids.

**Directions:** This project is designed to reinforce the previewing, reading, and notetaking skills you learned in Part 4. Assume that you are a student in Business 215 and your text for the course is *Business in Action*, 3rd ed., by Lester A. Bittel, Ronald S. Burke, and Charles P. Bilbrey. Now turn to Appendix B. There you will see a reprint of the introductory material and one complete chapter from this textbook. These materials will give you all the practice you need to preview, read, and take notes effectively in all your courses.

As you complete the project, be sure to follow the instructions carefully and answer the questions completely. Remember: Mastering previewing, reading, and notetaking skills will save you a lot of time and, more importantly, it will improve your ability to learn.

## Previewing the Book

In Chapter 8 you learned that previewing is a basic part of the reading process. Now practice your previewing skills by following these steps in sequence.

**Step 1.** *Read the title of the book.*

Then answer these questions:

- Does the title distinctly express the subject matter of the book?
- Have you had experience with the subject of business before?
- What do you know about business?

**Step 2.** *Skim the Preface.*

What does the Preface tell you about this book?

- How is the textbook organized?
- How is this edition different from previous editions of the book?
- What additional studying aids are available for students?

**Step 3.** *Read the Table of Contents.*

The Table of Contents shows you the arrangement and focus of the book. Answer these questions based on the contents pages:

- Is the subject material arranged chronologically?
- Why do you believe the authors chose this type of organization?
- What are the major subjects discussed in the textbook?

**Step 4.** *Identify the information contained in the back of the book.*

## Previewing a Chapter

Turn to Chapter 16. You are now ready to preview the chapter.

**Step 5.** *Skim the front material.*

The authors have provided a list of objectives and a chapter outline.

- Are these objectives useful to you as you preview? Why?
- What do you know about Chapter 16 after reading them?
- Is the outline useful to you as you preview the chapter? Why?

**Step 6.** *Skim the back material.*

Several miscellaneous parts appear at the end of the chapter to help you understand the information presented.

- List these parts.
- Skim the Key Concepts. Is this feature useful? Why?
- Note the Review Questions and Case Critiques listed at the end of the chapter. When you read, attempt to recall the information that is needed to answer these questions. The questions reflect the major points that were made in the chapter. The important terms you'll be reading within the chapter are also listed here. By skimming terms now, your reading will be easier.

### Step 7. *Skim the pages for heads.*

- How many levels of heads are shown in the chapter?
- For each subhead, write down its realtionship to the head.
- For each sub-subhead, write down its relationship to the sub-head and to the head.
- Turn each head into a question. Remember to use words such as *who, what, when, which, why,* and *how significant.* You will answer these questions when you read the chapter.

### Step 8. *Skim the pages for key words.*

- How can key words be identified in a passage?
- List a minimum of one key word you can locate on each page of narrative in the chapter.

### Step 9. *Preview the graphics.*

Six graphics appear in the chapter to help you understand the material.

- Name the graphics that appear in the chapter.
- Look at Figure 16–1. Read the caption and skim the information in the figure. What is the purpose of this graphic?
- Look at Table 16–2. Read the title, the column heads, and the explanatory note. What information is contained in this table?
- Look at Table 16–5. Read the title, the column heads, and the explanatory note. What is the purpose of this table?

### Step 10. *Identify how you will read the chapter.*

For Chapter 16, which one of the two basic approaches to reading the material will be better for you? Why?

Step 11. *Identify the main idea of each paragraph along with supporting information.*

■ Read each paragraph on each page of the chapter. Write down the main ideas of each paragraph.

■ Write down other important or supporting ideas in each paragraph. Look for defined terms, enumerations, repetition, words indicating importance, and words indicating transition.

Step 12. *Mark the material.*

You are now ready to mark your reading for notetaking purposes. Use a highlighter or abbreviated notations for marking (see Table 9–2 on page 151), or removable self-adhesive slips of paper.

■ Mark the main ideas.

■ Mark defined terms, enumerations, and other important material that shows the development of the subject matter.

## Taking Notes on the Chapter

Step 13. *Section your paper for notetaking.*

Use the 2½-inch by 6-inch column method.

Step 14. *Use the information presented in Chapter 9 ("Reading and Notetaking," pages 143–164), to take notes on Chapter 16 of* Business in Action.

Step 15. *After completing the notes, write a brief summary.*

Step 16. *Review your notes.*

■ Are they logical? Are they complete?

■ Fill in any incomplete material by referring to the chapter.

Step 17. *Write recall words in the left column of your paper.*

Step 18. *Quiz yourself on your mastery of the information presented by changing each recall note into a question.*

■ Write down the questions.

■ Answer the questions in writing without referring to your notes.

■ Check your answers and review any material you are having trouble with until you are satisfied with your understanding.

# PREPARING FOR TESTS

All the study skills you have learned so far—time management, taking notes, listening in class, previewing, and reading—are put to the test when you take an exam. How well have you carried out your routine studying? You'll find out when you start preparing for a test. In Part 5 you'll learn:

- **What to study.**

- **How to study for a test.**

- **How to minimize anxiety by thoroughly preparing.**

- **How to overcome stress during a test.**

- **Strategies for taking objective tests.**

- **Strategies for taking essay tests.**

# 10 STUDYING FOR TESTS

Ideally, studying for tests is an ongoing process that begins on the first day of the term and continues until your last exam. If you have been attending class, keeping up with the reading, taking notes, and doing assignments on time, you have been laying the foundation for test preparation. You should already have what you need to study—your notes and other materials. Now you must learn the steps involved in studying for a test.

## WHAT TO STUDY

Your notes on class discussions and readings are your most important source of information when studying for a test. Less important, although valuable, are other sources such as instructor handouts, past quizzes, study guides, and other textbook aids.

### Notes

Perhaps you are beginning to realize just how important it is to take notes in class and when you read. Taking notes forces you to sort out the important facts and ideas for each course. If you also review your notes regularly, adding recall notes and summaries, you have already learned much of what you need to know. A good set of notes will give you three major advantages when you start to prepare for a test:

**1.** *You have ready-made study aids.* A comprehensive set of notes means that you do not have to try to remember what went on in class or reread your textbook. In taking notes, you have recorded the important material, identified key terms and concepts, and put the subject into your own words.

**2.** *You have a self-test.* When you added recall words and phrases to your notes, you created a way to test yourself on the material. When you turn each recall note into a question and answer it, you test your knowledge as well as identify items likely to be included on the instructor's test.

**3.** *You have an overview of the material.* The summary statements you wrote after each set of notes can be used to gain an understanding of the course as a whole. As you read the summaries, you can see the relationships between the topics presented.

## Other Sources for Studying

Although your notes are the major source of information when you are studying for a test, there are other sources that you should not overlook. These include:

**1.** *Instructor handouts.* Many instructors give handouts during class sessions to illustrate key points. Reviewing these handouts provides you with an indication of what the instructor thinks is important.

**2.** *Past quizzes and tests.* Review your past quizzes and tests. What information was included? What types of questions were asked? What did you have difficulty with? Try to figure out what you could have done to prepare better for these tests and consequently, the test you are studying for at present.

**3.** *Chapter activities in the textbook.* Look at the activities at the end of chapters to be covered on the test. Since these activities are generally based on the most important information presented in the text, they can give you some insight about what may be included on the test.

**4.** *Study guides and workbooks.* Some texts have study guides or workbooks to help students master the textbook content. The activities and questions can be used to give an additional review of the course content.

## HOW TO STUDY

If you have a good set of notes from class sessions and reading assignments, preparing for a test need not be an anxiety-filled and rushed process. Start about a week before the test, and follow these steps:

**1.** *Determine what is to be tested.* This sounds so obvious that many students overlook it. What chapters will a quiz cover? If the test is a final, will you be tested on the whole course or the material covered since the midterm? Make sure you know what will be covered so that you can direct your studying efforts accordingly.

**2.** *Look at past quizzes and tests.* Look at the tests you have taken so far to determine which areas you need to do better in and to see what type of tests the instructor gives.

**3.** *Organize your notes and handouts.* Group according to subject matter your classroom notes, handouts, and notes from readings. If you have followed the notetaking suggestions in Chapter 4, this will be easy, since you will be able to remove and rearrange notes taken on one side of the paper within a loose-leaf binder. Arrange the topics in an organized sequence, usually the sequence of the classroom lectures. While you are organizing the notes, stay alert for notations indicating that the material might be on the test.

**4.** *Read through all your notes for an overview.* Block out enough study time to read all your notes, including the summaries, in one sitting. By doing this, you get an overview of the subject, a better understanding of relationships between major topics, and an idea of what topics you may need to spend more time on.

**5.** *Quiz yourself.* Turning each recall note into a question, quiz yourself on the contents of your notes. Respond to each question either orally or in writing, and then check your notes to see if you were correct. For the questions you get wrong or feel shaky about, study your notes again and repeat the quiz. As you finish each set of notes, read the summary for reinforcement. Look at your textbook's related chapter activities and study guide material, if any. Continue this process during the course of the week until you have tested yourself on all of your notes to your satisfaction.

**6.** *Drill with your vocabulary flash cards.* As you learned in Chapter 4, preparing and studying vocabulary flash cards is a good way to master the special language of each course. If the subject is scientific or technical, you can also use flash cards for formulas, equations, and so on.

**7.** *Guess what the instructor will ask.* As you work through your notes, keep asking yourself, "Would this be a good question for the test?" Jot down the questions you identify; then make sure you know the answers. Remember, your instructor has a limited amount of material upon which to base an examination. The more you quiz yourself, the more likely you are to anticipate at least some of the test questions.

# SUMMARY

Attending class, keeping up with the reading, taking notes, and doing assignments on time lay the foundation for test preparation. Your notes are the most important source of information when you study for a test. Other sources of studying material are instructor handouts, past tests, text chapter activities, and study guides or workbooks.

During the week before a test, follow these steps to prepare: (1) determine what is to be tested, (2) look at past tests, (3) organize your notes and handouts, (4) read all your notes for an overview, (5) quiz yourself, (6) drill with vocabulary flash cards, and (7) guess what the instructor will ask.

Name                                                          Date

# CHAPTER 10 ACTIVITIES

## CHECK YOUR UNDERSTANDING

**1.** What is the most important source of information when you study for a test? What are some other sources of information?

_____

_____

**2.** What three advantages do a good set of notes give you when you are studying for a test?

_____

_____

**3.** List the seven steps you should follow when studying for a test.

_____

_____

_____

_____

**4.** How should you organize your notes and handouts before studying them?

_____

_____

**5.** Describe how you can quiz yourself on the information in your notes.

_____

_____

_____

## APPLY YOUR KNOWLEDGE

### Case Study

Gus works in a convenience store to earn money to enable him to go to school. Because he has classes during the day, he has been working the night shift from 11 p.m. to 7 a.m. This arrangement is fine except on those days when the person who starts work at 7 a.m. comes in late. Gus has often had to stay until 8 a.m., or even later, waiting to be relieved.

Because of his schedule, Gus has missed his 8:50 a.m. biology class several times this semester. Even when he does attend class, he finds himself sleepy and not always attentive in taking lecture notes. He has, however, kept up with all of the reading assignments and has taken notes to use for studying.

As exam time draws near, Gus is concerned about his biology class. Gus asks you for advice on how to prepare for his biology final examination.

On a separate sheet of paper, write five questions you would ask Gus before giving him advice. Your questions should reflect the information presented in this chapter on how to prepare for an examination.

### Use Notes to Study

Pages 177 and 178 show notes Lori took in her U.S. History class. Since, most of the time, the lectures in the course parallel the course textbook, Lori has ruled her notebook pages with a left margin of 2 inches for recall notes, 5 inches for lecture notes, and 1½ inches for corresponding notes from the textbook.

Read through Lori's notes carefully. Then, on a separate sheet of paper, complete the following activities.

1. Write down the main topic for the day's lecture. State one or two points made in the lecture.
2. To study the contents of this day's lecture, you need to use recall notes. Looking at Lori's recall notes, write a question for each one.
3. Write an answer to each one of the questions you developed based on the recall notes. Could you answer each question without

| | **Lecture Ms Elliott** | |
|---|---|---|
| | *Econ impact of Civil War* | |
| | *q did war help or hurt* | |
| | *econ growth* | |
| | *q did war cause dec in* | |
| | *So wealth* | |
| *econ impact* | *Econ Indicators =* | |
| *of war-3* | *1. No lost more men* | *So lost* |
| | *2. So lost prop value* | *slaves/* |
| *So suffered* | *So suffered =* | *phys* |
| | *a. 1880 farm value ⅓* | *damage to* |
| | *below 1860 level* | *prop* |
| | *b. lack of livestock & farm* | |
| | *equip* | |
| | *c. demand for So cotton* | *1830–1860* |
| | *dropped* | *cotton boom* |
| | *Ex. = Britain bought* | *world demand* |
| | *from India even after* | *incd 5%/yr* |
| | *war* | *1866–1890* |
| | *d. agr did not modernize* | *demand* |
| | *quickly* | *dropped* |
| | | *5%→2%* |

Notes on U.S. Civil War (con't on following page)

referring to the notes a second time? Your response indicates how well you understood and concentrated on the notes.

**4.** Imagine that these are your notes to use in studying for a test in U.S. history. Write three questions that you would anticipate the instructor might use for the test.

| rr constr | 3. Damage to rrs | |
|---|---|---|
| delayed | rr constr interrupted | 1860 31,000 |
| | ex 9,000 mi built before | mi rr track |
| | war | 1900 200,000 |
| | 4,000 mi during war | mi rr track |
| | 16,000 mi after war | |
| rr-Key | RR Key to expansion | Cong. & |
| to expansion | 1. filled in gaps of sm | states gave |
| | lines | land to |
| | 2. connected sm lines w | rr |
| | lgr (consolidation) | |
| | 3. stl gauge dvlp (width | see p 93 |
| | of rr track) | |
| | 4. rr created natl mkt | jobs created |
| | for goods | |
| | 5. improved com | telegraph |
| | across country | co used |
| | | rr land |
| | | to put up |
| | | poles |

Summary:
    The Civil War caused econ probs
for the country esp the So/e.g., farm
values fell & cotton sales dropped.
The rr was the key to the growth
in the econ.

## IMPROVE YOUR WRITING SKILLS

**Pronouns:** *Pronouns* are words that take the place of nouns in phrases, clauses, and sentences. Some pronouns, called *personal pronouns*, have different forms to indicate whether they refer to the speaker (first person), the person spoken to (second person), or the person or thing spoken about (third person). In addition, these pronouns have different forms for singular and plural as well as different forms for use as subjects (called *nominative case*), objects (called *objective case*), and possessives. All personal pronouns in the English language are listed in the following chart.

| Person | Nominative Case | | Objective Case | | Possessive Case | |
|--------|-------|-----|-------|-----|-------|-----|
| | Sing. | Pl. | Sing. | Pl. | Sing. | Pl. |
| First | I | we | me | us | my mine | our ours |
| Second | you | you | you | you | your yours | your yours |
| Third | he she it | they | him her it | them | his her, hers its | their, theirs |

As the subject of a sentence or clause, the second-person personal pronoun *you* is always considered plural and is always used with a plural verb even though it may refer to only one person.

You are highly qualified for this position, Jack.
When you have completed your assignments, each of you should notify your immediate supervisor.

The following personal pronouns ending with *self* are known as *intensive* or *reflexive pronouns*: *myself, ourselves, yourself, yourselves, himself, herself,* and *itself.* Except for *yourself* and *yourselves,* which may refer to the understood subject pronoun *you,* each of these pronouns must have a stated antecedent (subject reference), as shown here:

I probably will have to do the work myself.
Perhaps we ourselves are at fault.

Don't blame yourself.
You will need to make your reservations yourselves.
The company produces products for itself and other firms.
Jeff injured himself while trimming some bushes.
Laura always takes good care of herself.
Several young kittens were left to fend for themselves.

As illustrated by the preceding sentences, a reflexive pronoun may be used as an object of a verb or a preposition, but not as the subject of a sentence or a clause.

## Practice

In each of the following sentences, determine which of the pronoun forms shown in parentheses is correct and underline it.

**1.** (*I, We*) am surprised that (*he, him*) objected to the change.

**2.** (*Her, She*) was confident of (*her, hers*) ability to do a good job.

**3.** All of (*them, they*) must have changed (*their, theirs*) minds.

**4.** Is (*it, its*) (*your, yours*) or (*him, his*)?

**5.** According to (*he, him, his*), the store is changing (*its, their*) policy.

**6.** Are you sure that (*us, we*) should submit (*our, ours*) reports today?

**7.** Is this copy (*mine, my*) or (*her, hers*)?

**8.** You may contact (*I, me*) at (*mine, my*) home address.

**9.** (*Them, They*) are not (*our, ours*).

**10.** Jane told (*us, we*) of (*your, yours*) offer to help (*her, hers*).

**11.** Did he offer to write the letter (*himself, hisself*)?

**12.** Speaking for (*me, myself*), I would accept their offer.

**13.** All of them can be proud of (*theirselves, themselves*).

**14.** Karen bought (*her, herself*) a new raincoat.

**15.** Jean and (*I, myself*) volunteered to assist them.

Can you remember a time when you were *not* anticipating—even worrying—about some kind of test? Probably not. Starting at a young age, people are tested for physical fitness and on their skills in school, sports, music, jobs, and so on. Being nervous about a test is a natural reaction. Indeed, a small amount of nervousness often improves your performance. What is important, however, is that you take steps, both before and during an exam, to keep stress under control so that it does not interfere with your performance.

## BEFORE A TEST

In the last chapter, you learned a method of studying for tests that should ensure you are prepared. Being—and feeling—prepared is the single most important thing you can do before a test to reduce anxiety. To prepare properly and avoid cramming, you must manage your time. Proper studying should leave you with a feeling of confidence and enough time to get ready for the test without rushing.

## Manage Your Time

In Chapter 3 you learned the importance of keeping monthly, weekly, and daily schedules. If you have been using these time management tools, you probably have been keeping up with your course work. In addition, you have been recording the dates of all tests on your monthly calendar so that you are always aware of when a test is coming up. In other words, you are managing your time. Inadequate time to prepare properly is a major cause of anxiety—and with good reason. You can't prepare as thoroughly for a test in one evening as you can over a longer period of time.

Organize your time so that a week before a test you can start the studying process described in Chapter 10. During that week, you'll attend all your classes and do all your assignments. Don't miss class or postpone assignments because of a test. However, you can put off other activities that are less critical to make some time to study.

## Have a Positive Attitude

At the mention of the word *test*, most people get anxious and worry about how they will do. Some students even experience anxiety attacks during which their minds seem to stop functioning. To overcome the fear of taking a test, you need to develop a positive attitude. Feel confidence in your ability to do well.

If you have followed the study suggestions in this book, you have all the tools you need to study effectively for an exam. Since you have made taking and reviewing your notes part of your study routine, you have much of the course information almost committed to memory. The chances are that you are well prepared even before you start the intensive review the week before the test. A feeling of confidence should arise from the feeling that you are well prepared.

As the time for taking the test approaches, you should develop a positive, confident outlook. You know the material, you understand the concepts of the course, and you are ready to demonstrate to your instructor how well you have mastered the material!

## Be Ready

Since you have been studying for a week, the night before the test should be free from time pressure. Review your notes once more, and then get a good night's sleep. Take a quick look at your notes again in the morning. If your exam is scheduled early in the day, you may get up a little earlier to go through your notes for the last time.

Make sure you know what materials you will need to take the test, and the day before, gather them together. You might need pens, pencils, paper, a calculator, a watch, or even your books and notes if it is an open-book test. If you are missing anything, you'll have time to obtain it. If you leave this task for the last minute, all your feelings of preparedness and confidence will be shaken as you try to borrow from or share with a classmate.

On the day of the test, make sure you leave enough time to get to class punctually. Rushing into the room or arriving late can be embarrassing, but more important, it will make you anxious.

## DURING A TEST

Finally, the moment has arrived. You have studied the material and are as prepared as you will ever be. Still, you are nervous about actually taking the test. What can you do to help yourself overcome this anxiety? First, use the few minutes before the test to collect your thoughts. Second, listen or read directions carefully. Last, pace yourself during the exam.

### Collect Your Thoughts

Before the test starts, do a few things to help you concentrate. Choose a seat where you can see and hear but where you will have few distractions. If you don't have a watch, make sure you can see a clock from your seat. Try not to talk to your classmates about the test— you don't want them to get you worried that your studying may have been inadequate. Use the few minutes before the test as "quiet time" to collect your thoughts.

### Pay Attention to Instructions

The test instructions may be written or oral, or both. Never start a test until you fully understand the instructions. Don't be so eager that you begin working while your instructor is talking; he or she may be giving you directions that don't appear on the test itself. If any instructions, oral or written, are unclear to you, ask for help.

If, after starting the test, you realize that you don't understand a direction, get it clarified immediately.

## Pace Yourself

Have you ever taken a test and, five minutes before the end of the period, realized you had not even started a 25-point essay question? To avoid running out of time and becoming anxious, you must learn to pace yourself as you take a test. Pacing yourself will also enable you to use the full amount of time set aside for the test. You do not want to set a record for finishing early, either.

There are two basic strategies for pacing yourself during an exam. First, you should glance over the whole exam to get an overview. Are the questions all of one type and given equal point value? Then you should give each about equal time. Are there two essay questions worth 25 points each, and 50 short-answer questions worth 1 point each? Then half the exam time should be given to answering the two essay questions, and half to the 50 short-answer questions.

Second, you should answer the "easy" questions first. This will enable you to make rapid progress and to maintain your feeling of confidence. Never allow yourself to get stuck on a question; simply make a mark in the margin and go on. Perhaps something later in the exam will trigger your memory and you will be able to answer the difficult question.

Pacing yourself will help you control your feelings of anxiety. If, after a while, you feel yourself rushing unnecessarily or becoming tense, stop working for a moment. Take a few slow, deep breaths, or try to yawn. Both will help you relax. Then resume your work.

## SUMMARY

Good study habits throughout the term and during the week before a test will ensure that you are prepared to do well. To study properly, you must manage your time. If you are well prepared, your anxiety level will decrease and you will develop a positive attitude. In addition, you will have time before the test to gather what you need without rushing.

During the test period, you can minimize anxiety by using the few minutes before the exam starts to collect your thoughts. Make sure you understand all the directions, both oral and written. Pace yourself during the test so that you give adequate attention to each question without rushing or running out of time.

Name                                                      Date

# CHAPTER 11 ACTIVITIES

## CHECK YOUR UNDERSTANDING

**1.** What is the most important thing you can do to reduce anxiety before a test?

_____

_____

**2.** How can managing your time help you reduce test stress?

_____

_____

**3.** What should you do the night before a test?

_____

_____

**4.** Why is it important to understand all the directions before you start taking a test?

_____

_____

**5.** Describe the two basic strategies for pacing yourself during a test.

_____

_____

## APPLY YOUR KNOWLEDGE

### Case Study 1

Paul has been a fairly good student; however, he is beginning to feel the need to get more A's in his classes. There are several scholarships that would be available to him if he had a higher grade-point average.

He has a major exam coming in one week in his sociology course— a course he enjoys very much. Paul prepares for this exam by studying all his notes from the class lectures and the outside readings carefully. He does everything he is supposed to do to prepare for an exam.

Paul feels very confident and ready to take the test when the day comes. He arrives at the classroom in plenty of time so that he can sit quietly and organize his thoughts before the exam is distributed. Everything seems to be just fine. Suddenly, in the middle of the exam, Paul gets excited. His heart is beating faster and his mind doesn't seem to want to concentrate on the test questions. He keeps telling himself that he knows this material, but at the same time he is reminding himself that he needs a good grade in this course. He can't seem to get the correct words together to write the responses to the test questions. The time is passing by, and he is far from finished with the test. Paul is scared—he is going to *fail* this test that he has prepared so well for all last week.

Think about Paul's situation and what he can do about it. Then respond to the following questions on a separate sheet of paper.

1. Have you ever panicked in a test situation? Describe how you felt. How did you overcome the feeling of anxiety and get on with the test? If you have never become upset during an exam, explain how you kept your emotions under control.

2. What is causing a problem for Paul? Can he deal with his emotions or should he accept the fact that he will fail the test? Should he allow himself to think about getting a good grade in this course while taking the test? Offer Paul a solution.

## Case Study 2

Gina has always been a good student, achieving A's and B's in all her classes. She knows how to organize her tasks so that part of each day is spent in reviewing class notes and preparing for her assignments. She maintains planning calendars to enable her to manage her time wisely. She takes good lecture notes and reading notes, which she uses to study for quizzes and exams. She seems to be a model student who knows how to study effectively.

This semester started out as usual. However, about midpoint in the semester, she caught a cold that turned into the flu. She missed classes sporadically over a period of three weeks. Gina was not able to maintain her study schedule. She kept up with her reading assignments and took good notes, but she did not have the energy to review her notes as she used to do.

The end of the semester is approaching, and all of her classes have set dates for the final examinations. Gina is panicked. How can she prepare? She is missing lecture notes and she has missed many days of studying from the notes she does have. Sometimes, when she attended classes, she was not feeling well, and her notes reflect it. They aren't as detailed as they should be.

On a separate sheet of paper, advise Gina on how to relieve her anxiety and help her prepare for her examinations. In offering advice, review the following:

**1.** What are the steps involved in preparing for an examination? Has Gina missed any of these, or has she completed them?

**2.** How do you overcome anxiety when the announcement of an examination is made and you don't feel organized for it?

## IMPROVE YOUR WRITING SKILLS

**More About Pronouns:** *Who, which,* and *that* are *relative pronouns.* They are used to connect dependent clauses to noun or pronoun antecedents in sentences. The relative pronoun *who* has the objective case form *whom* and the possessive case form *whose.*

> The person who interviewed her is Dr. Walsh.
> He who scores highest on the test will get the job.
> She is the candidate whom Ms. Miller interviewed.
> They are officers of a firm whose products are used everywhere.
> You should buy the model that is on sale.
> Your order includes two items which are out of stock.

Some pronouns, called *interrogative pronouns,* are used to introduce questions. These include *who, whom, whose, which,* and *what.*

> Who is in charge of the office?
> Whom did you wish to see?
> Whose responsibility is it to advise them?
> Which of the job openings appeals to you?
> What is your main objective?

Such pronouns as those listed below are classified as *indefinite pronouns* because they do not have stated antecedents.

| | | | |
|---|---|---|---|
| each | either | neither | anyone |
| everyone | everybody | anybody | nobody |
| someone | something | anything | nothing |
| somebody | no one | one | everything |

Indefinite pronouns that end in *one*, such as *everyone* and *no one*, or in *body*, such as *somebody* and *nobody*, have possessives formed by adding *'s*:

somebody's     nobody's     someone's     no one's

The pronouns *this*, *that*, *these*, and *those* are referred to as *demonstrative pronouns*. Note that *this* and *that* are singular and require singular verbs when they are used as subjects. *These* and *those* are plural and require plural verbs when they are used as subjects.

This is the equipment that you should buy.
These are the documents to be signed.
This was a mistake on their part.
Those over there were not found until yesterday afternoon.

## Practice

In each of the following sentences, decide which of the pronouns shown in parentheses is correct and underline it.

1. (*Who*, *Whom*) has the authority to approve it?

2. Do you know (*who*, *whom*) is likely to be the new director?

3. I am not sure (*whose*, *who's*) interests will be protected.

4. It is doubtful that (*anything*, *nothing*) will be done right away.

5. If (*any one*, *anyone*) can do that job, you can.

6. Mel, (*who*, *whom*) you probably have met, will be the keynote speaker.

7. (*Them*, *Those*) are the latest sales figures.

8. Are you sure (*these*, *this*) type will be satisfactory?

9. She is (*some one*, *someone*) (*who*, *whom*) has a lot to offer any employer.

10. (*That*, *Those*) seem more appropriate than the others.

Being well prepared and overcoming anxiety during a test are usually enough to ensure that you will do well. However, you can improve your performance even more by understanding how to take different types of tests. There are two basic test formats: objective tests, which contain short-answer questions that have right or wrong answers, and essay tests, which ask questions that require you to write out responses in your own words. The answer you select for an objective test question is either the correct one or an incorrect response. Answers to essay questions may be either wholly or partially correct.

## OBJECTIVE TESTS

The term *objective* is used to describe short-answer tests because each question has just one right answer, regardless of who scores the test. This does not necessarily mean that objective tests are easier than essay tests, which are subjective. Questions on objective tests can range in difficulty from simple recall of facts to analysis and interpretation of ideas and concepts. Therefore, studying for an objective test should be just as intense as studying for an essay test.

### Types of Questions

When taking an objective test, it helps to be aware of the types of questions that may appear and special strategies for taking objective tests. Objective tests may contain questions in one or more of the following formats: true-false, multiple-choice, matching, and fill-in-the-blank.

**True-False Questions.**   Most students rightly consider true-false questions the easiest type of questions to answer. After all, you have a 50 percent chance of being right since there are only two possible answers. The main consideration in answering true-false questions is to read carefully. Missing a critical word such as *not* or *always* may cause you to answer incorrectly.

**Multiple-Choice Questions.**   In the multiple-choice format, you are given four or five possible answers to each question, and you must select the correct one. Here, the odds of being right are not as favorable, but you can still improve your chance of answering correctly with a couple of techniques.

First, read all the responses before selecting one. For example, look at the following question:

When studying for a test, you should review your:
**a.** Notes
**b.** Instructor handouts
**c.** Past tests in the course
**d.** All of the above

Although *a* may be correct, if you had stopped reading there and marked *a* as your response, you would have been wrong. Since *b* and *c* are also correct, *d. All of the above* is the right answer.

Second, if you are having difficulty selecting the right answer, cross out responses that you can immediately eliminate as being wrong. You may be left with two choices rather than four or five, and it may be easier to choose the correct answer—or at least guess.

**Matching Questions.** In matching questions, you are given two columns of items in random order and asked to match them. Often there is a leftover item in the second column, so you can't be sure you have correctly paired every choice. Matching questions often test mastery of vocabulary, with defined terms in one column and definitions in the other.

There are a couple of techniques to help you answer matching questions. First, read through all the items before attempting to match the first item. Then, as you use an item in the second column for an answer, cross it out so that you do not accidently use it again.

**Fill-in-the-Blank Questions.** If they are well-written, fill-in-the-blank questions should have only one or two correct responses. You are given a sentence with a word or phrase omitted, and you must supply what's missing. This can be more difficult than the other types of objective questions because the answer does not appear on the test. You must think of it yourself.

If you can't readily fill in the blank, decide what type of word or phrase belongs there by reading the rest of the sentence. For example:

The first president of the United States was _____.

A name, or proper noun, is the type of response you are looking for; in this case, of course, the answer is *George Washington.* If you still can't think of the answer, skip the question and mark it in the margin. You may find the answer elsewhere on the test, or something on the test may spark your memory.

## Strategies for Taking Objective Tests

In addition to the techniques that are specific to the different types of objective questions, there are some general strategies for taking objective tests.

**1.** *Pace yourself.* Most important, pace yourself so that you are giving the right amount of time to each question (see Chapter 11). Start with the easiest questions—perhaps the true-false or multiple-choice questions, and then go on to the more difficult ones.

**2.** *Follow directions.* Make sure you read and follow the directions for each section of the test. For example, if the answer to a multiple-choice question is to be underlined, then underline it—don't circle the letter of the correct response. If your responses are to go on an answer sheet rather than the test itself, make sure that's what you do.

**3.** *Read each question very carefully.* Don't leap at the answer before you finish reading the question. If time permits, read each question twice to make sure you understand it.

**4.** *Don't make things more complicated than they already are.* Try not to read into a question more than the instructor intended. Generally, instructors aren't trying to trick you when they make up test questions. Don't ignore the obvious and straightforward answer in favor of one involving complex thinking.

**5.** *Guess only if you will be penalized for skipping a question.* In some grading systems, giving a wrong answer causes points to be deducted from your score, whereas skipping the question has no effect on your score. Guess only when a wrong answer and no answer are scored in the same way.

**6.** *Review the test when you have finished.* If you have time, go over the test again, making sure you have answered each question correctly and haven't made any sloppy mistakes such as putting the answers on the wrong lines. If you decide to change an answer as you review the test, think through why you answered as you did the first time. Be sure you have a good reason for making the change.

## ESSAY TESTS

An essay test often causes more anxiety in students than an objective test because students must provide information, rather than respond to information already on the test paper. When writing an essay, you have to provide facts, analyze and interpret those facts, and demonstrate an understanding of the subject matter. In addition to knowing the answer, you must be able to express it. The person grading the essay has only what you write to evaluate. He or she can't give credit for what you know but haven't expressed.

You can improve your performance on essay tests by using a few basic strategies outlined below. In addition, by paying attention to the mechanics of writing, you may be able to improve your score.

## Strategies for Taking Essay Tests

The following guidelines will help you take essay tests. Remember, these suggestions will improve your performance, but they aren't a substitute for being well prepared!

**1.** *Follow all the directions.* Read the directions carefully before you start, and do what you are instructed to do. Make sure you are answering the correct number of questions; often you are asked to choose a specified number. When responding to a specific question, make sure you are actually answering the question. For example, if you are asked to compare and contrast two things, do so. Don't discuss only one because you are biased toward it.

**2.** *Read all the questions before starting to write.* Reading all the questions gives you an overview of the test. You can select which one you will answer if you are given a choice, or you can decide which one you will respond to first. Sometimes questions are related, and it is helpful to be aware of that before you start developing your answers.

**3.** *Pace yourself.* Look at the point values and allocate your time accordingly. For example, if the exam lasts two hours and you must answer four 25-point questions, you would allow half an hour for each. However, if one question was worth 40 points and the remaining three were worth 20 points each, you would spend about 50 minutes on the 40-point question and about 25 minutes on each of the 20-point questions.

**4.** *Jot down ideas for each question.* Before you start writing the first essay, write down some facts and ideas about all the questions you'll answer. Why should you do this? Your subconscious mind is working all the time. As you write the first essay, your mind is working on the other responses as well.

**5.** *Organize your essay.* Before you write, make sure you have your response worked out. Perhaps the list you have jotted is sufficient for this, or perhaps you can write a quick outline. If your essay is not well-organized, you will lose points.

**6.** *Be direct and be specific.* Write a direct response to the question. In the first paragraph, tell the reader the main ideas you will develop. Subsequent paragraphs can present supporting statements and details. Be as specific as you can. Use dates, names, illustrations, facts, and examples to support the main ideas you present.

**7.** *Don't pad your answer.* Don't overwrite your essay, thinking that a longer response will be more favorably received. Quality, not quantity, is the key here.

**8.** *Provide a summary for each essay.* A complete answer to an essay question should close with a brief summary of its highlights.

## The Mechanics of Writing

Many instructors will also score you on the mechanics of writing. Present your ideas in a logical manner, leading from one point to another. Using transitional words and phrases will help (see Chapter 9).

Use correct spelling and word usage and good grammar, punctuation, and style. If you are permitted to use a dictionary or reference manual during the exam, do so. Last, be neat!

# SUMMARY

You can improve your performance on tests by understanding how to take different types of tests. There are two basic test formats, objective tests and essay tests.

Objective tests may contain true-false, multiple-choice, matching, and fill-in-the-blank questions. There are techniques to help you answer each of these types. In addition, general strategies for taking objective tests include pacing yourself, following directions, reading each question carefully, answering straightforwardly, guessing answers only when you will be penalized for skipping questions, and reviewing the test when you are finished.

Strategies for taking essay tests include following directions, reading all the questions before starting to write, pacing yourself, jotting down ideas for each question, organizing your answer, being direct and specific, not padding your answer, and providing a brief summary for each essay. You must also pay attention to the mechanics of good writing: logical development of ideas; correct spelling, grammar, punctuation, style, and usage; and legibility.

Name                                                                    Date

# CHAPTER 12 ACTIVITIES

## CHECK YOUR UNDERSTANDING

**1.** What is the difference between an objective test and an essay test?

_____

_____

_____

**2.** What are two techniques that can help you answer multiple-choice questions?

_____

_____

**3.** When should you guess at an answer on an objective test?

_____

_____

**4.** List four techniques for taking essay tests.

_____

_____

_____

**5.** Why are the mechanics of writing important on essay tests?

_____

_____

## PRACTICE YOUR TEST-TAKING SKILLS

### Test-Taking Strategies

**Directions:**   Take the following test based on the information in this chapter. The point value for each set of questions is shown. There are 20 total points.

You have ten minutes to complete the test.

**A.** *True-False*    One point per answer. Circle the correct answer.

**1.** Studying for an essay test is harder than studying for an objective test.    True    False

**2.** Before starting to write an essay, write down facts and ideas on all the questions.    True    False

**B.** *Matching*    Two points per answer. Match the correct answer in column 2 with an item in Column 1.

| Column 1 | Column 2 |
|---|---|
| ____ **a.** matching question | **a.** essay |
| ____ **b.** basic test format | **b.** four or five possible answers to each question |
| ____ **c.** multiple-choice question | **c.** provide facts |
| ____ **d.** true-false questions | **d.** match two columns of ideas |
| | **e.** 50 percent chance of being right |

**C.** *Multiple-Choice* Three points per answer. Circle the correct answer.

**1.** When writing an essay test, you should:

   **a.** provide facts

   **b.** analyze facts

   **c.** interpret facts

   **d.** all of the above

   **e.** none of the above

**2.** A strategy for taking objective tests is to:

   **a.** read each question carefully

   **b.** jot down ideas for each question

   **c.** organize your answer

   **d.** answer as rapidly as possible

**D.** *Fill-in-the-Blank* Two points per answer.

**1.** Use _____ words and phrases to lead the reader from one point to another in an essay test.

**2.** If you have time, _____ the test after you have finished.

What strategies did you use to complete this test? Did you use the ideas provided in this chapter? Were you successful in carrying out the strategies—what is your score? The correct responses are shown here.

**ANSWERS TO TEST**

*True-False*

**1.** False
**2.** True

*Matching*

**a.** d. match two columns of ideas
**b.** a. essay
**c.** b. four or five possible answers to each question
**d.** e. 50 percent chance of being right

*Multiple-Choice*

**1.** d. all of the above
**2.** a. read each question carefully

*Fill-in-the-Blank*

**1.** transitional
**2.** review

Total points = 20


*My Score:* _____


## Analyzing a Case Study

In this activity there are three parts. Follow the directions in each.

**A.** *Read the case study:* The instructor gave the following essay question to students after they had studied the chapter on how to take objective and essay exams.

There are two basic test formats: objective tests and essay tests. Describe the characteristics of an objective test and the strategies that should be used to take an objective test.

One of the students in the class submitted the following answer to this essay question:

There are several kinds of tests that are clasiefid as objective. Among these kinds of tests are the true/f; the multiply choice, the fill in the blank, and the matching tests. Probably the worst one to take is the fill in the blank because you have to think about the answer because the answer is not already on the test paper. An essay test is even harder, however, because you have to provide all of the information—at least in the objective tests only a few short answers have to be given back to the teacher.

The matching test usually asks you to pair up one column with another column, which is fun at times. But sometimes there is an extra answer in one column and then your not to sure if you paired all the right combinations. At least in the fill in the blank answer there is usually only one or two correct answers.

Essay tests take more thought since you have to state specific information and then analyze it.

Sometimes the fill in the blank causes the same problems because you have to remember a word or a phrase to answer the question. You can't spend too much time thinking about the right word because pacing yourself is one of the strategies to carry out in taking a test. Other types of objective tests are the multiple choice and the true false.

The true false test is good if you are lucky in guessing that's because you have a 50–50 chance of getting the answer right if your not sure. It pays to read these kinds of questions carefully before answering, which is a test strategy. I personally prefer the essay test, but my teachers usually give the objective tests. I'm glad you gave this essay test for the chapter. It gives me a chance to show everything I know about taking various tests. The last kind of objective test is the multiple choice. This one is a chalenge because you have to know which one of several answers is the right one and if that isn't enough sometimes all the answers listed are the right ones. So you have to read each answer very carefully and decide if it answers the question before you write down the right answer to the question. if you read the questions carefully, you will be able to do a good job on an objective test. I could write lots more but the time is up.

**B.** *Evaluate the student's response:* How well did the student carry out the strategies for taking an essay examination? Write your evaluation of the essay on a separate sheet of paper. Use the following questions to guide your evaluation.

1. Do you think the student jotted down ideas or prepared an outline before beginning to write the response?
2. Is the information presented in an organized way?
3. Has the student answered the two parts of the question?
4. Did the student stay on the subject and write information that related directly to the question?
5. Is the student careful with the mechanics of English, such as spelling, sentence structure, and grammar?

**C.** *Rewrite the student's response:* How would *you* answer the essay questions in part A? On a separate sheet of paper, write your response using the strategies you have learned about writing an effective essay test.

## IMPROVE YOUR WRITING SKILLS

**Adjectives and Adverbs:**   *Adjectives* are words that describe or modify nouns and pronouns. They answer such questions as these: "Which?" "What kind of?" "How many?"

As illustrated below, possessive nouns, possessive pronouns, indefinite pronouns, and numbers are often used as adjectives.

| | | |
|---|---|---|
| large company | happy employees | several candidates |
| your response | Lee's promotion | three telephones |
| her address | yellow flowers | company's bid |

Most words used as adjectives have three different forms.

| Positive Form | Comparative Form | Superlative Form |
|---|---|---|
| large | larger | largest |
| happy | happier | happiest |
| intense | more-less intense | most-least intense |
| impulsive | more-less impulsive | most-least impulsive |

The positive form of an adjective is used to describe a quality or characteristic without referring to any other person or thing. The comparative degree is formed by adding *er* to the positive degree or by using *more* or *less* with the positive degree. Use it when two persons or things are being compared. The superlative degree is formed by adding *est* to the positive degree or by using *most* or *least* with the positive degree; it is used when three or more persons or things are being compared.

Frank has a large office.
Pat's office is larger than Frank's.
Of all the offices in this building, yours is the largest.
She bought an expensive coat.
A leather coat is more expensive than a cloth coat.
What is the price of the most expensive coat in the store?

When using the articles *a*, *an*, and *the*, remember that *a* is used when the following word begins with a consonant or a consonant sound; *an* is used when the following word begins with a vowel or a vowel sound.

| | |
|---|---|
| a picture | an itinerary |
| a large box | an honest person |
| a new house | an officer |
| a high price | an effective manager |
| a uniform | an understatement |

## Practice

Decide which of the adjectives shown in parentheses is correct; then draw a line under it.

**1.** Please order (*a*, *an*) copy of the (*current*, *currenter*, *currentest*) edition of that reference manual.

**2.** Prospective students must take (*a*, *an*) entrance exam to enter (*a*, *an*) university or college.

**3.** Of the two machines, this one is (*easy*, *easier*, *easiest*) to use, and it is (*expensive*, *less expensive*, *least expensive*) than the other one.

**4.** Monday seems to be the (*long*, *longer*, *longest*) and (*busy*, *busier*, *busiesi*) day of the week.

**5.** Which of the twins is (*tall, taller, tallest*) and (*heavy, heavier, heaviest*)?

**6.** (*A, An*) union official emphasized the importance of (*comprehensive, more comprehensive, most comprehensive*) health insurance.

**7.** What is the (*valuablest, most valuable*) gem in the (*new, newer, newest*) display at the local museum?

**8.** In our area July is (*more hot, hotter*) and (*more humid, humider*) than August.

**9.** It seems (*shady, shadier, shadiest, more shady, most shady*) and (*clean, cleaner, cleanest*) on the other side of the street.

**10.** She is (*adept, adepter, adeptest*) at doing (*manual, manualer, more manual*) things.

*Adverbs*, many of which are formed by adding *ly* to adjectives, are words that modify verbs, adjectives, and other adverbs. An adverb tells *how, when, where, why,* or *to what extent or degree.*

| | | |
|---|---|---|
| stopped suddenly | arrived yesterday | quickly approved |
| very considerate | most helpful | unusually cold |
| more carefully done | waited quite patiently | dress less casually |

Most adverbs, like most adjectives, have different forms for use in comparisons.

| Positive Form | Comparative Form | Superlative Form |
|---|---|---|
| soon | sooner | soonest |
| lively | livelier | liveliest |
| neatly | more or less neatly | most or least neatly |
| easily | more or less easily | most or least easily |
| candidly | more or less candidly | most or least candidly |

**Practice**

In each of the following sentences, decide which of the adverb forms shown in parentheses is correct and underline it.

**1.** A (*neatly, neatlier, neatliest*) prepared report (*likely, likelier, likeliest*) will receive a good reception.

**2.** The reward should be divided (*equally, more equally, most equally*) among those who responded (*quickly, more quickly, most quickly*).

**3.** She (*usually, more usually, most usually*) dresses (*casual, casually, more casually, most casually*) during the summer than during any other season.

Name                                                                                    Date

# PART 5 PROJECT

**Directions:** You have completed studying a unit on human resource management. You have read and taken notes on the chapter "Human Resource Management."

A test has been scheduled in one week for this unit. You want a good grade on this test, so you know that you need to start your studying now. Let's complete the steps that are necessary to study for this test. You will be required to take an actual test at the end of this project.

Follow each of the steps in sequence.

## Studying for the Test

Follow these steps:

**1.** In your own words, what is the subject matter for this test?
**2.** What materials do you have that would provide the basis for the test?

Once you can identify the subject matter to be tested and what materials you have for studying, you are ready to prepare for the test. Remember to use your standard abbreviations whenever you have the opportunity to jot down notes.

**3.** Look at the Review Questions section at the end of the chapter "Human Resources Management." The questions focus on the important information in the chapter, and therefore, they provide a good clue as to what will be on the test. Can you answer questions 1–10? Your instructor may ask you to discuss your responses in class.
  **a.** Using either 3- × 5-inch or 4- × 6-inch cards, prepare flash cards for each one of the terms listed in question 1.
  **b.** Use these flash cards to memorize the special terminology from the chapter.
  **c.** Carry the flash cards with you. Whenever you have a few spare minutes, shuffle through the cards to review the terms.
**4.** Review your notes from the chapter.
  **a.** Turn each recall note into a question. Then write down the answer to each question. Check your notes to see if you were correct.

   **b.** Review your summary statement.

   **c.** Repeat this process until you feel comfortable with the material.

 **5.** Anticipate what the instructor will ask on the test by reviewing your notes from the handout and the chapter.

   **a.** Write down possible questions.

   **b.** Answer the questions you have identified.

You have now completed the essential steps in studying for a test.

## Handling Test Anxiety

Before taking a test, you should keep anxiety controlled so that you can perform well. Whatever subject you are being tested on, you need to take certain measures that will lessen any nervousness you have.

■ Write down everything you need to do to feel and know you are ready for the test before you walk into the room.

■ Prepare a self-assessment checklist that you can use before each test or quiz. Copy down on a 4- × 6-inch card the following "Self-Assessment Checklist to Lessen Test Stress."

■ Before taking the test that appears in this project, complete the self-assessment checklist.

### Self-Assessment Checklist to Lessen Test Stress

|  | Yes | No |
|---|---|---|
| **1.** I place dates for all tests and quizzes on a master calendar. | ___ | ___ |
| **2.** I attend all classes regularly. | ___ | ___ |
| **3.** I read, mark, and make notes for all reading assignments. | ___ | ___ |
| **4.** I take notes on each lecture. | ___ | ___ |
| **5.** I review my notes before each class. | ___ | ___ |
| **6.** I set aside time one week before a test to give high priority to studying for that test. | ___ | ___ |
| **7.** I study in an environment free of distractions. | ___ | ___ |
| **8.** I gather the materials I will need for the test the day ahead. | ___ | ___ |
| **9.** I review my notes again the night before the test. | ___ | ___ |
| **10.** I get a good night's sleep because I know I am prepared. | ___ | ___ |
| **11.** I plan my schedule to arrive at the room several minutes before the test is to start. | ___ | ___ |

**12.** I sit in a part of the room with the fewest
distractions, if possible.                                    ____  ____

**13.** I sit quietly to collect my thoughts for the test.      ____  ____

**14.** I understand all directions *before* starting the
test.                                                          ____  ____

**15.** I know how to pace myself during the test.             ____  ____

**16.** I have a positive, confident feeling about my
readiness to take the test.                                    ____  ____

## Taking Objective and Essay Tests

You know that there are certain test-taking strategies to keep in mind
whether the test is an objective or essay exam. Before taking your
test, review these strategies. Your instructor will direct you either to
write your answers or to be prepared to discuss your responses in
class.

**1.** What techniques can help you answer the questions on each type
of objective test:
  **a.** true-false
  **b.** multiple choice
  **c.** matching
  **d.** fill-in-the-blank

**2.** Identify the general strategies for taking objective tests.

**3.** List the guidelines to follow when taking an essay test.

**4.** Discuss the importance of the mechanics of writing when taking
an essay test.

## THE TEST ON "HUMAN RESOURCES MANAGEMENT"

The time has arrived to take the test on the material presented in the
chapter "Human Resources Management." Your instructor prepared
a test that uses both the objective and the essay formats to determine
how well you know the material.

Follow the directions provided for each part of the test.

TEST: Human Resources Management        Business 215
NAME: _____SCORE: _____
**Directions:** Complete the following questions. The point value for
each set of questions is shown. There are 100 points. You have 60
minutes to complete the test.

## Part 1. Matching Questions. 20 points (2 points per answer)

**Directions:** Match the correct answer in Column 2 with the items in Column 1.

| Column 1 | Column 2 |
|---|---|
| ____ Job Analysis | **a.** establishing a scale of pay for every level and type of job |
| ____ On-the-Job Training | **b.** locate qualified candidates for professional and managerial positions |
| ____ Executive Recruiter | **c.** formal programs designed to help managers increase their effectiveness |
| ____ Compensation | **d.** analysis of the performance of an employee |
| ____ Performance Appraisal | **e.** determination of the knowledge and skills needed to perform a specific job |
| ____ Affirmative Action Plan | **f.** things of value that employees receive in addition to their salary |
| ____ Job Pricing | **g.** the number of workers who leave their job permanently and must be replaced |
| ____ Employee Benefits | **h.** the way most employees are trained |
| ____ Management Development Programs | **i.** things of monetary value an employee receives in exchange for work |
| ____ Employee Turnover | **j.** specific actions a company will take to hire and promote a larger number of minorities and other groups |

## Part 2. True-False Questions. 10 points (1 point per answer)

**Directions:** Respond *True* or *False* to each statement.

____ 1. Human resource managers usually have responsibility for the training and development of employees.

———   **2.** A job specification is done to determine exactly what a person in a given job does and what qualifications are needed to do that job.

———   **3.** *Bona fide occupational qualification* is a legal requirement that bars employers from failing to hire because of age, sex, and other characteristics.

———   **4.** Apprenticeship training combines on-the-job training with classroom learning.

———   **5.** Employers are required by law to provide employees with safe and sanitary working conditions.

———   **6.** Job evaluation is the most common form of performance appraisal.

———   **7.** A two-tier compensation system usually specifies that employees hired after a certain date receive higher pay rates for the same work than those already on the payroll.

———   **8.** It is illegal for companies to force most employees to retire before the age of 70.

———   **9.** The concept of comparable worth compares the value of the work performed by different workers in different jobs.

———   **10.** Assessment centers are used by some companies to select candidates for supervisory positions.

### Part 3. Multiple-Choice Questions. 15 points (3 points per answer)

**Directions:**  Circle the correct answer (*a*, *b*, *c*, or *d*).

**1.** The form of compensation that pays employees based on the number of units produced is known as:
 **a.** commissions
 **b.** bonuses
 **c.** wages
 **d.** piecework

**2.** Which of the following is *not* considered an employee benefit?
 **a.** pension
 **b.** profit sharing
 **c.** guaranteed annual wage
 **d.** promotion

**3.** The process of selecting new employees to hire often includes all of the following except:
 **a.** face-to-face job interview
 **b.** physical examination
 **c.** investigation of the information given by the applicant
 **d.** job analysis

**4.** A job specification
    **a.** spells out the activities and responsibilities of a job as well as the skills and characteristics needed to perform the job.
    **b.** lists measurable information that describes an employee who would be suitable for a given job.
    **c.** sets the pay scale for each level and type of job.
    **d.** ranks jobs in order of difficulty and of their contribution to the company as a whole.

**5.** The Federal Wages and Hours Law requires most companies to
    **a.** pay a higher wage rate for any hours over 40 worked in a week.
    **b.** pay overtime for all work over 8 hours a day.
    **c.** pay employees no less than the current minimum wage.
    **d.** pay overtime for all work over 10 hours a day.

### Part 4. Fill-in-the-Blank Questions. 10 points (2 points per answer)

**Directions:** Select the correct word(s) to complete the sentence.

**1.** The legal requirement stating that questions asked during a job interview must be restricted to those undeniably relevant to job performance is known as _____.

**2.** _____ is a training method used to teach specific job skills such as machine and computer operation.

**3.** Formal programs designed to enhance the effectiveness of supervisors and managers are called _____.

**4.** _____ is a term used to specify the number of employees who leave work permanently and who must be replaced.

**5.** _____ administers the many regulations concerned with employee safety and health.

### Part 5. Essay. Point values are indicated for each response.

**Directions:** Respond to each statement as completely as possible.

10 points   **1.** Discuss the functions of the personnel department.

15 points   **2.** Explain the role of job analysis, job description, and job specification in determining the personal qualities and skills needed to perform jobs that must be filled.

20 points   **3.** The idea of employment quotas is a controversial one in many companies. Describe what employment quotas are and explain why they are controversial.

# PREPARING REPORTS

One of the most important skills you acquire as a student is the ability to write a good report. Report writing is not confined to school. Required in many types of businesses, it is a valuable skill that you will draw on throughout your career.

When you write a report, you should approach it as a process, rather than as an end product. Report preparation has many steps; preparing the final copy is just one. In Part 6 you will:

■ **Find information in the library and select a topic.**

■ **Prepare a preliminary outline.**

■ **Take notes while developing the content of the report.**

■ **Prepare a final outline.**

■ **Write and revise the first draft of the report.**

■ **Format the final copy.**

# 13 USING THE LIBRARY

**WHAT'S IN THE LIBRARY?**

**FINDING INFORMATION**
The Card Catalog
Indexes to Periodicals
Computerized Databases

**SUMMARY**

As a student, you will have many occasions to use the library. You may need to do research in order to prepare a report. Your instructors may direct you to do extra reading that's not in your text. You may want to read the newspaper or skim some recent magazines. Or you may find that the library is a good place to study. To help you get the most out of the library, you should make yourself familiar with its resources and how to use them to find information.

## WHAT'S IN THE LIBRARY?

Most people think of books when they think of libraries. Libraries do have lots of books, but they have information in many other forms as well.

The reference section of the library contains encyclopedias and dictionaries, both general and specialized, and other types of reference books. Atlases, almanacs, and yearbooks can be found here. There are telephone books and other directories. Libraries have indexes and bibliographies to help you locate information on a particular subject.

Since most of the books in the reference section are expensive or hard to replace, they can't be checked out. They must be used in the library.

In addition to books, libraries collect periodicals—newspapers, magazines, and journals. The selection of periodicals varies from library to library, depending on the needs of the school, city, business, or association that runs it. Libraries also have files of clippings from periodicals and pamphlets. Many libraries have maps and artwork.

In recent years, libraries have expanded their collections to include information stored in forms other than paper. Many libraries have slides, records, CDs, audiocassettes, videocassettes, computer software, computerized databases, and microfilm. They usually have the equipment needed to use these forms of information—slide projectors, record and CD players, cassette players, VCRs, computers, and microfilm readers.

## FINDING INFORMATION

One of the most important resources in the library is the librarian. He or she is trained to help you find information in the library. If what you are looking for isn't available there, the librarian can often order an item from another library, through a system called *interlibrary loan,* or can direct you to another source. The librarian can also help you learn to find information on your own.

Libraries have different types of systems to help you locate information. The most important of these are the card catalog, indexes to periodicals, and computerized databases.

### The Card Catalog

The card catalog is a file containing at least three index cards for each book in the library. One card is filed alphabetically by the last name of the author, one by the book's title, and one or more by subject headings, as shown on page 212. All the cards provide you with the *call number* of the book—the number under which the book is filed on the shelves.

If you are looking for a specific book, you can look either under the author's name or under the title. If you are looking for books on a specific subject, look under the subject heading, and you will find

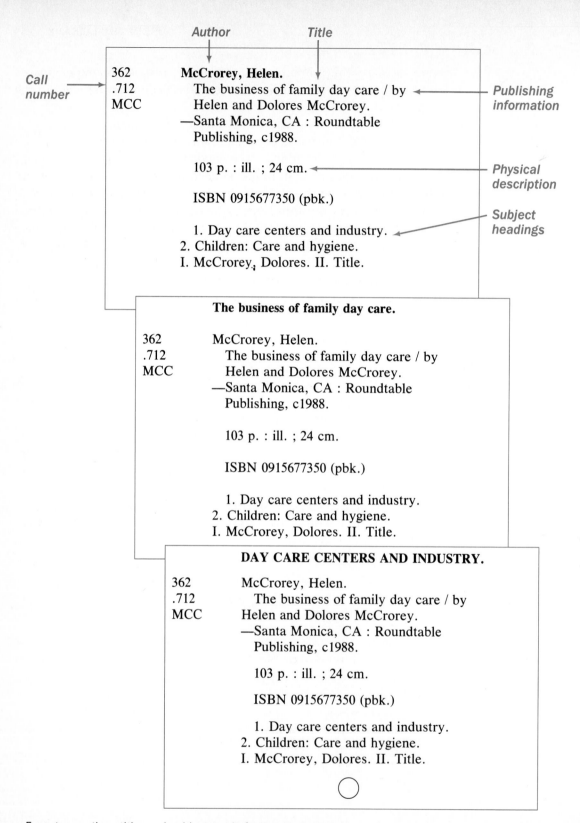

*Author*

*Title*

*Call number*

362
.712
MCC

**McCrorey, Helen.**
The business of family day care / by
Helen and Dolores McCrorey.
—Santa Monica, CA : Roundtable
Publishing, c1988.

103 p. : ill. ; 24 cm.

ISBN 0915677350 (pbk.)

1. Day care centers and industry.
2. Children: Care and hygiene.
I. McCrorey, Dolores. II. Title.

*Publishing information*

*Physical description*

*Subject headings*

**The business of family day care.**

362
.712
MCC

McCrorey, Helen.
The business of family day care / by
Helen and Dolores McCrorey.
—Santa Monica, CA : Roundtable
Publishing, c1988.

103 p. : ill. ; 24 cm.

ISBN 0915677350 (pbk.)

1. Day care centers and industry.
2. Children: Care and hygiene.
I. McCrorey, Dolores. II. Title.

**DAY CARE CENTERS AND INDUSTRY.**

362
.712
MCC

McCrorey, Helen.
The business of family day care / by
Helen and Dolores McCrorey.
—Santa Monica, CA : Roundtable
Publishing, c1988.

103 p. : ill. ; 24 cm.

ISBN 0915677350 (pbk.)

1. Day care centers and industry.
2. Children: Care and hygiene.
I. McCrorey, Dolores. II. Title.

*From top:* author, title, and subject cards from a card catalog all the books in the library on that subject. It is also helpful to read and use the subject headings at the bottom of the card to find books on related topics.

## Indexes to Periodicals

There are many indexes to periodical literature, many of which specialize in particular subjects. The most common general index is the *Reader's Guide to Periodical Literature*, which lists articles from over one hundred popular magazines by subject and author.

A typical entry from the *Reader's Guide to Periodical Literature* is shown below. Once you know the magazine, date, and page number, you can locate the article in the back issues or on microfilm. If the library doesn't own the periodical, the librarian can generally find out where it can be located.

## Computerized Databases

Many libraries have different types of computerized databases, or collections of related information, to help you locate information quickly.

In some libraries, the card catalog has been replaced by a computer system that can do quick searches of the library's collection. Sometimes the database also includes the collections of other libraries in the interlibrary loan system. Instead of flipping through index cards, you use a computer terminal to key author, title, or subject information into the system. The computer responds by displaying the information

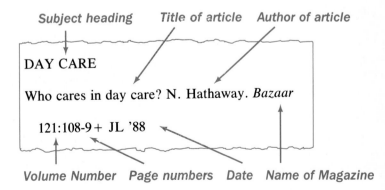

Entry from the *Reader's Guide to Periodical Literature*

you need to locate the book. In many cases, the computer also tells you whether the book is on the shelf or has been checked out.

Other computerized databases can provide abstracts or summaries of articles on various subjects, the full text of newspaper articles, legal citations, financial information, and so on. Ask the librarian which databases, if any, are available and what the guidelines for use are.

## SUMMARY

In addition to books and reference works, libraries have periodicals, clippings, pamphlets, maps, and artwork. Many libraries also have slides, records, CDs, audiocassettes, videocassettes, computer software, databases, microfilm, and the equipment to use these items.

The library has different systems for finding information. The most common of these are the card catalog, indexes to periodicals, and computerized databases.

Name                                                    Date

# CHAPTER 13 ACTIVITIES

## CHECK YOUR UNDERSTANDING

**1.** What types of books can be found in the reference section of a library?

_____

_____

**2.** List five items you can find in a library other than books.

_____

_____

**3.** How would you find this book (*Study Skills*) in the library?

_____

_____

**4.** What is the *Reader's Guide to Periodical Literature*?

_____

_____

**5.** How do you get information from a computerized card catalog?

_____

_____

## BUILD YOUR RESEARCH SKILLS

**1.** Locate in your library each item from the list that follows. Write down the location.
   **a.** encyclopedias
   **b.** dictionaries
   **c.** yearbooks
   **d.** *Reader's Guide to Periodical Literature*
   **e.** newspapers
   **f.** magazines

2. What other material is available and where?

3. On a separate sheet of paper, describe the types of holdings in your library, using the following list as a guide:
   a. Name three sets of encyclopedias.
   b. Identify three dictionary titles.
   c. Name at least two yearbooks published by different sources.
   d. Name four newspapers that are available.
   e. Identify five magazine titles.
   f. List any type of audiovisual equipment that is available.

4. Talk with your librarian to determine how to use the interlibrary loan system.

5. Referring to the three library cards shown on page 212, write the answers to the following questions:
   a. Is Helen McCrorey's material published in a book or a magazine?
   b. How many pages are in this publication?
   c. When was McCrorey's material published?
   d. What subject headings could be used to locate information on family day care?
   e. What company published McCrorey's material?
   f. What are the call numbers to locate the book?

6. Each of the following books should be in your library. Using either the card catalog or the computerized database, write the answers to the following questions for each book.
   - *Beyond Feelings: A Guide to Critical Thinking* by Vincent Ryan Ruggiero; subject heading, Critical Thinking
   - *The Physiological Bases of Motivation* by Jack E. Hokanson; subject heading, Motivation (Psychology)
   - *Patterns of Intention: On The Historical Explanation of Pictures* by Michael Baxandall; subject headings, Painting-Expertising; Art and History
   - *John F. Kennedy* by Judy Mills; subject headings, Kennedy, John F.—(John Fitzgerald), 1917–1963; Kennedy Family; Presidents—United States-Biography

   a. How many pages are in the book?
   b. What is the publication date?
   c. Is the book illustrated?
   d. Where was the book published?

**e.** What is the call number?

**f.** What company published it?

**7.** If you used the computerized database in your library, explain how you accessed the system to find the information for each book.

## IMPROVE YOUR WRITING SKILLS

**Conjunctions:** *Conjunctions* are words that connect words, phrases, and clauses in sentences. *Coordinate conjunctions* connect grammatically equal words, phrases, or clauses, for example:

| | |
|---|---|
| and | Bob and Sue are graduates of Columbia University. |
| but | This carton is small but heavy. |
| or | Please call him before 10 a.m. or after 1:30 p.m. |
| nor | John was not present for the meeting, nor was Claude. |

Some coordinate conjunctions, known as *correlative conjunctions*, are used in pairs. Note that *either* is used with *or* and that *neither* is used with *nor*.

| | |
|---|---|
| both . . . and | She seemed both surprised and disappointed. |
| either . . . or | You may select either green or blue carpeting for your office. |
| neither . . . nor | The material is neither informative nor entertaining. |
| not only . . . but also | Such activities are not only dangerous but also illegal. |
| whether . . . or | We do not know whether she will do the work herself or hire someone to do it for her. |

*Subordinate conjunctions* are words used to connect dependent clauses to independent clauses. The following are examples of commonly used subordinate conjunctions:

| | | | |
|---|---|---|---|
| after | although | because | before |
| since | if | until | when |
| while | unless | as soon as | why |

We learned of the problem after the plane landed.

The company canceled her insurance because she did not pay the premium on time.

When using coordinate conjunctions, including correlative conjunctions, it is important to remember that they must connect elements that are functionally alike and parallel in construction.

Steve, Jean, and I have submitted our applications.

This cereal is neither appealing nor nutritious.

The train is scheduled to leave here at two and to arrive there at four.

We stopped using their products because their prices are too high and their delivery service is often unreliable.

## Practice

Study each sentence to determine whether it contains the correct conjunction(s) and whether the elements joined by the conjunction(s) are parallel. If the sentence contains an error, revise it as necessary.

1. Customers expect salesclerks not only to be helpful but also courteous.

2. The supervisor told us to order those supplies and that we should do so before the end of the month.

3. Either you should plan to be here or ask someone to substitute for you.

4. Neither they or we were aware of all the details.

5. Planning and obtaining information for a report is often more time-consuming than to write it.

6. We wish we could assist you, and it is doubtful that we can.

7. The reason we arrived late is because our flight was delayed an hour.

8. Did you read in the newspaper where construction of another office building will begin in April?

9. This office neither has carpeting nor drapes.

10. She has neither the experience nor has she the training the position requires.

**SELECTING THE TOPIC**
    Choose a Broad Subject
    Brainstorm Ideas
    Gather Background
      Information
    State the Purpose of the
      Paper

**DEVELOPING THE PRELIMINARY OUTLINE**

**SUMMARY**

**CHAPTER 14 ACTIVITIES**

**CHECK YOUR UNDERSTANDING**

**APPLY YOUR KNOWLEDGE**

**IMPROVE YOUR WRITING SKILLS**

Preparing a report can be difficult and unpleasant, or it can go smoothly and be rewarding. What makes the difference? The answer is, *organization.* If you understand and follow the steps involved in writing a paper, you will find that the process can be painless and even stimulating. Whether your report is 3 pages or 20, there are several basic steps involved in preparing it:

- Selecting the topic
- Preparing the preliminary outline
- Developing the content
- Preparing the final outline
- Writing
- Revising
- Formatting the final copy

In this chapter you will learn about selecting a topic and drafting a preliminary outline, the two steps in the planning stage of report preparation.

## SELECTING THE TOPIC

Your instructor has given you an assignment to write a paper, but she hasn't given you a specific subject. Perhaps she wants you to explore a topic related to the objectives of the course. Or maybe the topic is wide open because she wants to see how well you communicate in writing. Whatever the situation, you need to identify a topic for your paper.

Few people can come up with a good topic when they first start thinking about it. The best way to identify a topic is to proceed from the general to the specific. First, choose a broad subject. Then, through brainstorming and gathering background information, narrow the topic until you can state the purpose of your paper.

### Choose a Broad Subject

When you first start thinking about your assignment, settle on a general subject. When you consider the possibilities, keep in mind that preparing the paper will be easier if you:

- *Pick an interesting topic.* Try to select a topic that is interesting to you so that you have built-in motivation for working on the paper.

- *Pick a topic with which you are slightly familiar.* If you are somewhat familiar with the topic you select, you will feel confident when you begin your research.

- *Pick a manageable topic.* Choose a topic that stretches you a little—but not too much. For instance, don't choose a topic like "Laws Governing Sale of a Partnership" if you have never taken a law course.

### Brainstorm Ideas

Once you have a general subject in mind, try brainstorming ideas. To do this, jot down or keyboard what you know about the topic. Then write questions about what you *don't* know. As you write, let your mind wander to create as many questions as possible. Don't worry about spelling or grammar; concentrate on getting as many ideas on paper as you can.

As you write, you will find you have identified various aspects of the broad topic. For example, for his sociology class, Robert was assigned to write a paper on changes in society by the year 2000. Robert first chose a broad topic—how people will be employed in the year 2000. When he brainstormed ideas, he came up with narrower topics such as employment in service jobs, loss of manufacturing jobs overseas, increase in technology-oriented employment, and changes in the composition of the labor force.

## Gather Background Information

With a narrower, tentative topic in mind, you are ready to do some preliminary investigating to refine the topic further. Go to the library to skim the sources you might use when researching the paper. For example, the encyclopedia might give you an overview of the topic. The card catalog, computerized database, and periodicals index can give you further direction. Jot down additional questions and ideas.

When Robert went to the library to see what he could find about changes in the makeup of the labor force by the year 2000, he discovered a lot of material. In particular, he was interested by the fact that women will account for the majority of new entrants to the labor force and will make up about 50 percent of all workers by the year 2000. He decided to focus on women workers in the year 2000.

Before making a final decision about your topic, you might want to consult with your instructor, who is in a position to give you advice and guidance about research. When Robert met with his instructor, they discussed issues relating to women in the work force. Robert learned that 80 percent of women between the ages of 25 and 54 will be in the work force by the year 2000. What will happen to family life and children? Robert decided to focus on the increased need for day care by the year 2000.

## State the Purpose of the Paper

Now that you have narrowed your topic and found a focus for your paper, it is time to write a statement of purpose. Briefly, in a sentence or two, write down what the paper will be about.

In Robert's case, the purpose of the paper is to discuss the types, quality, and location of day-care facilities and the alternatives to day care that might accommodate the increase in women workers by the year 2000.

## DEVELOPING THE PRELIMINARY OUTLINE

With a statement of purpose, you have decided the direction your paper will take. Now put your thinking into action by drafting an outline to serve as a guide when you do research for the paper.

The draft outline can be as detailed as the knowledge you possess at this point. Because you haven't yet conducted your research and don't know all the information that exists about your topic, the outline will not be complete. Develop main points and fill in subheads with questions. Try to make the draft outline as organized as possible.

Robert's draft outline was sketchy, since he did not know much about his topic. However, he was able to write this much:

   I. The need for day care as more women enter the work force
  II. Basic types of day care
 III. The role of business in supporting day care
 IV. The role of government in supporting day care
  V. Alternatives to day care
     A. Telecommuting (working at home)
     B. Flexible hours for men and women

All the major topics of his outline are aspects of Robert's narrowed subject. Note that he didn't have sufficient information at this point to provide subtopics under the first four major topics. He will identify subtopics as he develops the content of the paper.

## SUMMARY

The basic steps in preparing a report are selecting the topic, preparing the preliminary outline, developing the content, preparing the final outline, writing the paper, revising the paper, and formatting the final copy.

When you select a topic, pick something that is interesting, somewhat familiar, and manageable. The steps involved in selecting a topic are choosing a broad subject, brainstorming ideas, gathering background information, and stating the purpose of the paper.

Once you have a statement of purpose, you can draft an outline, which may be sketchy, to serve as a guide for doing research.

Name                                                          Date

# CHAPTER 14 ACTIVITIES

## CHECK YOUR UNDERSTANDING

**1.** List the seven steps involved in preparing a report.

_____

_____

_____

**2.** What characteristics should you be looking for when you are considering a topic for a paper?

_____

_____

_____

**3.** What is the purpose of brainstorming?

_____

_____

_____

**4.** When are you ready to write a statement of purpose for your paper?

_____

_____

_____

**5.** What is the purpose of writing a preliminary outline?

_____

_____

_____

## APPLY YOUR KNOWLEDGE

1. You are in the course Consumer Economics 210 and are studying consumer behavior. The instructor assigns a paper on a phase of this broad topic.

   a. What do you know about consumer behavior? Using a keyboard or your longhand with abbreviated notes, list at least five things you know on the subject. (Keep in mind, you are a consumer.)
   b. Jot down at least five questions that occur to you as you think about the topic of consumer behavior. Do this either at the keyboard or with your abbreviated longhand system.
   c. Go to the library. Use the encyclopedia, card catalog, computerized database system, indexes, or any other help you can locate in your library to get additional ideas on the topic of consumer behavior. You are attempting to narrow this broad topic to a specific one that could be used as the topic of a research paper. Identify one research topic that emerges from your search.
   d. In a sentence or two, write a statement of purpose for your paper.

2. Using the information you have gathered so far, prepare a preliminary outline of your paper on consumer behavior.

## IMPROVE YOUR WRITING SKILLS

**Commas:**   If the parts of a compound sentence are joined by a coordinate conjunction, use a comma before the conjunction to separate the clauses.

> The company promised delivery of our order by May 4, but we did not receive it until May 12.

> Sally knows the wholesale business inside and out, and I am confident that she would do a great job for your company.

But if the parts are very short and very closely related, no comma is necessary:

He didn't receive an invitation or he simply forgot about it.

I wrote the letter and the manager signed it.

When two or more adjectives separately modify a noun, use commas between the adjectives—but not after the last adjective and the word it modifies.

We stopped to get a drink of clear, cold spring water.

The car broke down in the middle of a long, damp, dark tunnel.

Use a comma after an introductory word. These are some of the most frequently used introductory words:

| | | | |
|---|---|---|---|
| accordingly | first | next | otherwise |
| consequently | however | therefore | nevertheless |
| furthermore | further | yes | no |

However, we need more information in order to make a decision.

Yes, a new model will be available in September.

Also use a comma after a long prepositional phrase, after any phrase that includes a verb form, and after introductory clauses that don't stand alone (often these begin with words such as *if* and *when*).

Of the many new trade publications, yours is the most informative.

After checking it, please initial and return it to Tom.

If you would like to attend, be sure to return the enclosed card.

## Practice

Insert commas wherever necessary in the following sentences.

1. She planned to take her vacation in July but her supervisor asked her to postpone it until the middle of September.

2. To maintain their share of the market they will have to lower their prices.

3. Naturally we hope you will be able to go with us.

4. Yes there is a valid reason for delaying a decision.

5. After swimming they lay in the sun for a half hour or so.

6. Tom was there but Dick and Harry were absent.

7. However we can finally see the light at the end of the tunnel.

8. Ms. Mack gave a short interesting informative talk at the fall meeting in Des Moines.

9. If I were she I would apply for the job in Atlanta.

10. Rita is from Las Vegas and Lewis is from Reno.

# 15 NOTETAKING FOR REPORT PREPARATION

Armed with a topic, preliminary outline, and familiarity with the library's resources, you are ready to dig in and get information for your paper. It is very important to approach this task in an organized way. The more organized your research notes are, the easier it will be to write the paper. In this chapter you will learn what materials you will need to take notes, how to prepare a list of sources of information, or bibliography, and how to take organized notes.

## PREPARING NOTETAKING MATERIALS

Before you go to the library, buy a quantity of 3- × 5-inch or 4- × 6-inch index cards and a couple of pens. You will take all your notes on index cards, rather than in a notebook. The reason for this is that it is easy to sort and rearrange index cards, which contain small amounts of information, into the order you will follow when you start writing.

During the course of your notetaking, you will accumulate a large number of cards. It is important to decide at the outset how you will safeguard them. You may decide that rubber bands are sufficient to keep them together. Or you may want to buy a special card file or envelope to store cards. When you make your first trip to the library, have your rubber bands or card file with you.

## DEVELOPING THE BIBLIOGRAPHY

Before you start reading and taking notes, you should prepare a "working bibliography." As you search the card catalog, computerized database, periodicals index, and other reference sources, record bibliographic information about *each* likely reference you find on separate index cards.

The information you record now will be used in several ways. First, you will use the bibliography cards to locate material in the library. Later, when you write, you will use the information in footnotes or endnotes to document the source of specific material in the paper. Last, you will use the bibliography cards when you prepare the bibliography page, which lists all the references you consulted.

You can see that it is important to be complete and accurate when preparing the bibliography cards. For each book you find, record the author(s), title, publisher, place of publication, year of publication,

---

| | |
|---|---|
| *More women enter labor force* | *Jenson, June; Elisabeth Hogen; and Ceallaigh Reddy (eds.)* <u>*Feminization of the Labor Force:*</u> <u>*Paradoxes and Promises*</u> *New York: Oxford Press, 1988*<br>    *HD6053*<br>    *F43*<br>    *1988* |

Bibliography card for a book

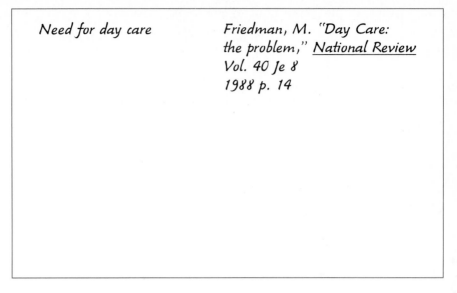

*Need for day care*          *Friedman, M. "Day Care:*
                             *the problem," National Review*
                             *Vol. 40 Je 8*
                             *1988 p. 14*

Bibliography card for an article

and call number in the upper right-hand corner of an index card, as shown on page 228. For each article you find, record the author(s), title, name of publication, volume number, date, and page numbers, as shown above. In the upper left, record the topic covered in the source.

When you have recorded all the possible sources of information for your paper, you should organize your bibliography cards. Using your working outline as a guide, sort the cards by topic. Then place them in an order that parallels the topics in your outline. Of course, if your outline has changed during the course of your research, order the cards accordingly. Don't be afraid to change your outline, if it is necessary. When the cards are in rough order according to the outline, you are ready to look up information, starting with the first major topic.

## TAKING NOTES

By this time you no doubt have acquired a small pile of bibliographic index cards representing many sources to be read. Finding, reading, and taking notes on all these references may seem an overwhelming task. To make the job manageable, you must first preview the readings, develop a system for taking notes on the cards, and organize your note cards.

## Previewing

Should you read and take notes on all your sources? No. As you find each source, use the previewing skill you developed in Chapter 8 to decide whether it is worth reading. If your preview indicates that the material is not relevant to your paper, then don't waste time reading it. Write *No* on the bibliography card to indicate that you checked the reference and it wasn't usable. If you don't mark the card to show you have looked up the material, you may return to it later and waste time looking it up again.

## A Notetaking System

You should take notes on any material you decide is worth reading. To make this process efficient, here are guidelines to help you create a good notetaking system.

- *Write legibly on one side of the card.* Use ink and write legibly, making sure not to crowd your handwriting. Ink will not smudge as you handle the cards, and it is more legible than pencil.

- *Place only one subject from one source on a card.* Each card should contain information on one topic from a particular source. When you change topics or sources, use a new card.

- *Label each card.* Label each card with the topic in the upper left and the source (abbreviated) in the upper right (see page 231). Number each card in sequence from a particular source. Also record the number of the page in the book or article from which the information on the card was taken. You will need the page numbers to prepare footnotes or endnotes.

- *Record quotations accurately.* If you wish to quote directly from a source, copy the quotation and place quotation marks around it. Check twice to make sure you have recorded it accurately. Be selective about using quotations; your paper should not be a series of quotations.

- *Record partial quotations using ellipsis marks.* Sometimes you may wish to quote only part of a sentence in your paper. Use *ellipsis marks,* or three spaced dots, to indicate omitted words. For example:

  "The role of the secretary changed over the decade of the '80s . . . with more assuming a mid-management position."

---

*Role of government—*               *DeBlois* ③
*tax credits*                                   *p. 402*

         *Tax credits for day-care expenses benefit*
         *middle class, not working poor.*

---

Note card labeled with topic, source, page number, and card number

If the omission of words comes at the end of the sentence, use three ellipsis marks followed by a period (four dots):

"During the past twenty-five years we have witnessed a change in buying habits . . . ."

- *Paraphrase.* If you choose not to use a direct quotation but you want to use the information, record it in your own words.
- *Credit the source of information.* In your paper you will credit the source of all quotations and special information. For information commonly known, you don't need to cite a reference. Ask yourself if you could find the material in at least two other sources. If you can, you need not credit the reference.
- *Mark your own thoughts.* As you read, you may get ideas or make observations of your own. Record these, but indicate they are your own by bracketing them and writing *me* or *mine.*
- *Use photocopies sparingly.* Students often photocopy articles or pages from a book when preparing a report. This isn't usually a good idea. You still have to take notes from the photocopy, and you have wasted time standing in line for the machine. If, however, you wish to quote a long passage, photocopying is a good idea. Make sure you label the copy with the same information you would record on a note card.

## Organizing the Note Cards

After you have completed your notetaking for the day and before leaving the library, check your note cards. Did you label each card? Are page numbers shown for the source of the information? Can you read your writing? If you answer no to any of these questions, correct the problem immediately. Backtracking while you are still in the library is easier than trying to fill in missing information when you are writing.

When you are satisfied that the cards are complete, sort them by topic. Either fasten all cards with the same topic with a rubber band or place cards in the file according to subject. Since you will be working with many notes and probably making several trips to the library, it is important to make sure your notes are complete and organized at the end of each session.

# SUMMARY

When taking notes for a report, index cards are used to make sorting and rearranging information easier. In addition to index cards, you need pens and either rubber bands or a card file to hold the cards.

Make a bibliography card for each possible source of information you find in the library. The cards are used to (1) locate material in the library, (2) provide information for footnotes or endnotes, and (3) provide information for the bibliography page of the final report. When you have found all the possible sources of information for your paper, organize the bibliography cards according to the sequence of topics in your outline.

You should preview each book or article to see if it is worth reading. If it is, take notes, following these guidelines: write legibly on one side of the card, place only one subject from one source on a card, label each card, record quotations accurately, record partial quotations using ellipsis marks, paraphrase, credit the source of information, mark your own thoughts, and use photocopies sparingly. After each library session, check the cards to make sure they are complete and organize them by topic.

Name                                                    Date

# CHAPTER 15 ACTIVITIES

## CHECK YOUR UNDERSTANDING

**1.** When preparing a paper, why are index cards, rather than a notebook, used for notetaking?

_____

_____

**2.** Describe three ways bibliography cards are used.

_____

_____

_____

**3.** What information is recorded on a bibliography card for a book? for an article?

_____

_____

_____

_____

_____

**4.** List five guidelines for taking notes when preparing a report.

_____

_____

_____

**5.** What should you do with your note cards at the end of each library session?

_____

_____

## APPLY YOUR KNOWLEDGE

1. **Directions:** Use the statement of purpose on consumer behavior that you developed at the end of Chapter 14. Get index cards and a couple of pens to prepare to work on your paper in the library.

   a. Locate two articles and two books that would contain information related to your statement of purpose.
   b. Prepare bibliography cards for each one of the articles and for each one of the book sources you located. Label your cards according to the information in this chapter.
   c. Organize your bibliography cards according to the sequence of topics in your outline.

2. Complete note cards for each source you identified in the previous activity. Use longhand abbreviations in your notes as much as possible to speed your writing. Label the cards with the subject and the source of the notes. Number consecutive cards from the same source according to the directions in this chapter.

3. Before leaving the library, check that all note cards contain complete information. Then organize your note cards according to topics.

## IMPROVE YOUR WRITING SKILLS

**More Practice with Commas:** Use commas to set off parenthetic expressions—those that interrupt or break the flow of the sentence and are not essential to the meaning or completeness of the sentence.

It is possible, however, to customize this program.

Harry will, I am sure, be happy to assist you.

Keyboarding, for example, requires manual dexterity.

There seems to be little that we can do about it, however.

Miss Lewis, whom you probably have met, will be the main speaker.

Also use commas to set off names or titles used in direct address; the year when it follows the month and day; the name of the state when it follows the name of a city; a degree or title or similar term after the name of a person.

Thank you, Anne, for your assistance.

Are you sure you have the correct number, sir?

The first conference was held on May 12, 1990, in Topeka, Kansas. Ella Stern, M.D., and Floyd Hawkes, director of admissions, served on the panel.

Did they move to Albany, New York, or to Albany, Georgia, Roger?

## Practice

Insert commas wherever they are needed in the following sentences.

1. Please remember to tell them about our new model Dick.

2. Unfortunately it will be delayed at least two months.

3. She was born on June 6 1978 in New Orleans Louisiana.

4. It was good to see you Mike and I'm happy to learn that you'll be moving back to the city within the near future.

5. George Weaver director of marketing will be in charge of the show.

6. Whatever you do Sally please be sure to give him my message.

7. Mr. Stern whom you have met recommended Carol Russo Ph.D.

8. What in your opinion would be the best procedure?

9. The increase won't become effective until January however.

10. Mark the time has come for us to make a firm commitment.

# 16 WRITING AND REVISING

When your research and notetaking are finished, you will have a stack of note cards and a preliminary outline that may no longer be entirely useful. What is the best way to proceed to the next major step, writing the paper?

First, you must realize that writing is a process with several steps. When you are ready to sit down and write, you should follow these steps:

■ Prepare the final outline.

■ Write the first draft of the paper.

■ Revise what you have written.

## PREPARING THE FINAL OUTLINE

Throughout the research process, the statement of purpose and preliminary outline served as your guides. Typically, as you collected more information, the outline changed. You may have rearranged the order of topics, changed a subhead to a major head, added topics, or dropped topics. In addition, your grasp of the topic is much more detailed now, and your original statement of purpose is probably too vague or general to be very useful. You must rewrite the statement of purpose, revise the outline, and transfer the outline numbers to the note cards.

### Rewriting the Statement of Purpose

At this stage, you are ready to write a more focused and detailed statement of purpose for your paper. If you recall, Robert's initial statement of purpose for his paper was:

> To discuss the types, quality, and location of day-care facilities and the alternatives to day care that might accommodate the increase in women workers by the year 2000.

After his notetaking was complete, Robert developed a more detailed statement of purpose for his paper:

> With four out of five women between the ages of 25 and 54 in the work force by the year 2000 and with the growing presence of two-worker families, day care and day-care alternatives are issues needing attention from society and government.

The revised statement of purpose is called the *premise* of the paper. The final outline should be a detailed breakdown of the premise.

### Revising the Preliminary Outline

As you review your preliminary outline and note cards in order to prepare the final outline, ask yourself these questions:

- Can any topics be omitted?
- Must major new topics be added?
- What subtopics relate to each major topic?
- Do I have enough information to justify each subtopic and major topic?

■ Is the sequence of major topics logical?

■ Is the sequence of subtopics under each major topic logical?

As you think about the answers to these questions, you will be developing the final outline of the paper. Write the outline down using the traditional format:

I. Major topic
  A. Subtopic
    1. Subtopic
      a. Subtopic
        (1) Subtopic
          (a) Subtopic

This format allows you to show the relationship of topics to one another and the sequence of material. Although your outline may not have so many levels of topics, try to be as detailed as possible to make the writing task easier.

## Posting Outline Numbers on the Note Cards

The last step in preparing the final outline is to arrange the note cards in outline order and write the appropriate outline number on each card. You may have more than one card with a particular outline number. Or you may have an outline number with no card, which indicates a gap in your notetaking. Either go back to the library to find the missing information or delete the topic from the outline, if you think the paper can do without it.

## WRITING THE FIRST DRAFT

As you have by now realized, writing is a process with many steps. When you sit down to write, be aware that you will not write a perfect paper the first time. Rather, you will write a first draft on which the final paper will be based. Since the first draft does not have to be perfect, relax and get words down on paper without worrying about grammar, sentence structure, spelling, and so on. The important thing now is to concentrate on the content of the paper, not the form.

There are different ways of approaching the writing of a first draft. Some people like to start at the beginning and work through in sequence to the end. Others choose an easy section to write first. A common method, explained here, is to write the main discussion of the paper first and then to write the introduction and conclusion. Drafting the introduction and conclusion last is easier because after writing the main part of the paper you have a solid grasp of the topic.

## Writing the Main Discussion

Take your sequenced and numbered note cards and begin writing. If possible, use a keyboard or shortcuts to write more quickly. Remember, you should not be copying what is on the cards. You must develop and link the ideas and facts you are presenting.

Try to focus on what you are saying, not how you are saying it. If a sentence doesn't sound right but you can't immediately think of a way to fix it, just move on. You will come back to it when you are revising the paper.

When you use a direct quotation or paraphrase special information from one of your sources, mark it with an asterisk and briefly note the author and page number in the margin. Later you will credit the source of the information with a footnote or endnote.

## Writing the Introduction

The introduction of the paper should state its premise. It should also provide some background information on the general subject you have researched. In just two or three paragraphs, the introduction should tell the reader what the paper is about.

The introduction also serves to capture the reader's attention. If there are statistics or facts that are little known but important, you can present them. Perhaps there is an interesting anecdote or case study that would nicely lead into the body of the paper. Whatever you choose to include, remember that you want the reader to be interested in reading more.

## Writing the Conclusion

What do all the ideas and facts you have presented mean? What should be concluded from them? In the last part of the paper, you should provide a concluding statement that flows logically from the main discussion. In the conclusion, you may summarize the main points that have been discussed and then move beyond to discuss the implications of the information covered in the paper. Depending on the length of the paper, the conclusion can be a few sentences or a few paragraphs.

## REVISING THE PAPER

By the time you complete the first draft of a paper, you may feel that you have lived too long with your subject. That isn't unusual, since you have spent a good deal of effort to get to this point. But remember, a good writer is a good rewriter. The first draft may be quite rough and full of errors. It isn't suitable to be submitted to your instructor. If you have planned your time wisely, you can spare the time to let the paper sit for a day or two so that you can get a fresh look at it.

When you revise the first draft of your paper, you are looking at it in two basic ways. First, you are reading it critically to make sure it is complete and makes sense. Second, you are proofreading it to make sure that your grammar, punctuation, word usage, and spelling are correct. The checklist on page 244 shows what to pay attention to when revising a first draft.

### Checking the Content

Reading your own writing critically can be hard, but it helps to distance yourself by pretending you are a reader who knows nothing about the subject. From this point of view, read through what you have written—but don't fix anything yet. Ask yourself the following questions: Does it make sense? Is the premise clear? Does one paragraph lead logically into the next one, with smooth transitions? Does each paragraph have a topic sentence and supporting details? Has something been omitted? Is there information that does not contribute to the understanding of the topic and that can be deleted? Is there unnecessary repetition? Does the conclusion flow logically from the content of the paper?

As you read, jot down problem areas. By the time you get to the end of the paper, you may have quite a few items that require more work. Once you know what needs revising, you can go back and start to rewrite the portions of the paper that need to be improved.

### Proofreading

After you have revised the content of your paper, it is time to read it again, this time as a proofreader. When you proofread, you are looking at the mechanics of writing: grammar, punctuation, word usage, and spelling. During this step, you should have a dictionary handy to look up the spelling of words. In addition, you should have a manual such as *The Gregg Reference Manual* by William A. Sabin (McGraw-Hill

Book Company, New York, 1985) to look up rules of grammar, usage, and punctuation. A reference manual will also offer guidance on *style*, or consistency in presenting items such as lists, numbers, and abbreviations.

Proofreading is a very demanding task; you need to look at every word you write. If you read your paper slowly out loud, you have a better chance of finding errors than if you read it silently. Check all quotations and numbers against your note cards to make sure they are accurate. If you are unsure of something, look it up in the dictionary or reference manual. Remember, your paper will be judged not only on its content but on the mechanics of writing as well.

## SUMMARY

There are three basic steps in the writing process: preparing a final outline, writing the first draft, and revising the paper.

When you prepare the final outline, you first rewrite the statement of purpose to make it more detailed and focused. Then you should review and revise the preliminary outline, updating it and adding as much detail as possible. Last, you should post the outline numbers to the note cards.

The purpose of writing a first draft is to get ideas and facts on paper without worrying about grammar and spelling. A common method of writing a paper is to write the main discussion of the paper first, going through the note cards in sequence. Then you can go back and write the introduction and conclusion.

The revision process has two steps. First, you must read critically to make sure the paper is complete and accurate and that it makes sense. Then you can rewrite the portions that need improvement. Last, proofread the paper for errors in spelling, grammar, punctuation, style, and usage.

Name                                                    Date

# CHAPTER 16 ACTIVITIES

## CHECK YOUR UNDERSTANDING

**1.** Why is it important to revise the preliminary outline before starting to write?

_____

_____

**2.** When you write the first draft of a paper, what should you concentrate on?

_____

_____

**3.** Why does it make sense to write the introduction and conclusion after the main discussion of the paper?

_____

_____

**4.** List four steps involved in checking the content of the first draft.

_____

_____

_____

**5.** Name four items you check when you proofread.

_____

_____

_____

## APPLY YOUR KNOWLEDGE

**1.** In Chapter 14 you developed a statement of purpose for your paper on consumer behavior. Now, based on the readings you completed and the note cards you prepared from two books and two magazines (in Chapter 15), revise your original statement of purpose.

2. In Chapter 14 you also developed a preliminary outline for your paper on consumer behavior. Because you gained more information on your topic from your library readings, no doubt your outline needs to be revised. Prepare a final outline for your paper using the traditional outline format as illustrated in this chapter.

3. Using your final outline, write the appropriate outline number on each note card.

4. You are now ready to write a first draft of your paper on consumer behavior. With the information you have on your note cards, write a first draft of the introduction, main discussion, and conclusion.

5. Revise the draft of the paper that you just completed. Review the many items that need to be checked when going through the revision process (refer to the checklist below).

6. Proofread your revised draft looking at grammar, punctuation, spelling, and word usage. Make corrections as needed.

### Checklist for Revising the Draft of a Paper

Reviewing the Content

☐ The premise is clear.
☐ The introductory statement is interesting.
☐ Ideas are presented in a logical sequence.
☐ If headings are used, they are logically related to one another, with correct subordination.
☐ Transitions are used between paragraphs.
☐ Each paragraph has a topic sentence.
☐ Each topic sentence has supporting details.
☐ No necessary information has been left out.
☐ No unnecessary information has been included.
☐ There is no unnecessary repetition.
☐ The conclusion flows logically from the body of the paper.
☐ The paper makes sense as a whole.

Proofreading

☐ Words are spelled correctly.
☐ Grammar is correct.
☐ Punctuation is correct.
☐ Word usage is correct.
☐ Lists, numbers, abbreviations, and other items are treated consistently.

## BUILD YOUR PROOFREADING SKILLS

**1.** Each word in Column 1 is spelled incorrectly. Write the correct spelling in Column 2.

| Column 1 | Column 2 |
|----------|----------|
| alot | _____ |
| allready | _____ |
| balott | _____ |
| colegue | _____ |
| colum | _____ |
| defered | _____ |
| accomodate | _____ |
| eligable | _____ |
| acadamic | _____ |
| excede | _____ |
| fullfil | _____ |
| ocassion | _____ |
| bookeeper | _____ |
| Febuary | _____ |
| recieve | _____ |
| comittee | _____ |
| asisstent | _____ |

**2.** Not all the words listed below in Column 1 are spelled correctly. Find the misspelled words, and write their correct spellings in Column 2.

| Column 1 | Column 2 |
|---|---|
| oblige | _____ |
| priviledge | _____ |
| proceedure | _____ |
| preception | _____ |
| referred | _____ |
| exhilirate | _____ |
| deceive | _____ |
| exercize | _____ |
| liaison | _____ |
| seperate | _____ |

## IMPROVE YOUR WRITING SKILLS

**Semicolons:**   When the parts of a compound sentence are not joined by a coordinate conjunction, use a semicolon between them.

The conference will begin at noon on Monday; it will end at noon on Wednesday.

If I remember correctly, construction is scheduled to begin June 5; however, it probably will be delayed until the middle of August.

Also, if at least one of the items in a series is punctuated with commas, use a semicolon to separate the items.

The tour includes stopovers in Madrid, Spain; Paris, France; and Rome, Italy.

### Practice

Insert semicolons and commas wherever they are needed in the following sentences.

1. Two of our secretaries will be retiring in June however we do not plan to replace them until the first of next year.

2. He is the choir director she is the organist.

3. We have meetings scheduled for Green Bay Wisconsin Marquette Michigan and Duluth Minnesota.

4. Paul is the president Mary the treasurer and Jennie the secretary.

5. Please try to obtain a copy of the May 11 1989 June 14 1989 and July 25 1990 issues of that magazine.

6. She became ill late yesterday afternoon consequently we must find someone to take her place on the panel.

7. There are rumors that the company will be sold they can't be confirmed however.

8. Samuel Harris Ph.D. Emily O'Connor M.S. and Roger Daley B.S. will be on this special advisory committee.

9. To want something is one thing to get it is another.

10. It sounded too good to be true and it was.

**Colons and Dashes:**   Use a colon after a statement that introduces a series or a listing of items.

> You will need such supplies as these: letterheads, envelopes, memo forms, and address labels.

> Please be sure to provide the following data:
>
> 1. Social security number
>
> 2. Permanent home address
>
> 3. Home telephone number

Also use a colon after *remember, note,* or a similar word that introduces a statement requiring special emphasis.

> Remember: Reservations for rooms at this reduced rate must be made before June 10.

In personal-business and business correspondence, use a colon after the salutation of a letter.

> Ladies and Gentlemen:      Dear Mr. Walters:      Dear Ms. West:

Always use a dash before a summarizing word following a series of items.

> Towels, sheets, bedspreads—all will be included in this special sale.

> Hammers, saws, chisels—everything you need for your home workshop is available at Hagstrom Hardware.

For greater emphasis, use dashes instead of commas to set off a repeated statement or a contrasting statement.

> You can be proud—very proud indeed—of your achievement. (Instead of "You can be proud, very proud indeed, of your achievement.")

> I'm sure the author meant to say a fetal—not a fatal—position! (Instead of "I'm sure the author meant to say a fetal, not a fatal, position!")

## Practice

Insert colons and dashes wherever they are needed in the following sentences.

1. This stand sells apples, peaches, pears fruits of all kinds.

2. Remember This offer will not be repeated anytime soon!

3. She is fluent in several languages Spanish, French, Italian, and English.

4. They tried really tried to get us to go along with them.

5. Rain, sleet, snow nothing seems to prevent her making it to the office on time.

6. The best bargains are these shoes, handbags, and suede jackets.

7. We should never forget this There is more than one way to do a job.

8. He was sorry truly sorry that he forgot their anniversary.

9. The one thing we don't know is this the cost of a replacement.

10. It is the governor not the mayor who is supporting that group.

# CHAPTER

# 17 FORMATTING THE REPORT

Until this point, it hasn't mattered whether you have been keyboarding or handwriting the first draft and revisions of the report, because only you have been reading it. Now, however, you need to prepare the final copy of the report for submission to your instructor. The final copy should be typed on a typewriter or keyboarded on a personal computer with word processing software.

Reports can be formatted in several ways. Formal reports are generally long; they have front matter and back matter in addition to the body of the report. Informal reports have no front matter and only endnotes and a bibliography in the back matter. Whether your report is formal or informal, you must follow certain basic keyboarding guidelines. In addition, you must decide how to handle references to sources from which you are citing information. Some instructors will give you specific guidelines for formatting your report. If not, you can follow the guidelines in this chapter for preparing the final copy. And remember, the last but very important step in preparing the final report—proofreading.

## FORMAL REPORTS

Formal reports have three basic parts: front matter, body, and back matter. Each of these basic parts may contain one or more types of material in the order presented here.

### Front Matter

The front matter of a report consists of the pages that precede the body of the report. This includes:

- *Title page.* The title page of a formal report includes the title, author (you), instructor's name, course title and number, and date. There are many ways to set up the elements of the title page, one of which is shown on page 251.
- *Table of contents.* If the report is divided into chapters or sections, each having a title, then a table of contents page is prepared. This shows the parts of the report, including the parts of the back matter (see page 252). If the body of the report has not been divided into chapters or sections, then a table of contents is not necessary.

The front matter pages are not numbered with the body of the report. The title page never has a number. The contents page is labeled with a small roman numeral two (*ii*).

### Body

The body of the report is the part you have already drafted and revised. If the report is long, it can be divided into chapters or sections. As you recall, the body (main discussion or part) of the report contains:

THE NEED FOR CHILD CARE FACILITIES
IN THE UNITED STATES
BY THE YEAR 2000  ↓ 6

By ↓ 2

Robert Durfey ↓ 6

Prepared for ↓ 2

Mrs. Charlene Romsky
Sociology 101 ↓ 2

December 19, 199—

Title page of a formal report

↓ 13 CONTENTS ↓ 13

ii

Contents page of a formal report

- *Introduction.* The introductory material may consist of the first few paragraphs, or in a long report, it may be chapter 1.
- *Main discussion.* The main discussion is the bulk of the report. It may be divided into chapters.
- *Conclusion.* The conclusion may be the last few paragraphs or the last chapter if the report is divided into chapters.

Remember, these three elements may run together without being formally labeled.

## Back Matter

The back matter contains at least one element: the bibliography. However, it may have other items in it as well:

- *Appendix.* If you have tables, charts, or other materials that you feel are too specific to be included in the body of the report, you can place them in the appendix.
- *Endnotes.* If you have not used footnotes or parenthetical citations in the body of the report when you cited specific sources of information, then you would prepare a page of endnotes. Endnotes are discussed further on page 257.
- *Bibliography.* The bibliography is a list of all the sources you consulted when you prepared the paper. It is arranged in alphabetic order by each author's last name. How to prepare the bibliography is discussed on page 258.

Note that each item in the back matter occupies one or more separate pages. These are numbered consecutively with arabic numerals following the last page of the body of the report.

## INFORMAL REPORTS

Although you may set up a long or important term paper as a formal report, more often you will be submitting shorter reports that can be formatted informally.

An informal report has no front matter. There is no title page, because the information that would appear on the title page appears

```
                                                    Robert Durfey
                                                    Mrs. Romsky
                                                    Sociology 101
                                                    December 19, 199—


                   THE NEED FOR CHILD CARE FACILITIES
                          IN THE UNITED STATES
                            BY THE YEAR 2000


INTRODUCTION

     The participation of women in the work force has continued to grow. By the year

2000 it is estimated that women will make up over 50 percent of the work force. In

fact, four out of five women between the ages of 25 and 54 will be working. With so

many women working, who will mind the children?
```

First page of an informal report

on the first page of the report instead (see above). A table of contents is not necessary, because an informal report is not divided into chapters.

With the exception of the first page, the body of an informal report looks like the body of a formal report. It may or may not contain headings to divide the material.

An informal report sometimes contains no back matter at all. However, it may contain endnotes and a bibliography (see page 255).

## BASIC KEYBOARDING GUIDELINES

Whether the report is formal or informal, there are some specific guidelines for formatting it. When you keyboard the paper, keyboard the body first and then the back matter. Once you know the page numbers of a formal report, you can prepare the table of contents. Last, keyboard the title page with the date.

↓ 13 BIBLIOGRAPHY ↓ 13

Day, Kathy H., and C. William Day. ''Will Schools Meet the Need?'' <u>American Schools and Universities</u>, Vol. 60, July 1988, p. 57. ↓ 2

DeBlois, Therese. <u>Industry and Family Life</u>. New York: Seminar Press, 1989.

Forbes, Malcolm S., Jr. ''Who Will Care for the Children?'' <u>Forbes</u>, Vol. 142, July 25, 1988, p. 29.

Friedman, M. ''Day Care: the Problem.'' <u>National Review</u>, Vol. 40, July 1988, p. 14.

Garland, Susan B., and Joseph Weber. ''America's Child-Care Crisis: the First Tiny Steps Toward Solutions.'' <u>Business Week</u>, July 10, 1989, p. 64.

Hall, Francine S. <u>The Two-Career Couple</u>. Reading, Mass.: Addison-Wesley Publishing Company, 1979.

Hamilton, Joan O'C. ''California Makes Business a Partner in Day Care.'' <u>Business Week</u>, June 8, 1987, p. 100.

Haskins, Ron, and Hank Brown. ''The Day-Care Reform Juggernaut.'' <u>National Review</u>, Vol. 41, March 10, 1989, p. 20.

Hathaway, N. ''Who Cares in Daycare?'' <u>Bazaar</u>, Vol. 121, July 1988, pp. 108-109.

Hochschild, Arlie Russell. <u>The Second Shift: Working Parents and the Revolution at Home</u>. New York: Viking, 1989.

Jenson, June, Elisabeth Hagen, and Ceallaigh Reddy (eds.). <u>Feminization of the Labor Force: Paradoxes and Promises</u>. New York: Oxford Press, 1988.

McCrorey, Helen, and Dolores McCrorey. <u>The Business of Family Day Care</u>. Santa Monica, Calif.: Roundtable Publishing, 1988.

1

Bibliography

Here are some formatting guidelines. Note that further guidance on formatting can be found in a good reference manual or style book.

■ *Paper.* Use good quality paper—at least 20 pound bond. The proper size is 8½ × 11 inches.

■ *Margins.* Generally, use a 1-inch margin at the top, bottom, and sides of the page. Use a 2-inch margin at the top of the first page of (1) each element of the front and back matter, (2) each chapter, (3) an informal report.

■ *Spacing.* Double-space the report. When you are typing a quotation of 4 or more lines, leave 1 blank line, indent 5 spaces from the left and right margins, and type it single-spaced. Do not use quotation marks. Leave 1 blank line before resuming the double-spaced text.

■ *Order of material.* Assemble the paper in this order: title page, contents, body, appendix, endnotes, bibliography.

■ *Numbering.* Number the front matter at the bottom of the page with lowercase roman numerals, starting with *ii* for the first contents page. Number the body and back matter of the report with arabic numerals in the upper right-hand corner of each page. On the opening page of each body and back matter element, the page number should appear at the bottom of the page.

## BIBLIOGRAPHIC REFERENCES

The purpose of bibliographic references is to give credit where credit is due. Whenever you cite specific information or quote from a source, you must cite it in a note. Whenever you consult a source in the course of doing research for a paper, you must list it in the bibliography. The information you need to format notes and the bibliography is on the bibliography and note cards prepared when doing research.

### Notes

Notes are references that identify the source of specific information or quotations in the body of the paper. They may take one of three forms: footnotes, endnotes, or textnotes.

**Footnotes.** When notes appear at the bottom of the page on which the information is cited, they are called *footnotes*. Footnotes are generally keyed by number to the item cited in the text. After citing an idea or quotation, key a raised number in the text, like this.[1] If your word processing system doesn't have the capability of formatting raised numbers, type the footnote number in parentheses or brackets after the cited information, like this: *(1)* or *[1]*. Then at the bottom of the same page, key the numbered footnote.

A footnote for a book contains the footnote number, author(s), title, place of publication, publisher, year of publication, and page number in the following format:

> 1. Richard Bolling and John Bowles, America's Competitive Edge: How to Get Our Country Moving Again (New York: McGraw-Hill, 1982), p. 63.

A footnote for an article in a magazine or journal contains the author(s), article title, title of magazine or journal, volume number (if given), issue number (if given), date, and page number in the following format:

> 1. Gary Weiss, "A Down-Home Approach to Savvy Investing," Business Week, No. 3093, February 27, 1989, p. 20.

**Endnotes.**  *Endnotes* are citations that are grouped together at the end of a report. Endnotes are easier to prepare than footnotes, and they are becoming more acceptable as a way to document sources. As with footnotes, endnotes are keyed by number to the information cited in the text. However, endnotes don't appear at the bottom of the page on which the information is cited; they appear on a separate page in the back matter.

The format for book and article endnotes is the same as that for footnotes. The endnotes appear in consecutive order on a separate back matter page entitled "Notes." The notes page does not take the place of a bibliography page; you will still have to prepare a bibliography page when using the endnotes system.

**Textnotes.**  A third method of citing information is to use textnotes. A *textnote* is a brief reference in the text to the full citation in the bibliography. The basic format is to give the author's last name and the page number on which the information appears *(Bolling, p. 63)*. If the bibliography contains more than one work by Bolling, you would include either an abbreviated title *(Bolling, Edge, p. 63)* or the year of publication *(Bolling, 1982, p. 63)*. The interested reader can then refer to the full entry for Bolling in the bibliography.

## Bibliography

The bibliography lists all sources you consulted, including those already cited in the notes. The sources are listed alphabetically by the author's last name. A publication with no author is listed alphabetically by title.

There are many formats in use for the bibliography page. If your instructor doesn't tell you how to set up the bibliography, you can consult a reference manual or style book for details. The basic formats for bibliographic references to books and articles are shown here:

Hennig, Margaret, and Anne Jardim. The Managerial Woman. New
York: Pocket Books, 1976.

Hof, Robert D. "Why MIPS Is the One to Beat." Business Week, No.
3093, February 27, 1989, pp. 40–41.

Note that the arrangement of information and the punctuation differ from those of the footnote format.

## PROOFREADING

Before you hand in your report, proofread it. Give it the same careful reading you did in the revision stage. Make sure there are no typographic, spelling, grammar, punctuation, usage, and style errors.

# SUMMARY

Formal reports have front matter, consisting of a title page and contents page; a body, consisting of an introduction, main discussion, and conclusion; and back matter, which may contain an appendix, endnotes, and bibliography. An informal report has no front matter, but it may have endnotes and a bibliography.

When keyboarding, follow standard guidelines for paper quality and size, margins, spacing, order of material, and page numbering.

Notes are references that identify the source of specific information in a report. They may take the form of footnotes, endnotes, or textnotes. A bibliography is an alphabetic list of all sources consulted during the course of research.

Before submitting the final report, carefully proofread it.

Name _____     Date _____

# CHAPTER 17 ACTIVITIES

## CHECK YOUR UNDERSTANDING

**1.** Name the items in the (a) front matter, (b) body, and (c) back matter of a formal report.

_____

_____

_____

**2.** How does an informal report differ from a formal report?

_____

_____

**3.** What is the purpose of a note?

_____

_____

**4.** What is the difference between footnotes and endnotes?

_____

_____

**5.** What does a bibliography contain?

_____

_____

## APPLY YOUR KNOWLEDGE

**1.** You have completed a formal report to submit to your instructor, Mr. R. J. Clark, in Consumer Economics 210. Your report is entitled: "Do Consumers Shop Wisely?" Type a title page for the report.

**2.** Your report on consumer behavior contains several sections that need to be shown in a table of contents. Prepare a contents page with information taken from the headings within the report.

**3.** In Chapter 16 you prepared a draft of your paper on consumer behavior. You now need to put it into final form as an informal report for the course Consumer Economics 210. Type the final draft of the first page of your informal report using the format shown in this chapter.

**4.** Russ used the following sources to prepare his report on consumer behavior.

  **a.** Herrmann, Robert O. Consumer Choices in the American Economy. Cincinnati: South-Western Publishing Company, 1988.

  **b.** O'Shaughnessy, John. Why People Buy. New York: Oxford Press, 1987.

  **c.** Bloom, Paul N., and Ruth Belk Smith (eds.). The Future of Consumerism. Lexington, Mass.: Lexington Books, 1986.

  **d.** Engel, James F., Roger D. Blackwell, and Paul W. Miniard. Consumer Behavior. 5th ed. Chicago: Dryden Press, 1986.

  **e.** Settle, Robert B. Why They Buy: American Consumers Inside and Out. New York: Wiley, 1986.

  **f.** Foxall, G. R. Consumers Choice. New York: St. Martin's Press, 1983.

  **g.** Langer, Judith. Consumers in Transition: In-depth Investigations of Changing Lifestyles. New York: AMA Membership Publications Division, American Management Association, 1982.

  **h.** Ewen, Stuart, and Elizabeth Ewen. Channels of Desire. New York: McGraw-Hill, 1982.

  **i.** Assael, Henry. Consumer Behavior and Marketing Action. Boston: Kent Publishing Company, 1981.

  **j.** Warden, C. "Power to the Consumers." Consumers' Research Magazine, Vol. 72, June 1989, p. 19.

**k.** ———. "Your Shopping Personality." <u>Glamour</u>, Vol. 87, January 1989, p. 30.

**l.** Cooper, J. C., and K. Madigan. "Do Factories and Consumers Have Too Much Vim and Vigor?" <u>Business Week</u>, November 28, 1988, pp. 25–26.

**m.** Stewart, M. Lee. <u>Consumer Economics: The Consumer in Our Society</u>. 10th ed. Columbus: Publishing Horizons, 1990.

In completing his report, Russ cited several sources in the text of the paper. He is using the endnotes method to reference his sources of information. He cited material in his paper by the following authors in the following order (1) Assael, (2) Warden, (3) O'Shaughnessy, (4) Settle, (5) Foxall, (6) Bloom.

**a.** Type a "Notes" page for Russ.
**b.** Type a Bibliography for Russ.

**5.** Type a title page for the report you drafted in Chapter 16 on consumer behavior.

**6.** Type a bibliography page with the sources you used in gathering information for your report on consumer behavior.

## IMPROVE YOUR WRITING SKILLS

**Quotation Marks:** Use quotation marks to enclose a *direct quotation*, that is, a statement written or spoken by someone else. Note that a comma is used to separate the rest of the sentence from the quotation.

Tom said, "A merit increase can't be less than 5 percent."

"The company will employ between 100 and 150 people," according to a spokesperson for the firm.

If a direct quotation is interrupted, use quotation marks around the quoted works only and use commas to set off the interrupting words.

"If there is any change," the manager commented, "each of you will be notified well in advance."

Dave's question, "Who will be in charge of the project?" will not be answered for a few weeks.

(Note that question mark or an exclamation point replaces a comma at the end of the quotation.)

As illustrated below, a question mark or an exclamation point is not placed before a closing quotation mark unless it is part of the quotation itself.

Bill asked, "When may I expect to see a revised version?"

Did Adam say, "The company can be held liable"?

The fire warden shouted, "Everybody out!"

No one here said, "Maybe so"!

Well-known sayings, proverbs, and quotations that are not direct are not enclosed in quotation marks.

As everyone knows, a penny saved is a penny earned.
An apple a day, or so it has been said, keeps the doctor away.
Phyllis wanted to know who would serve as chairperson.

## Practice

Insert quotation marks wherever they are needed in the following sentences.

1. Sharon is the one who asked what the new salary range would be.

2. Your question, the spokesperson replied, can't be answered fully at this time.

3. Remember: A stitch in time saves nine.

4. This statement appears on every page of the catalog: Prices are subject to change without notice.

5. The manager replied, Further staff reductions are not anticipated.

6. We expect to resume negotiations later this month, Ms. Downs said.

7. Mr. Farrell asked, if I remember correctly, Why would you like to work for our company?

8. The question of how much the increase will be can't be answered at this time.

9. Would you like for him to return your call, the receptionist asked.

10. The more favorable exchange rate, according to the article, will result in more foreign tourists this summer.

Name _____     Date _____

# PART 6 PROJECT

Chapters 13 through 17 presented the information you need to write a concise, complete, and orderly paper. This project will allow you to demonstrate your ability to utilize this information to write a good paper.

Your assignment is to write a formal report on a topic of your choice. You need to refer to Chapters 13 through 17 as you develop the paper to review each part of the writing process.

**Directions:** Follow the outline presented here. It will lead you sequentially through the entire formal reporting procedure for your paper. Do not skip a step. Review examples and information in the chapters as you carry out each activity.

## Outline of Project

**I.** IDENTIFY TOPIC OF PAPER
  **A.** Choose a Topic
    **1.** topic should be interesting
    **2.** topic should be at least slightly familiar
    **3.** topic should be manageable
  **B.** Brainstorm
    **1.** jot down or keyboard questions on topic
    **2.** develop a narrowed listing of potential topics
  **C.** Go to Library
    **1.** search for information on potential topics
    **2.** use all library resources in search
    **3.** select a narrowed-down topic as subject of paper
  **D.** Write Statement of Purpose
    **1.** put topic of paper in focus
    **2.** answer question: "What will the paper be about?"
  **E.** Develop Preliminary Outline
    **1.** jot down information from personal knowledge
    **2.** jot down information gleaned from library search
**II.** START SET OF NOTE CARDS
  **A.** Determine Method of Organizing Cards
  **B.** Prepare Bibliography Cards
    **1.** search all sources in library for information
    **2.** write down bibliographic information for each source

          **3.** organize bibliography cards
    **B.** Begin to Take Notes
          **1.** look up material for each bibliography card
          **2.** organize notes

**III.** PREPARE FINAL OUTLINE
    **A.** Write Concise Statement of Purpose
    **B.** Revise Preliminary Outline
          **1.** use statement of purpose as basis for outline
          **2.** prepare outline according to traditional format
          **3.** arrange note cards to agree with outline sequence

**IV.** WRITE FIRST DRAFT
    **A.** Write Main Discussion of Paper
          **1.** use sequenced and numbered note cards
          **2.** mark parts that will require reference notes
    **B.** Write Introduction
          **1.** tell what paper is about
          **2.** capture interest of reader
    **C.** Write Conclusion

**V.** REVISE PAPER
    **A.** Read for Content
    **B.** Proofread for Mechanics of Writing

**VI.** FORMAT REPORT
    **A.** Format Front Matter
          **1.** title page
          **2.** table of contents
    **B.** Format Body
          **1.** introduction
          **2.** main discussion
          **3.** conclusion
    **C.** Format Back Matter
          **1.** appendix
          **2.** endnotes (if used)
          **3.** bibliography
    **D.** Follow Guidelines to Format Paper
          **1.** use quality paper
          **2.** use appropriate margins
          **3.** double-space
          **4.** sequence pages
          **5.** number pages

**VII.** PROOFREAD ENTIRE REPORT

**VIII.** SUBMIT REPORT TO INSTRUCTOR

# MAKING ORAL PRESENTATIONS

Although most of your assignments, tests, and reports will involve reading and writing, on occasion you may be called upon to make an oral presentation in class. Although the prospect of having to make a speech strikes fear into many people's hearts, it need not be such a difficult and stressful event. As with most other challenging tasks, the key is to be properly prepared.

In Part 7 you will learn the skills you need to prepare and deliver an oral presentation. You will learn:

■ **How to plan a presentation.**

■ **How to prepare materials, including notes and visual aids.**

■ **What makes a good speaker.**

■ **How to rehearse your presentation.**

■ **How to control your anxiety.**

# 18 PREPARING ORAL PRESENTATIONS

No doubt you have heard the old saying that the second greatest fear of most people is death; their first fear is having to speak before an audience. If you are nervous at the thought of giving a presentation, you aren't alone. However, you can reduce your anxiety to a more manageable level if you learn how to plan and organize an oral presentation. Preparedness is the key to speaking effectively.

## PLANNING THE PRESENTATION

Any activity you undertake requires a plan of action. Even a simple shopping trip requires decisions about what you need to buy, where you will buy it, and when you will shop. Similarly, an oral presentation requires planning. Very few people can give a good speech off the top of their heads.

When you plan an oral presentation, you must decide what you are going to say, what points should be illustrated with visual aids, and how much time you should allot to the speech.

## Content

An oral presentation needs to be well organized so that information flows smoothly and is easy to understand. Because the audience hears the presentation just once, the ideas communicated should be clear and straightforward. If you are adapting a written report for your presentation, you will have to consider how the change from reading to hearing affects the content of the presentation.

**Simple Organization.** Most presentations are simple in their organization. First, you tell the audience the purpose of your speech; you then give the main ideas; and you finish with a conclusion or summary.

The organization of the content can be explicitly stated in the speech. For example, if you are giving a presentation on the changing role of women in the work force, you might say:

> First, I want to trace the history of women entering the work force. Second, I will present my analysis of why women assumed low-level, low-status jobs in business for many years. And finally, I'll give you my views on the changing role of women in the work force as we approach the twenty-first century.

Remember, your audience will hear the speech only once. Make it easy for them to understand the subject of your speech.

**Adapting a Written Report.** After completing a written report for a class, you may be asked to share the information you gathered by giving an oral presentation. The information you present orally will differ from the information in the written report in several ways. When you plan an oral presentation based on a written report, you should consider these points:

■ *Select the most important ideas.* Your audience can absorb only a few ideas in the time you will have to present your information, so emphasize the most important ones. What do you want your audience to know and remember? Answer this question, and highlight those ideas in your written report.

■ *Repeat the important points.* Though not usually acceptable in a written report, some repetition *is* considered appropriate in a speech. This doesn't mean that you should say the same words over and over. Rather, you should repeat important points by using different words or perhaps by using a visual aid to illustrate and amplify what you're saying.

■ *Address the audience directly.* In your written report, you probably did not use *I* and *you.* Instead, you wrote in an impersonal, objective way. When you give a speech, however, you want to connect personally with each member of the audience. To do this, you should plan to recast your presentation to use words such as *I, me, myself, you, yourself,* and *we.*

■ *Use transitional words.* A listener can't go back through your speech to pick up a lost train of thought. Therefore, you must give the listener as many transitional clues as possible. For example, tell the audience what you will discuss. When you move to the next topic, say so: "Next, I want to . . . ." Tell them when you are listing things: "There are three reasons for . . . ." Then tell them which reason you are stating: "The first reason . . . ." In other words, be explicit about the relationship between ideas in the presentation.

## Visual Aids

Some material is easier to explain visually than orally, and good visual aids are an important part of almost every speech. A visual aid may take the form of a simple list of points, a chart, a graph, a diagram, or a picture.

If you are adapting a report that included visual aids such as charts, graphs, or illustrations, consider using them when giving the presentation. If not, review the content of your presentation and decide what material, if any, could be conveyed better with the help of a visual.

## Time

When you plan a presentation, you must consider the amount of time you have so that you can judge how much information you can communicate. Although this is difficult for the inexperienced speaker to do, you should try. For example, will you allow time for a question-and-answer period? Do you need extra time to explain the visual aids? How much detail will you have time to explain? Perhaps the best way to get a sense of time is to rehearse the presentation (discussed in Chapter 19) and then make it shorter or longer if necessary.

## ORGANIZING YOUR MATERIAL

If you are like most speakers, you want your audience to think you are delivering your speech with little effort and great enjoyment. Although this may seem impossible for the inexperienced speaker, you can give yourself a boost in the right direction by organizing your material so that the speech is as easy to deliver as possible. This is done by means of note cards and carefully prepared visual aids.

### Note Cards

Good speakers use notes. Why? Notes can serve several purposes when you are giving a speech:

- Notes remind you what needs to be said.
- Notes keep your ideas organized and in sequence.
- Notes keep you from going off on an unrelated topic.
- Notes help you stay within the allotted time for the speech.

Properly formatted notes can be used to guide the speaker on content and also to provide cues.

**Format of Notes.** The best way to prepare notes for an oral presentation is to use 4- × 6-inch or 5- × 7-inch index cards. The notes can be written in one of three ways: in sentences, in phrases, or in topics.

If you use sentence form, you write out your entire speech using complete sentences. Using the sentence form for note cards may make the inexperienced speaker more comfortable because the entire speech is written down. However, sentence form has several disadvantages. First, there is a lot of material to write down and a lot of cards, which may be hard to manage. Second, it is difficult to glance at a note card for the next idea, since there are so many words written down. And last, having the entire speech written down makes it easy to give in to the temptation of reading it word for word. This generally results in a flat, too-rapid delivery.

If the notes are written using phrases, the note cards contain the key words to keep the speaker on track. The major advantage of this method is the ease with which you can glance at the card and see the next idea. A disadvantage is that the speaker may think it necessary to memorize the full text of the speech, using the phrases as reminders.

The last format involves writing one or two words, typically nouns, that identify each topic in the presentation. The topic method has the advantage of resulting in few cards, so it is easy to prepare the cards and to use them during the presentation. The major disadvantage of this method is that the speaker must be very familiar with the material or must memorize a great deal in order to deliver the speech.

Of these three methods, the phrase format is probably the best for most people. The note cards are easy to read yet contain enough detail to help the speaker move easily through the presentation.

**Using the Note Cards.** In addition to containing the content of your speech, the note cards can provide additional help. You can number them, highlight them, and add cues to yourself about the presentation.

When you prepare the note cards, you should number them consecutively, just in case they become disorganized when you are making the presentation. You can quickly shuffle the cards into the correct order if they are numbered.

If you have used the phrase format for your notes, you can give yourself additional guidance by highlighting or underlining key words on each card. This gives you the advantages of both the phrase and topic formats when you are delivering the speech.

You may also want to add "cues" to yourself on the note cards. These can be reminders about posture or gesturing, or they can be references to the visual aids you are using.

## Visual Aids

Once you have prepared the note cards, you can decide where the visuals will fit into the presentation. Ask yourself how the information can be presented best. Then decide whether to use transparencies, flip charts, posterboard, slides, or the chalkboard.

Remember that your speech will be given in a classroom. Prepare visual aids that can be handled easily in the classroom and that can be used on the equipment and in the time period you have. Most important, make sure that your visual aids can be seen by all members of your audience.

If you anticipate that you will have to step away from the desk or podium when using the visuals, leaving your note cards behind, you should prepare some notes to yourself on the visuals themselves. You can make small notations on the visual that can be seen by you, but not by your audience. Use the margin of the posterboard or flip-chart paper or the holder that frames the transparency. These notes will keep you moving smoothly through the presentation until you return to the desk or podium and resume using your note cards.

# SUMMARY

Giving a good oral presentation requires planning. The content of the presentation should be simply organized so that the audience will understand it after one hearing. If you are adapting a written report, you should select only the most important ideas, repeat important information, address the audience directly, and use transitional words to guide the audience. When planning a presentation, it is also important to use good visual aids and to consider the amount of time you have been allotted.

Organizing your material will help you deliver the presentation smoothly. Write your notes on index cards, using phrases with key words to keep yourself on track. Note cards should be numbered sequentially and may contain cues about your appearance or the visual aids. Prepare visual aids with both classroom and time limitations in mind. Most important, they should be easily seen by all members of the audience.

Name                                                                                    Date

# CHAPTER 18 ACTIVITIES

## CHECK YOUR UNDERSTANDING

**1.** What basic organization should be used for most oral presentations?

_____

_____

**2.** What four factors should you consider when you convert a written report into an oral presentation?

_____

_____

_____

**3.** What are two reasons for using notes when giving an oral presentation?

_____

_____

**4.** What are the advantages and disadvantages of writing notes in phrase format?

_____

_____

**5.** What should you consider when deciding on the format of your visual aids?

_____

_____

## BUILD YOUR SKILLS

**1.** Tom developed an outline for an oral presentation in his psychology class. He will be speaking on several theories related to behaviorism. Revise his outline to make his speech flow smoothly and logically.

I. Behaviorism in the Twentieth Century
   A. Ivan Pavlov
      1. experiments with dogs
      2. classical conditioning
   B. John Watson
      1. experiment with "little Albert"
      2. classical conditioning
   C. Edward Thorndike
      1. law of effect
      2. operant conditioning
   D. B. F. Skinner
      1. experiment with pigeons
      2. operant conditioning
II. Review of Theories in Behaviorism from the Nineteenth Century
III. Summary
IV. Comparison and Contrast of Classical Conditioning and Operant Conditioning

2. Tish prepared the following outline for a presentation on nonverbal communication for her speech class. She hasn't done a good job organizing the sequence of topics she is going to present. If she uses this outline, her speech will ramble. Organize the sequence of topics in the outline so that she can make an effective, well-organized speech.

I. Nonverbal Communication in the Environment
   A. Public transportation
   B. Public meeting places
II. Definition of Nonverbal Communication
III. Nonverbal Communication Devices Used by People
   A. Hands
      1. accessories
   B. Face
   C. Appearance
      1. clothing
      2. skin
      3. hair
   D. Gestures
      1. posture
   E. Business offices
IV. Summary

3. Read this report on behaviorism, and answer the questions that follow.

Catherine O'Connell
Mrs. Wojta
Psychology 123
April 23, 19—

BEHAVIORISM IN LEARNING

Advocates of the Behaviorism Theory

Behaviorism as a theory developed through work with animals where behavior is observed and conclusions are drawn from what is seen, i.e., a stimulus/response association occurs. The results of many studies with animals were then transferred to understanding how humans learn. Behaviorism was shaped as a theory from work done by Ivan Pavlov and John Watson, who put forth the classical conditioning theory; and Edward Thorndike and B. F. Skinner, who were advocates of operant conditioning.

Pavlov.  In the early twentieth century, Pavlov revolutionized the understanding of animal and human intelligence. He is considered the "father of classical conditioning," in which an organism learns to make a reflex response to some stimulus that was previously neutral. He experimented with dogs to show that the dog's salivary reflexes had been conditioned to respond to a tone. In the experiments, an association was learned between tone and food.

Watson.  One of the most famous examples of classical conditioning is a child known in literature as "little Albert." Watson, the "father of behaviorism," believed that infants were born with three basic emotions: fear, rage, and love. He applied the principles used to measure animal behavior to children. One of his experiments was with "little Albert" who was about two years old. He put little Albert in a room with toys and a white rat. One day while Albert played with the rat, Watson banged two metal bars together. Albert soon became fearful of the rat. Fear became attached to a previously neutral stimulus, the rat.

Thorndike.  Thorndike emphasized three laws of learning in his behavioral theory. They were (1) the law of contiguity, (2) the law of exercise, and (3) the law of effect. The law of effect was an important foundation for the principles of operant conditioning. Thorndike put hungry cats inside locked "puzzle" boxes. The cats could see food that was placed outside the boxes, but they could not get to the food unless they learned how to escape from the boxes. Eventually, the cats learned to pull a rope that would open the box; then they could reach the food. The cats had learned by trial and error to pull the rope. Once they learned that the rope provided the means to get the food, they no longer repeated other methods they had originally tried to get to the food.

Skinner.  Another leader in operant conditioning of behavior was Skinner. He believed that behaviorism was based on operant learning techniques, where the organism must do something for the consequence to occur. Rewards are used to encourage a behavior, and unpleasant events take place to terminate a behavior. In each case, the giving of the reward, the removal of the reward, or the presentation of unpleasant consequences take place immediately after the behavior.

Summary

Behaviorists believe that learning takes place when there is a stimulus/response activity. This type of learning represents a case in which an association is formed between two events. Two types of associative learning are classical conditioning and operant conditioning.

Classical conditioning involves reflex behavior. In classical conditioning, an animal or person learns to make a response to some previously neutral stimulus paired repeatedly with an unconditioned stimulus. The principles of classical conditioning were demonstrated by Pavlov in his experiments with dogs.

In operant conditioning, the organism emits a response known as operant. The organism learns that by responding in a certain way, a particular outcome is likely to occur. When a response is rewarded, it probably will be repeated. When a reward is withheld, the response will not be repeated. The basic principles of operant conditioning were developed by Skinner and Thorndike.

**a.** You will be using the report on behaviorism for your oral presentation in class. Highlight important items in the report that you will want to use in the oral presentation.

**b.** What transitions in the written report would you consider using in your oral presentation? Highlight them.

**c.** Prepare note cards for your presentation, using both the phrase format and the topic method.

**d.** Taking the note cards you prepared with the phrase format, highlight key words and number the note cards.

**e.** What visuals can you use for the oral presentation based on this short report?

**f.** Sketch two visuals you have identified from the written report that you could use in giving your presentation on Behaviorism in Learning.

## IMPROVE YOUR WRITING SKILLS

**More Practice with Quotation Marks:** Although words referred to as words are usually italicized in printed copy, they may be either underscored or enclosed in quotation marks in typewritten copy.

She intended to write diary but wrote dairy. OR: She intended to write "diary" but wrote "dairy."

If a word is accompanied by a definition, underscore (or italicize) the word and enclose the definition in quotation marks.

The word <u>prodigal</u> means "recklessly extravagant."

Similarly, underscore a foreign expression and enclose the translation in quotation marks.

The Latin term <u>e pluribus unum</u> means "one out of many."

When slang, humor, or poor grammar is deliberately used for effect, enclose the expression in quotation marks.

We decided the best thing to do was just to "let it all hang out."

She told their representative that "we don't want no more excuses" for delayed deliveries.

Enclose in quotation marks the titles of chapters or parts of books, lectures, magazine articles, newspaper columns, and short poems; underscore the titles of complete works: books, magazines, newspapers, long poems, and so on.

Is "Heard on the Street" a column in <u>The Wall Street Journal</u>?

Chapter 12 of <u>Modern Business Management</u> is entitled "Managerial Compensation."

Use apostrophes to enclose a quotation within a quotation.

"This package should be marked 'Fragile,' " he said.

She said, "I don't believe Jack said, 'It's none of their business.' "

## Practice

Insert quotation marks and underscores wherever they are needed in the following sentences.

1. She recorded the message verbatim ac litteratim, which means word for word and letter for letter.

2. Everyone considers Vicky to be an eager beaver because of her willingness to work overtime and to do jobs that others don't want to do.

3. The words principal and principle are frequently confused.

4. As an adjective, principal means main.

5. The opening sentence was, Are you a regular reader of Newsweek?

6. This job, she exclaimed, has me ready to climb the walls!

7. The last chapter of Business Communication is entitled Employment Letters.

8. Remember, he said, early to bed and early to rise will make you healthy, wealthy, and wise.

9. Molly said, At least a dozen passengers ran down the platform shouting Wait for me!

10. Did you know that the plural of famulus, which means a private secretary or attendant, is famuli?

# 19 DELIVERING ORAL PRESENTATIONS

**WHAT MAKES A GOOD
SPEAKER?**
Appearance
Posture
Eye Contact
Gestures
Voice

**PRACTICING THE
PRESENTATION**

**CONTROLLING ANXIETY**

**SUMMARY**

Your note cards are in order, and your visuals have been prepared. Do you feel ready to give your oral presentation? Probably not! What is still missing from your preparation is attention to the delivery of the speech. Let's review the characteristics of a good speaker and then consider some techniques you can use to rehearse the presentation and control anxiety.

## WHAT MAKES A GOOD SPEAKER?

You have, no doubt, listened to many oral presentations, both in school and outside. Have you ever wondered why some speakers were so good that they could hold your attention no matter what they were talking about? or why others could not hold the audience's interest even though the subject of the speech was fascinating? If you have thought about this, you realize that interesting content isn't enough to guarantee the success of a presentation. The speaker's appearance, posture, voice, eye contact, and gestures all contribute to the success—or failure—of a presentation.

## Appearance

The first thing an audience notices about a speaker is his or her appearance. Therefore, it is important to look good and dress appropriately. This doesn't mean you should overdress; you don't want to distract people's attention from your speech to your appearance. Rather, you should dress tastefully so that you look and feel good without being flamboyant.

## Posture

As you stand—not sit—in front of your audience, rest your notes and perhaps a microphone on the desk or podium. Don't grab or lean on the desk or podium to give yourself a feeling of security. Rather, place equal weight on both feet and stand authoritatively before your audience.

Try to avoid pacing, shifting your weight from one foot to another, and jingling coins or keys. All these movements are distracting to the audience. Any movement you make should be related to what you are saying.

## Eye Contact

When you talk to your friends, you look at them. When you give a speech, you should think of the people in the audience as your friends and look directly at them. A person in the audience wants the speaker to talk to him or her even though there are many other people in the room.

You can create this one-to-one feeling by making eye contact as you speak. Eye contact creates a bond between the speaker and the listener. Scan the room, looking at people to the left, center, and right for a few seconds each. The audience will feel you care about them as you speak. In addition, you will feel more comfortable; as you look at people in the audience, you will realize that they are actually interested in you and your message.

## Gestures

Watch people conversing. Notice how frequently they gesture with their hands and how the expressions on their faces are animated and constantly changing. Communicating through facial expressions and body movements is perfectly natural. Gestures and expressions are important to a presentation, because they help you communicate and they increase the attention of the audience.

Why, then, do some people freeze when they have to speak in front of an audience? The answer, of course, is that they are nervous and self-conscious. When you are speaking in front of an audience, try to think of it as speaking with one or two friends. Don't try to make "false" or self-conscious gestures. If you can relax enough to feel as though you are communicating with a few receptive individuals, your face will become expressive, and you will gesture with your hands without even thinking about it.

## Voice

Your voice can convey expression, emotion, and meaning as well as words. An effective speaker uses the voice to create an atmosphere, gain and hold attention, and convey meaning. All of the following voice characteristics contribute to the effectiveness of a speaker:

- *Pitch.* The level of a sound on a musical scale is called *pitch*. People with high-pitched, low-pitched, or monotonous voices aren't easy to listen to. Speakers with the most pleasing voices are those who can vary their pitch to help convey meaning. Record yourself reading a passage, and then play it back listening to the pitch of your voice. Do you vary the pitch so that your voice is musical and pleasant to listen to?

- *Volume.* No presentation is effective if it can't be heard. When you speak, adjust the *volume,* or loudness and softness, of your voice so that people in the back of the room can hear you. Volume can be used to emphasize words or ideas. By making your voice louder or softer, you can convey meaning. If you make your voice softer, be careful; even a soft voice has to be heard in the back of the room.

- *Pronunciation.* The term *pronunciation* refers to the sound you make when you say a word. Since many people are listening, you should make sure you are pronouncing the words in your speech correctly. Check any words you are unsure of in the dictionary. If more than one pronunciation is given, the first one listed is generally preferred.

- *Enunciation.* The clarity with which you speak is called *enunciation.* Enunciate all your words clearly and distinctly. Don't drop the ends of words or run them together so that they are indistinguishable. For example, don't say "wadja say" for "what did you say." Good enunciation will help listeners understand your message.

- *Rate.* Speak slowly enough to allow the audience to understand what you are saying. If you speak too rapidly, words will run together and the audience will not be able to keep up with you. You can vary the rate, slowing down to emphasize important words, and speaking faster when saying unimportant words.

- *Pauses.* Don't be afraid of brief silences; they are better than filling in the pauses with "uh," "okay," or "umm." Pauses occur naturally in the course of a speech. The audience uses them to think about what you have just said and to anticipate what you will say. The speaker uses pauses to collect himself or herself and to mentally organize the next section of the presentation.

- *Tone.* Is your voice flat and dull or full of enthusiasm and energy? A good speaker can use the tone of his or her voice to project positive feelings. Your tone of voice can convey the feeling that you are interested in your subject and excited about sharing it. If you demonstrate enthusiasm for your topic, your audience will feel it too.

## PRACTICING THE PRESENTATION

Having note cards and visuals and understanding the characteristics of a good speaker are still not enough preparation for an oral presentation. Just as if you were in a play or film, you must rehearse. Regardless of the number of times you have given a speech, you should practice each new presentation.

There are several methods you can use, either singly or in combination, to practice your oral presentation:

- *Deliver the speech in front of a mirror.* Stand in front of a full-length mirror and give your presentation. Use your note cards and visuals as you would during the actual speech. Pay attention to the sound of your voice and your appearance. Make sure you are gesturing, look animated, and are controlling and varying the pitch, volume, tone, and rate of your voice.

- *Use a tape recorder.* Play the tape back to analyze the effectiveness of your voice. Are you enthusiastic? Do you enunciate clearly? Can you be heard?

■ *Use a video camera.* A videotape of your presentation will give you excellent feedback on both your appearance and your voice. Of course, you will need some help to set this up.

■ *Rehearse in a room set up for an audience.* If you have the space, you may want to arrange a room with chairs—and a friend or two, if possible—to simulate the actual presentation room. Go through the entire presentation including visuals, and ask your friend to critique your performance.

■ *Rehearse in the actual presentation room.* The best rehearsal would take place in the room in which you will give the presentation. You can run through the presentation, using visuals, equipment, and a podium as you would during the actual speech. You can also practice controlling the volume of your voice so that it can be heard in the back of the room.

When you rehearse, you should time yourself. If the presentation is too long or too short, you may have to modify it to accommodate the amount of time you have allotted.

When you practice the speech, try not to memorize it word for word until it becomes a meaningless series of sounds. You will be much better off if you are thoroughly familiar with the topic. If you get stuck, your note cards will prompt you with the next idea.

## CONTROLLING ANXIETY

Speaking in front of an audience creates anxiety even in people who are accustomed to doing it all the time. A good speaker will try to use the feeling of anxiety to convert it to extra energy and produce a better presentation. The first-time speaker, however, may allow anxiety and stress to dominate the speaking situation and may not perform successfully.

The best relief from feelings of anxiety is to feel prepared. This means you look good, have your note cards and visuals, have practiced, and are as ready as you will ever be. You can use the checklist on page 234 to make sure you have prepared thoroughly.

Remind yourself that you are the expert on this topic. You have researched it and studied it, and now you are ready to tell people what you have found out. Also remember that the audience is eager to hear you. If you can communicate a positive point of view about your topic, your audience will be with you.

## Checklist for Preparing for an Oral Presentation

Planning
- ☐ Ideas are well-organized and logically arranged.
- ☐ Written report has been adapted to needs of an oral report.
- ☐ Appropriate ideas have been selected for visual aids.
- ☐ Presentation is timed properly.

Organizing
- ☐ Note cards are prepared.
- ☐ Note cards are numbered in sequence.
- ☐ Note cards contain appropriate cues.
- ☐ Visual aids are prepared.
- ☐ Visual aids have notes, if necessary.

Practicing
- ☐ Appearance is appropriate.
- ☐ Posture is good.
- ☐ Eye contact is being made.
- ☐ Gestures are natural.
- ☐ Pitch varies.
- ☐ Volume is controlled.
- ☐ Pronunciation is correct.
- ☐ Enunciation is clear.
- ☐ Rate is neither too fast nor too slow.
- ☐ Pauses are used well.
- ☐ Tone of voice is enthusiastic.

# SUMMARY

Good speakers have a good appearance and posture, make eye contact with the audience, and gesture with their hands. They control the pitch, volume, rate, and tone of their voices. They pronounce words correctly and enunciate clearly, and they use pauses to collect their thoughts and move on to the next section of the presentation.

To practice a presentation, you can deliver the speech in front of a mirror, use a tape recorder or video camera, or rehearse in a room set up for an audience or in the actual presentation room.

Good speakers turn their natural anxiety into energy to produce a better presentation. You can use the checklist below to ensure that you are well-prepared. Being prepared is the best relief from feelings of stress.

Name                                                                    Date

# CHAPTER 19 ACTIVITIES

## CHECK YOUR UNDERSTANDING

**1.** Why are appearance and posture important to a speaker?

_____

_____

**2.** What is the purpose of making eye contact with an audience?

_____

_____

**3.** List seven qualities of the voice that must be controlled by the speaker.

_____

_____

**4.** What are two techniques for rehearsing an oral presentation?

_____

_____

**5.** What is the best way to control feelings of anxiety before a speech?

_____

_____

## BUILD ORAL PRESENTATION SKILLS

**1.** Do you know how you sound when you speak? Practice reading a passage from a magazine, book, or newspaper. Then tape-record the passage as though you were making a presentation. Play back your tape and listen to your voice.

Complete the following checklist to evaluate how well your voice conveys emotion, expression, and meaning. For each *No* answer, practice improving your speaking voice and work at overcoming the weakness. Select additional passages to record, play back, and evaluate.

| **Voice Checklist** | **Yes** | **No** |
| --- | --- | --- |
| **a.** My voice is pleasant sounding. | —— | —— |
| **b.** My voice shows interest in the subject matter. | —— | —— |
| **c.** My voice projects a positive message. | —— | —— |
| **d.** My voice varies in pitch. | —— | —— |
| **e.** My voice varies in loudness. | —— | —— |
| **f.** My voice is loud enough to be heard by an audience. | —— | —— |
| **g.** My voice is expressive. | —— | —— |
| **h.** I vary the rate of speaking to place emphasis on words. | —— | —— |
| **i.** I avoid fillers such as "uh" and "okay." | —— | —— |
| **j.** I use pauses effectively. | —— | —— |
| **k.** I speak at a rate that allows an audience to understand me. | —— | —— |
| **l.** I enunciate words clearly. | —— | —— |
| **m.** I pronounce all words correctly. | —— | —— |
| **n.** I need to record my voice again for additional practice. | —— | —— |

**2.** Interview a teacher who is a good role model for speaking before a group. Ask that person:

   **a.** How did you develop your speaking skills?

   **b.** Do you prepare notes before you speak to a class or to another audience? If yes, (1) What format do you use for your notes? (2) Do you highlight words on your note cards?

   **c.** Do you rehearse a presentation before giving it to a class or to another audience? If yes, how do you rehearse?

    **d.** Are you nervous before you speak to a group? If yes, how do you control anxiety? If no, how did you develop this positive feeling about appearing before an audience?

    **e.** What helpful hints can you share about speaking before a group?

**3.** Interview one or two people who often make presentations to groups. Using this listing as a guide, gather information on how successful presenters prepare for a speech.

- Are there a few anxious moments before going on stage? If so, how is this dealt with?
- Are visuals used during the presentation?
- What kinds of visuals are the best to use with an audience?
- Are there helpful hints on using visuals?
- Is it important to use eye contact and gestures?
- How are note cards prepared?
- How are notes handled during a presentation?
- What is the appropriate dress for a presentation?
- Is rehearsing important before making a presentation?
- What is the best way to prepare for a speech?
- Are there key items to think about and to do before making the speech?

**4.** Use the information you gathered in the previous activities to have a class discussion. What did your classmates discover in their interviews? What have you learned from the interviews that will help you become an effective speaker?

**5.** Five methods to practice an oral presentation were discussed in this chapter: stand in front of a mirror, use a tape recorder, use a video camera, rehearse in a room set up for an audience, and rehearse in the actual presentation room.

    **a.** List what specific aspects of a presentation can be seen or heard and, thus, evaluated by using each one of these five methods.

    **b.** Have you used any one of these five methods before to practice a presentation? Discuss what you learned from using the method.

**6.** You have to make a presentation in your psychology class based on the information in the short report on behaviorism shown on pages 275–6 and the notecards you prepared on page 276 (see Chapter

18). Your instructor has given you a time limit of three to five minutes for your presentation.

**a.** Rehearse your speech using one of the practice methods you learned in this chapter. Time yourself.

**b.** How did you feel about your presentation after the first rehearsal? Did you sense anxiety? Rate yourself on this scale:

| 1 | 2 | 3 | 4 |
|---|---|---|---|
| Very Satisfied | Satisfied | Not Satisfied | Very Unsatisfied |

**c.** Why did you select the particular rating for yourself? Are there any areas that need to be improved on in the second rehearsal? Did you stay within the three to five minutes? What can you do to improve any aspect of the presentation?

**d.** Now, rehearse your speech again using a different method.

**e.** Rate yourself after the second rehearsal.

| 1 | 2 | 3 | 4 |
|---|---|---|---|
| Very Satisfied | Satisfied | Not Satisfied | Very Unsatisfied |

**f.** Did you improve your performance? Were you on time? Do you feel better prepared to make the presentation? Use the following checklist to analyze your feelings of preparedness.

### Performance Checklist

- ☐ Ideas are logically arranged.
- ☐ Presentation is timed properly.
- ☐ Note cards contain appropriate cues.
- ☐ Posture is good.
- ☐ Gestures are natural.
- ☐ Eye contact is being made.
- ☐ Pitch varies.
- ☐ Volume is controlled.
- ☐ Pronunciation is correct.
- ☐ Enunciation is clear.
- ☐ Pauses are effective.
- ☐ Tone of voice shows interest in the subject.

# IMPROVE YOUR WRITING SKILLS

**Number Style:**   As a general rule, write the numbers 1 through 10 in words and the numbers over 10 in figures.

There are only nine or ten typos to be corrected in this report.

I believe 11 or 12 of our employees will be eligible to retire this year.

A number at the beginning of a sentence is always written in words.

Four applications have been reviewed so far.

Twenty-four students have enrolled in the beginning keyboarding course.

Use words to express a fraction that stands by itself, but use figures to write a mixed number (a whole number plus a fraction) or a decimal amount.

Nearly three-fourths of the voters are in favor of it.

Actual sales are about 2½ times the original estimate.

If I remember correctly, pi equals 3.1416.

An increase of 0.025 is likely. (Note the zero before the decimal point.)

Express related numbers and numbers in a series in the same manner. If one of the numbers must be written in figures, write all the numbers in figures. If one of them must be written in words, write all of them in words.

Twelve of the fifteen machines require minor repairs.

This carton contains 8 cups, 11 saucers, and 12 dinner plates.

A general period of time is usually written in words. However, the time of day is written in figures when accompanied by a.m. or p.m. or in either words or figures when accompanied by o'clock.

She has been with the company nearly twenty years.

Does your flight leave at 7 a.m. or at 7 p.m.?

We have an appointment for 11 o'clock (OR: eleven o'clock).

Use figures for a time period related to discount, payment, or similar terms and for amounts of money and percentages.

We applied for a loan of $250 for 30 days at 14.5 percent interest.

We bought 12 at a unit cost of $1.02, 15 at a unit cost of $0.97, and 8 at a unit cost of $1.18.

The price ranges from 12 cents to 18 cents.

In addresses, write the house number *One* and the numbered street names *One* through *Ten* in words; use figures for all other numbers in addresses.

The company's new address is One Park Place, Rego Park, NY 11374.

They moved from 11 West Tenth Street to 402 East 11 Street.

Frank lived at 4460 Caldwell Court, Tampa, FL 33615 for two years.

Numbers in the millions and billions are usually written partly in figures with the word *millions* or *billions*.

The city has a population of approximately 1.2 million.

The budget for the next fiscal year is $2.5 billion.

When two numbers appear consecutively and one is part of a compound modifier, write the shorter number in words and the other number in figures.

Please put two 25-cent stamps on this envelope.

This set contains 12 five-piece place settings.

In a month-day or a month-day-year date, always spell out the name of the month, write the day in figures without an ordinal ending (*st, nd, rd, d,* or *th*), and write the year as four figures.

July 4 is a national holiday.

She joined the company on September 1, 1988, as an accountant.

When the day stands alone or when the day precedes the month, write the day either in figures with an ordinal ending or in words.

He usually bills us by the 3rd or 4th of each month. (OR: third or fourth)

The wedding will be on the 22nd of June. (OR: twenty-second)

Years indicating class graduation and well-known historical events are often written in abbreviated form, as illustrated here.

The class of '90 donated a set of art encyclopedias to the school.

Occasional reference is still made to the blizzard of '88.

When they have special significance or when stated in years-months-days form, write ages in figures.

At age 62 you can begin to draw social security benefits.

On March 10 she will be 53 years 8 months old.

BUT: Some members of the class are six, but a few are four or five.

Centuries and decades may be written in the following forms:

the 1900s   OR: the nineteen hundreds   OR: the twentieth century

the 1990s   OR: the nineties   OR: the '90s   OR: the nineteen-nineties

When used with abbreviations and symbols, write numbers in figures.

$100    75%    45#    2 ft    30 yd    No. 330    10″

## Practice

For each number that is expressed incorrectly, write the number correctly in the space provided.

**1.** The 3 firms employ a total of 1,620 production workers.    _____

**2.** 48 of the 65 applicants passed the test.    _____

**3.** The complex includes three ten-story apartment buildings.    _____

**4.** Some members of the class of 80 met on April 10th to plan the next class reunion.    _____

5. A few of the 1000 copies were delivered by the printer on the 2nd. _____

6. An increase of 12% puts the new price at $18.48. _____

7. Please order 15 50-pound bags of lawn fertilizer. _____

8. The items are priced at $1.25, $1.10, and 85 cents. _____

9. Nearly ¼ of the employees are enrolled in the plan. _____

10. Flight No. 10 is scheduled to arrive at seven p.m. _____

11. I have been with this company four years 11 months and 15 days. _____

# PART 7 PROJECT

**Directions:** You have been assigned a five-minute oral presentation to give to your class. Your instructor has asked that you include at least one visual aid during your talk to enhance this presentation. You have selected the topic of physical fitness, and you have prepared a first draft of your talk.

Using the draft on pages 294–296, follow the eight steps listed here, which will lead you to the actual presentation of your information to your class.

**1.** Edit the draft so that it is organized, interesting, and informative for an audience. Include these four items in your editing exercise:

    **a.** Determine the major topics of the presentation.

    **b.** Organize the material in a logical order for presentation.

    **c.** Decide what details are necessary to support the major topics.

    **d.** Identify what content would make a good visual to use during the presentation.

**2.** Determine if the draft contains sufficient information. Are there enough details to support the main topics? If you believe additional data should be included in the presentation, go to the library to obtain it. Or perhaps you would want to adapt the notes to your interests and knowledge. If so, include that information as you edit the material.

**3.** Practice and time your presentation. Edit the material further if your talk is longer than the five minutes allotted to you. If you are short of five minutes' time, consider what material could be added. Then rehearse and time your presentation again.

**4.** Prepare note cards for your presentation. Use one of the three methods discussed in Chapter 18.

**5.** Prepare your visual aid. Determine what part of your content would be easier for the audience to understand if they were able to see it in a visual form.

**6.** Review the characteristics of a good speaker as discussed in Chapter 19. This would include your appearance, posture, eye contact, gestures, and voice.

**7.** Practice the presentation as you would give it to the audience using your note cards and your visual aid. Several techniques were discussed in Chapter 19 to help you rehearse; select one or more of these techniques for your practice. Again time your presentation to determine if it is within the five-minute guideline.

**8.** Deliver your presentation as directed by your instructor. You will be able to deliver your talk confidently and with poise because you have conscientiously followed the procedures that are necessary for delivering an oral presentation.

The following material represents the first-draft copy of a potential five-minute presentation on physical fitness.

## PHYSICAL FITNESS

### Introduction

Good health implies a feeling of well-being in mind and body. The way you live, what you eat, what activities you do, as well as your attitude, all influence your overall health. I believe people care about their health and want to have a long, enjoyable life. However, not all people actually make the effort to keep themselves in good mental and physical health. My objective today is to discuss with you the ways you can keep physically fit through using aerobic exercises.

The term *aerobic* means "with oxygen." Thus all aerobic exercises use oxygen. Oxygen is breathed in through the lungs as a person carries out some vigorous exercise over a period of several minutes. A broad range of health benefits, such as weight loss, lower blood-pressure and cholesterol levels, and reduction in stress levels, are said to come about by using an aerobic exercise program.

Exercise can help you cope with stress brought on by the pressures of the fast-paced world we live in. Stress these days is costing business lots of money. Some experts estimate that lower productivity and employee absenteeism are costing the economy as much as $150 billion a year. Many large corporations spend more than $200 million a year on medical benefits for their employees. Americans are filing a record number of stress-related workers' compensation claims. Nowadays, these claims can account for 14 percent or more of the occupational-disease claims, up from less than 5 percent in 1980.

*Can you exercise too much?* Even though exercise throughout your life is good, you can overdo a good thing. Too much exercise can depress the immune system and increase the risk of injury. Orthopedic specialists report that their business is up recently in the treatment of injuries such as pulled muscles, tendinitis, ligament sprains, and stress fractures. Thus the saying, "No pain, no gain" may not be so.

According to experts, people reach a point at which a maximum amount of oxygen is being pushed out to all parts of the body; after that, additional effort does not pay. This maximum level may be reached in only 20 to 45 minutes of aerobic activity carried out three or four times a week.

*How many people exercise?* Some 15 to 25 percent of the adult population exercise regularly. Many are joggers or runners; others get aerobic benefits from walking, swimming, bicycling, calisthenics, cross-country skiing, or participating in exercise programs shown on videotape or television. The U.S. Public Health Service hopes to involve more than 60 percent of adults ages 18 to 65 in aerobic exercises in the next few years.

### Types of Aerobic Exercises

I would like to discuss briefly with you four types of aerobic exercises that you may be familiar with already. These are walking, biking, jogging, and swimming.

*Walking*. Walking is a good starter among the variety of aerobic exercises for the beginner. A version of walking is race walking, a form of high-speed walking that imposes a discipline on body performance. The amount of energy used in race walking is similar to that consumed in running. Hiking is also a version of walking. It must be done briskly to get the aerobic benefits.

*Biking*. Biking is an efficient form of transportation. It demands less energy to move a moderate weight over a given distance than other methods. The beginner should work hard enough to sweat a little, but easily enough to continue a conversation.

*Jogging*. Jogging has become very popular in the last few years, probably because it is convenient and affordable. Anyone who is reasonably fit can enjoy jogging. It is convenient since you can fit it into your schedule without making a reservation at some fitness center. Jogging can be done anytime and anywhere even when you are traveling across the country. Jogging leads to improved functioning of the cardiovascular and respiratory systems. It increases strength in the legs. It is also an excellent calorie-burning activity. Jogging may help you cope better with the stress and frustrations of everyday life.

*Swimming.* Swimming is a good way to get lots of aerobic exercise in a short period of time. As you swim you are moving against the water rather than against gravity; thus the risk of injury to body muscles and joints is low. Not everyone can swim, therefore this is one exercise that is not an option to all people.

### Summary

In summary, health and vitality are goals most people want to achieve, but these are not easily obtained without effort. It is so easy to sit in a chair, ride an elevator, or take a car to travel a few blocks. But if you want to sleep well at night and feel good about yourself during the day, exercise is important to your health.

### References Used

Englebardt, Stanley L. "Are You Over-Exercising?" *Reader's Digest,* March 1989, pp. 135–139.

"Getting Fit, Staying Fit," *The Complete Manual of Fitness and Well-Being,* Reader's Digest Association, Inc., New York, 1988, pp 95–116.

 NOTETAKING
ABBREVIATIONS

## MONTHS OF THE YEAR

| Month | Abbreviation |
|---|---|
| January | Jan |
| February | Feb |
| March | Mar |
| April | Ap or Apr |
| May | May |
| June | J or Jun |
| July | Jl or Jul |
| August | Aug |
| September | Sept |
| October | Oct |
| November | Nov |
| December | Dec |

## DAYS OF THE WEEK

| Day | Abbreviation |
|---|---|
| Monday | Mon |
| Tuesday | Tues |
| Wednesday | Wed |
| Thursday | Thurs |
| Friday | Fri |
| Saturday | Sat |
| Sunday | Sun |

## STATES

| State | Abbreviation | State | Abbreviation |
|---|---|---|---|
| Alabama | AL | Nebraska | NE |
| Alaska | AK | Nevada | NV |
| Arizona | AZ | New Hampshire | NH |
| Arkansas | AR | New Jersey | NJ |
| California | CA | New Mexico | NM |
| Colorado | CO | New York | NY |
| Connecticut | CT | North Carolina | NC |
| Delaware | DE | North Dakota | ND |
| District of Columbia | DC | Ohio | OH |
| Florida | FL | Oklahoma | OK |
| Georgia | GA | Oregon | OR |
| Hawaii | HI | Pennsylvania | PA |
| Idaho | ID | Puerto Rico | PR |
| Illinois | IL | Rhode Island | RI |
| Indiana | IN | South Carolina | SC |
| Iowa | IA | South Dakota | SD |
| Kansas | KS | Tennessee | TN |
| Kentucky | KY | Texas | TX |
| Louisiana | LA | Utah | UT |
| Maine | ME | Vermont | VT |
| Maryland | MD | Virgin Islands | VI |
| Massachusetts | MA | Virginia | VA |
| Michigan | MI | Washington | WA |
| Minnesota | MN | West Virginia | WV |
| Mississippi | MS | Wisconsin | WI |
| Missouri | MO | Wyoming | WY |
| Montana | MT | | |

## GEOGRAPHICAL LOCATIONS

| Place | Abbreviation |
|---|---|
| Boston | BOS |
| Chicago | CHIG |
| Long Island | LI |

| Place | Abbreviation |
|-------|--------------|
| Los Angeles | LA |
| New Orleans | NO |
| New York | NY |
| San Francisco | SF |
| United States | US |
| United States of America | USA |

## PROPER NAMES

| Name | Abbreviation |
|------|--------------|
| Charles | Chas |
| Gilbert | Gib |
| James | Jms |
| Joseph | Jos |
| Robert | Robt |
| Thomas | Thos |
| William | Wm |

## GENERAL ABBREVIATIONS

| Abbreviation | Item |
|--------------|------|
| abbr | abbreviation   abbreviated |
| abs | absent   absolute |
| acad | academic |
| acct | account   accountant |
| actg | acting   accounting |
| adj | adjective   adjourned   adjustment |
| adv | advisory   against   advance   advertise(ment)   adverb |
| advg | advertising |
| aft | afternoon |
| agcy | agency |
| agr | agriculture |
| agt | agent |

| Abbreviation | Item | | | |
|---|---|---|---|---|
| AI | artificial intelligence | | | |
| alt | alternate | alternative | alteration | altitude |
| Am | America | American | | |
| a.m. | morning | | | |
| amt | amount | | | |
| anal | analogy | analysis | analytic | |
| ann | annual | annuity | | |
| anon | anonymous | | | |
| app | approved | applied | appointed | appendix |
| | apprentice | | | |
| approx | approximate(ly) | | | |
| appt | appointment | | | |
| apt | apartment | | | |
| arr | arrange(d) | arrangements | arrival | |
| art | article | artificial | | |
| asap | as soon as possible | | | |
| assoc | associate(s) | association | | |
| asst | assistant | | | |
| astron | astronomer | astronomy | | |
| atm | atmosphere | | | |
| attn | attention | | | |
| atty | attorney | | | |
| av | average | | | |
| AV | audiovisual | | | |
| ave | avenue | | | |
| B & B | bed and breakfast | | | |
| B & E | breaking and entering | | | |
| b & w | black and white | | | |
| bch | bunch | | | |
| bd | board | | | |
| bdl | bundle | | | |
| bf | boldface | | | |
| bk | book | bank | | |
| bkpg | bookkeeping | | | |
| bldg | building | | | |
| blvd | boulevard | | | |
| bsmt | basement | | | |
| bur | bureau | | | |

| Abbreviation | Item | | |
|---|---|---|---|
| bus | business | | |
| bx | box | | |
| C | century | | |
| cap | capacity | capital | capitalize |
| capt | captain | | |
| cf | compare | | |
| chg | change | | |
| chp | chapter | | |
| cit | cited | citation | citizen |
| cl | carload | center line | |
| | claim | class | clause |
| | cloth | clearance | civil law |
| clk | clerk | | |
| clsrm | classroom | | |
| cmd | command | | |
| Cmdr | Commander | | |
| co | company | | |
| C/O | care of | | |
| coed | coeducational | | |
| coef | coefficient | | |
| C of C | Chamber of Commerce | | |
| COLA | Cost of Living Adjustment | | |
| com | committee | common | communication |
| comp | compare | comparative | compiled |
| | composer | compound | composition |
| con | against | continued | |
| conf | conference | | |
| Cong | Congress | | |
| constr | construction | | |
| coop | cooperative | | |
| cpi | characters per inch | | |
| CPL | Corporal | | |
| cmp | cycles per minute | | |
| cu | cubic | | |
| dbl | double | | |
| dec | decrease(d) | declaration | |
| dept | department | | |
| df | definition | | |

| Abbreviation | Item | | | |
|---|---|---|---|---|
| Dr | doctor | | | |
| dvlp | develop | | | |
| e | east | eastern | | |
| ea | each | | | |
| econ | economy | economic(s) | | |
| ed | editor | edited (by) | | |
| educ | education | | | |
| e.g. | for example | | | |
| equip | equipment | | | |
| equiv | equivalent | | | |
| esp | especially | | | |
| est | established | | | |
| et al. | and others | and so on | and the rest | |
| etc. | and so forth | | | |
| ex | examined | example | exchange | executive |
| | express | extra | | |
| exp | expenses | experiences | experiment | |
| F | Fahrenheit | | | |
| | father | | | |
| | female | | | |
| FBI | Federal Bureau of Investigation | | | |
| fdn | foundation | | | |
| fl | fluid | | | |
| freq | frequency | frequent | | |
| ft | foot | feet | | |
| FY | fiscal year | | | |
| fyi | for your information | | | |
| gal | gallon | | | |
| govt | government | | | |
| gr wt | gross weight | | | |
| hd(s) | head(s) | | | |
| hdbk | handbook | | | |
| hdqrs | headquarters | | | |
| hf | half | high frequency | | |
| hgt/ht | height | | | |
| HS | high school | | | |
| HV | high voltage | | | |
| hwy | highway | | | |

| Abbreviation | Item | | | |
|---|---|---|---|---|
| ibid. | in the same place | | | |
| ID | identification | | | |
| i.e. | that is | | | |
| illus | illustrate(d) | illustration | | |
| imp | imperative | impersonal | imperfect | |
| inc | increase | including | inclusive | income |
| | incorporated | | | |
| indef | indefinite | | | |
| indiv | individual | | | |
| info | information | | | |
| int | interest | | | |
| intro | introduction | | | |
| IQ | intelligence quotient | | | |
| jct | junction | | | |
| k | carat | karat | kilogram | |
| lang | language | | | |
| lb | pound(s) | | | |
| lc | lower case | | | |
| lg | large | | | |
| liq | liquid | | | |
| lit | literature | | | |
| M | male | | | |
| mag | magazine | magnitude | | |
| math | mathematics | mathematical | mathematician | |
| max | maximum | | | |
| mdse | merchandise | | | |
| mem | member | | | |
| memo | memorandum | | | |
| mf | manufacture | | | |
| mfd | manufactured | | | |
| mfg | manufacturing | | | |
| mfr | manufacturer | | | |
| mgr | manager | | | |
| mngmnt/mgmt | management | | | |
| mi | mile(s) | | | |
| min | minute(s) | minimum | | |
| mkt | market | | | |
| mo | month(s) | | | |

| Abbreviation | Item | | |
|---|---|---|---|
| mpg | miles per gallon | | |
| mph | miles per hour | | |
| mtg | meeting | | |
| mtn | mountain | | |
| NA | not applicable | | |
| natl | national | | |
| nc | no charge | | |
| no | number | north | northern |
| nsf | not sufficient funds | | |
| o | o'clock | | |
| obj | object | objection | objective |
| obs | obscure | obsolete | observation |
| oc | of course | | |
| OK | all right | correct | |
| opp | opposite | opposed | |
| org | organize(d) | organization | |
| orig | origin(al) | | |
| oz | ounce | | |
| P & L | profit and loss | | |
| pg | page | | |
| phil | philosophy | | |
| phys | physical | physician | physics |
| p.m. | afternoon | noon to midnight | |
| PO | Post Office | | |
| ppd | postpaid | prepaid | |
| pres | president | | |
| prob | problem | probable | probably |
| prod | product(ion) | produce(d) | |
| prof | professor | | |
| prop | property | proper(ly) | proprietor |
| ps | postscript | | |
| psych | psychiatric | psychiatry | psychological |
| | psychology | | |
| ptg | printing | | |
| q | question | | |
| Q & A | question and answer | | |
| qt | quart | | |
| qty | quantity | | |

| Abbreviation | Item |
|---|---|
| R & D | research and development |
| R & R | rest and recuperation    rest and relaxation |
| rcd | received |
| rcpt | receipt |
| rd | road |
| ref | reference    referee |
| Rep | Representative    Republic    Republican |
| req | request    require(d) (s) |
| res | research |
| restr | restaurant |
| rev | revise(d)    revision |
| Rev | Reverend |
| rr | railroad    rural route    Right Reverend |
| RSVP | please reply |
| rte | route |
| Rx | remedy    cure    prescription |
| S & L | savings and loan |
| sci | science    scientific |
| Sgt | sergeant |
| shpt | shipment |
| sm | small |
| so | south(ern) |
| sq | square |
| SS | social security |
| St | saint    street |
| std | standard |
| subj | subject(ive)    subjunctive |
| syn | synonym(ous) |
| tab | table |
| tbsp | tablespoon(s) |
| TD | touchdown |
| tech | technology    technical(ly) |
| temp | temperature    temporary |
| TGIF | Thank God It's Friday |
| tit | title |
| TLC | tender loving care |
| TM | trademark |
| tng | training |

| Abbreviation | Item |
|---|---|
| tp | township |
| tpke | turnpike |
| tsp | teaspoon(s) |
| TV | television |
| twp | township |
| vb | verb |
| vet | veterinarian        veteran |
| voc | vocational |
| vocab | vocabulary |
| vs | versus |
| w | with        west(ern)        watt(s) |
| wk | week |
| w/o | without |
| wpm | words per minute |
| x | by        extra |
| YB | Yearbook |
| yd | yard(s) |
| yr | year(s)        your        younger |
| z | zero        zone |

# B TEXTBOOK CHAPTER SELECTION

The material in this appendix consists of the Contents, Preface, To the Student, and Chapter 16 from Business in Action, 3rd edition, by Lester R. Bittel, Ronald S. Burke, and Charles P. Bilbrey; it is reprinted here with permission of the Glencoe Division of Macmillan/McGraw-Hill Publishing Company.

# Contents

# *Preface*

This third edition of *Business in Action* further refines its uniquely flexible, adaptive approach to the study of business. The textbook has been expanded and enhanced for its use as a fully comprehensive, independent study resource. It now can be supplemented by adopting either a traditional student *Activity and Study Guide* or an experiential business model and student activity guide entitled *SSweetco: Business Model and Activity File*. This has as its core element a simulated model of a realistic company (SSweetco, the Shenandoah Sweets Company). A comprehensive package of instructional resources is also available to help the instructor achieve his or her course objectives.

## THE TEXTBOOK

The uniquely designed textbook is especially easy to read and comprehend. Each chapter systematically enumerates and links its learning objectives and chapter overviews with its major descriptive sections and summary highlights. These are arranged in an easy-to-follow outlining structure to help students in their study. Extensive business examples, case studies, news reports, role models, and end-of-chapter review questions make this textbook, by itself, a complete and well-rounded teaching and learning resource.

## Organization and Contents

The textbook has been carefully reorganized into 7 major units and 24 chapters. Each unit is an independent entity. Therefore an instructor can tailor the sequence of units and contents to match his or her own course of study.

The textbook has been substantially revised and updated. Chapter 4, on small business, has been expanded, providing more in-depth coverage of entrepreneurship and franchising. Unit 3, "Marketing of Products and Services," now includes a separate chapter (Chapter 10) on "Pricing Strategies for Profit." The importance of computers and technology in our rapidly changing information economy is recognized in Chapter 12 titled "Information and Computer Systems." Chapter 15 dealing with human relations now includes an expanded discussion of productivity.

## Textbook Features

Each chapter of the textbook integrates a set of learning devices that promote an understanding of how business operates.

*PICTOGRAPHS.* Pictographs are previews, or advance summaries, of the chapter presented in pictures and words. They are used to simplify and speed up the absorption of complex ideas. Similar illustrations are widely used in news magazines, such as *U.S. News and World Report*, to convey ideas readily and save readers precious time.

*LEAD ARTICLES AND PHOTOGRAPHS.* Each chapter is introduced by an article and related color photograph dealing with an issue, trend, company practice, or development in business. Each article, rewritten from popular business sources, serves as a springboard and dramatic lead-in to the subject matter and issues raised in a chapter.

*KEY TERMS.* Significant terms are highlighted in bold type at their point of definition in the textbook. They are also listed in the Review Questions at the end of each chapter with convenient cross-referencing to the pages on which they are defined.

*TABLES AND FIGURES.* Tables presenting arrays of data, and figures that illustrate concepts and ideas, are widely used throughout the text.

*ACTION BRIEFS.* Short anecdotes are interspersed in the margins of the text, providing a representative sampling of business practices, commendable or otherwise. There are over a hundred Action Briefs throughout the text; most are new to this edition.

*BILLBOARDS.* These features are found in specially chosen chapters of the text. Billboards are divided into two parts: readings that focus on business issues, and Profiles. The readings are based mainly on current events. They focus primarily on thought-provoking, business-related social issues and aim to stimulate students to form their own opinions about those issues. Profiles are vignettes that highlight the role, characteristics, and contributions of men and women who are succeeding in the business world.

**KEY CONCEPTS.** At the end of each chapter, the ideas presented in the pictographs and main headings are summarized. The concepts are keyed by number to the pictographs, objectives, and the major text headings—a system that helps link all major learning elements together.

**REVIEW QUESTIONS.** Each chapter concludes with a list of questions testing students' understanding of text material.

**CASE CRITIQUES.** Each chapter is supplemented with two documented and/or hypothetical case studies illustrating practical applications of key concepts and key terms. These case studies are designed to encourage students to develop critical judgments in assessing business actions.

**TECHNOLOGY IN THE WORKPLACE.** Also, at the end of each unit is another special feature: Technology in the Workplace provides a sampling of how careers and work are changing because of the development of new technologies, such as robotics, electronic mail, compact disks, and, of course, computers.

Lester R. Bittel
Ronald S. Burke
Charles P. Bilbrey

# To The Student
## Guidelines for Study With Business in Action

The following steps constitute an effective way to study the materials in each chapter. The key to effective study is making maximum use of the numbers that identify each pictograph, objective, major text heading, and key concept. If you are not already familiar with these features, you should read the discussion of "Textbook Features" starting on page v of the Preface.

**STEP 1.** Study the pictograph. Spend two or three minutes to be sure you get the whole picture. Then read the learning objectives that precede each chapter.

**STEP 2.** Now skim through the entire chapter reading only the main headings and subheadings. These headings provide an outlining structure for each chapter. They reinforce and extend the ideas presented in the pictograph. (These headings also may be used as your outline structure for notetaking from the text.)

**STEP 3.** Read the Key Concept summaries and glance at the list of key terms at the end of the chapter. Be alert for definitions of these terms as you read the chapter.

These first three steps, which make up a "three-part linked learning system," will help you quickly summarize the basic concepts in a chapter by skimming it in about 10 to 15 minutes. You are now prepared to read the chapter for details that will help you flesh out the Key Concepts.

**STEP 4.** Read the chapter carefully for detail. Devote an hour or more to this. Keep notes of important facts. Write down the definition of any terms that are necessary for understanding the topics under discussion. Key terms are in bold type for ease of identification.

As you read each chapter for detail, be certain to study each table and figure to be sure of its meaning. Also read the Action Briefs in the margins of the text

to get a feel for what *actually occurs* in business as opposed to what *ought* to happen.

**STEP 5.** Answer the Review Questions. It is a good idea to make a note of the pages on which the answer appears.

**STEP 6.** Read each of the Case Critiques. Try to make a connection between what has occurred in the cases and what you have just read in the text. Answer the questions associated with each case.

If your instructor has assigned the *Activity and Study Guide*, move to the corresponding chapter in that supplement and complete the assignments provided there. Be sure to self-check your answers to identify content areas that require further study.

*Only if your instructor has assigned material from the student supplement, SSweetco: Business Model and Activity File for Business in Action, Third Edition, should you continue with Steps 7 and 8 in the study plan as described below.*

**STEP 7.** If your instructor has included the SSweetco supplement in your course materials, move to the corresponding chapter in the activities section of *SSweetco: Business Model and Activity File*. Read the performance objectives that precede the two levels of achievement. Then complete the exercises and activities for the first level of achievement, the "Application Level."

**STEP 8.** Proceed to the next, higher level of achievement, "Analysis and Interpretation," by completing the decision-making and case problem assignments.

Rigorous follow-through on these study procedures will lead to good study habits that can have a positive effect on what you learn in this introductory business course and may, as a result, help to improve your grades.

**CHAPTER
16**

# Human Resources Management

## Learning Objectives

The purpose of this chapter is to show how the varied activities associated with personnel administration are essential to sound human resources management.

As evidence of general comprehension, after studying this chapter you should be able to:

**1.** Explain the objectives of human resources management and the role human resource managers play in it.

**2.** Describe the process of human resources planning and work force estimating.

**3.** Outline the sequence of the employment process and explain the role of recruitment, selection, and orientation.

**4.** Identify the principal methods used in employee training and management development.

**5.** Understand the purpose of personnel records and distinguish among transfers, promotions, and separations; and describe management's approach to accident prevention and health protection.

**6.** Explain how pay rates are determined and differentiate between the basic compensation plans.

**7.** Outline some of the more common employee benefit plans and evaluate their cost to and impact on business in general.

If your class is using SSweetco: Business Model and Activity File, see Chapter 16 in that book after you complete this chapter. There you will find exercises and activities to help you apply your learning to typical business situations.

## 1 HUMAN RESOURCES MANAGEMENT

is concerned with

obtaining

and

maintaining

the most effective work force

## 2 HUMAN RESOURCES PLANNING

makes plans for future employee requirements in terms of

Size      Quality

## 3 THE EMPLOYMENT PROCESS

establishes procedures for

Recruitment    Selection    Orientation

## 4 EMPLOYEE DEVELOPMENT

focuses on

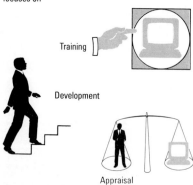

Training

Development

Appraisal

## 5 PERSONNEL ADMINISTRATION

maintains personnel records

Job changes

| S | M | T | W | T | F | S |
|---|---|---|---|---|---|---|
|   | X |   | X | X |   |   |
|   |   | X | X | X | X |   |
|   |   |   |   |   |   |   |
|   |   |   |   |   |   |   |

Attendance

monitors safety and health programs

OSHA OK

## 6 COMPENSATION PROGRAMS

provide financial rewards.

A.B.C. COMPANY PAYROLL

Job evaluation

Job pricing

Compensation systems

Legal compliance (wages, hours, EEO)

## 7 EMPLOYEE BENEFITS

add significantly to compensation.

Group life
   and health insurance
Pensions
   and profit sharing
Nonfinancial
   benefits and services

## *BALANCING PART-TIME AND FULL-TIME EMPLOYMENT*

*At tiny LyphoMed Inc. in Chicago, human resources director Edward Khamis tries to avoid layoffs of the company's permanent employees. To do so, he hires 35 or more temporary workers to handle the surges in the company's production requirements. When business for this pharmaceutical manufacturer slackens off, Khamis can let the part-time workers go with little regret. At large-sized Packard Electric Division of General Motors Corp. in Warren, Ohio, the company promises its 8,900 full-time employees jobs for life. When production schedules go up, GM fills the open positions with part-time employees, up to a limit of 10 percent of the total permanent work force. After that, if production requires it, the company fills the jobs with permanent employees. Why do companies handle employment this way? It's a reflection of their concern for human resources management. Full-time employees represent a long-term, and often expensive, commitment on a company's part. As a consequence, it makes economic sense to hold down the level of permanent employees. In return, most companies will extend great care in recruiting, selecting, and training these employees. A company will also be prepared to pay better wages and provide more side benefits for these employees than for those who are hired mainly to fill temporary gaps during production peaks or vacation periods.*

*While the practice of making a distinction between permanent and part-time or temporary help is not new, the use of this technique in human resources planning and management has been growing. Roughly 20 percent of the United States work force, or 12 million employees, are affected by it. Many workers, of course, seek part-time or temporary employment as a convenience or to accommodate their choice of life-style. Many others are part-time employees not by their own choice. Involuntary part-timers made up 4.1 percent of the workforce in 1976; today their numbers are up to 5.5 percent. It is evident that businesses increasingly make a conscious decision about this phase of human resources management. They are concerned with not only the surface economies involved but also the long-term effect such employment practices have on their total work force, permanent and temporary. Will, for example, full-time employees relax because their jobs are assured? Are part-time employees likely to be less motivated and more careless about their work because*

*the company has made no long-term commitment to them? How should pay scales and benefit programs be proportioned between the two kinds of employees? These and many other questions must be resolved in deciding upon such a personnel policy.*

*The emerging profession of human resources management plays a prominent role in such decisions. Human resources, as indicated in earlier chapters, account for a significant portion of the cost of doing business. This figure is pegged at anywhere from 20 to 80 percent of all expenses, according to the nature of a business's operation. Furthermore, the quality of a firm's human resources, not just its quantity or cost, is a pivotal element in a company's strategy. A first-rate work force can contribute unique competitive advantages. On the other hand, if flawed or poorly managed, a company's work force can become a fatal weakness.*

---

*SOURCE: Deborah C. Wise and Alice Z. Cuneo, "Part-Time Workers: Rising Numbers, Rising Discord,"* Business Week, *April 1985, pp. 62–63.*

---

# 1  HUMAN RESOURCES MANAGEMENT
## *Making the most effective use of people*

As seen in Chapter 6, the way in which a business organizes internally greatly affects the jobs that people are required to do and how well they do them. As the awareness of the value of the human contribution to profits has intensified, so too has the need grown for managing these human resources wisely.

**Human resources management** is the function that is concerned with obtaining and maintaining an employee work force that is most appropriate in size and quality for a business's internal organization structure. Every manager, regardless of his or her particular specialty, is concerned with this responsibility. Nevertheless, this task is so pervasive and vital to an organization that a special type of manager has evolved to coordinate human resources management. This manager may actually be called a **human resources manager** (or a personnel administrator or personnel director).

## RELATIONSHIP TO LINE MANAGEMENT
### *Service, advice, and control*

Robert Townsend, the former president of Avis Rent-A-Car Company, once recommended that executives should "fire the whole personnel department." He was emphasizing the point that the responsibility for people management belongs to every manager, not just to those who specialize in human resources management. This is true, but it fails to recognize that every manager also needs help in this area. There are innumerable details to take care of (like placing advertisements in newspapers for help) and records to keep (about promotions and pay, sicknesses and accidents, for example). There is also the need for expertise in finding new ways to motivate, train, and counsel employees. Human resources managers are the experts in these matters. Accordingly, their role in relation to other managers in a business is threefold:

■ *They provide specialized services to assist other managers as they engage in human resources management.* Personnel managers take care of recruiting and screening new employees and placing them on the payroll. They may provide training and development for these employees. The personnel department will certainly maintain the legal records of attendance, illness, accidents, compensation, and the like. Other managers may intervene in this process, such as making final decisions about whom to hire and whom to promote, but they will expect the specialist to provide assistance and prepare the paperwork.

■ *They offer informed advice in their specialized function.* Because they devote their entire efforts toward a concern for the effectiveness of people, human resources managers are especially helpful in advising other managers about motivational or disciplinary problems. They provide objectivity when personality problems arise. They can do so because they may know what is happening broadly throughout an entire company rather than focusing on the operation of a single department, as so many other managers are required to do.

■ *They exercise control over certain activities in order to ensure consistency in a company's human resources management.* A personnel department must make certain that all managers conform to legal requirements of hiring, promoting, training, compensating, and the like. It must also establish companywide procedures so that there is genuine equity in dealing with employee concerns and compensation matters. Line managers often feel that these controls are restrictive. This leads to the attitude characterized by Robert Townsend when he advises firing the personnel department. Without such controls, however, most companies would not be able to live up to their legal obligations or obtain optimum performance from their human resources.

## FUNCTIONS OF PERSONNEL DEPARTMENTS
*Numerous and varied* ━━━━━━━━━━━━━━━━━━━━━━━━━━━━

Over the years, the functions performed by personnel departments have grown in number and variety, as illustrated in Figure 16-1. Not every personnel department performs them all. Sometimes, the responsibilities are split between departments. In general, however, human resources managers will have responsibility for the following functions:

■ Work force planning, which is concerned with the number of employees and their performance capabilities and potential

■ The employment process, including recruitment, selection, and placement of new employees

■ Training and development of all employees, incumbents as well as new ones, blue-collar and white-collar, nonmanagerial and managerial

■ Appraisal of employee and managerial performance in relation to training and development, pay, promotion, and discipline when necessary

■ Administration and control of personnel movement, including the coordination of and record keeping of job changes, illnesses, accidents, and compliance with job safety and health requirements

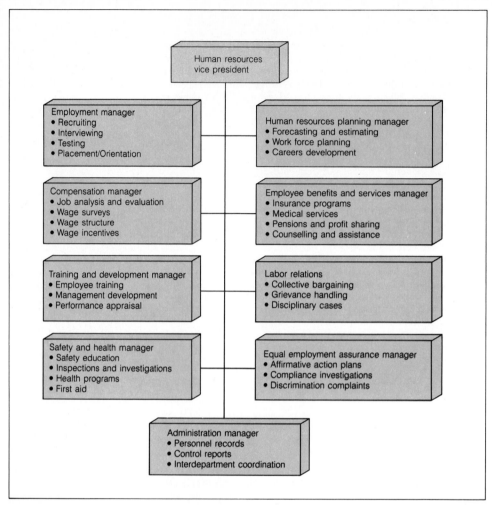

- Design and supervision of the financial reward systems, including compensation and employee benefit programs
- Relationships with labor unions, as discussed in Chapter 17

Figure 16-1 Typical jobs and functions in a human resources department.

## 2 HUMAN RESOURCES PLANNING
### *Establishes size and nature of the work force*

A basic responsibility of human resources management is to estimate a company's personnel needs. The two most important features of this estimate are the number of employees needed and their characteristics or performance requirements. When a company divides its tasks and responsibilities, it establishes the qualifications and skills needed to perform each task. Based upon this division of labor (described in Chapter 6), the human resource manager can make a projection of how many people will be required to perform each of these tasks to meet established production and operation schedules. The combination of the two features provides the basis for hiring, training, and developing of personnel.

## QUALITIES NEEDED IN EMPLOYEES
*Job analysis, job description, and job specification*

The rough division of labor used to design a company's internal organization structure is used as a starting point in determining the personal qualities and skills needed to perform the jobs that must be filled. Each job requires a different combination of physical, mental, creative, social, and personal knowledge and skills. The determination of the specific combination required for each job is accomplished through a systematic study of the job's characteristics and activities. Such a study is called *job analysis.* It is usually performed by a specialist who observes the job as it is being performed and who also interviews the person doing the job and that person's supervisor. The objective of the study is to find out exactly what a person in a given job does and what qualifications are needed to do that job. This information is summarized in a *job description,* which spells out the activities and responsibilities of each job and the skills and other characteristics needed to do the job. A *job specification* is often used when actual hiring is done. It generally lists measurable information—years of schooling, length and type of experience, physical characteristics, and others—that would most likely describe an employee who would be suitable for a given job. Table 16-1 shows a typical job description and job specification combined.

## ESTIMATING THE SIZE OF WORK FORCE
*Planning around uncertainties*

Companywide plans usually include specific targets for the quantity of goods and services to be produced. These can be used to make estimates of future work force needs. In a company that has been in operation for some time, it is possible to estimate fairly accurately how much production can be expected from one person. With this information, the number of staff members needed to meet production goals can be projected.

A number of complicating factors make these projections more difficult in practice. Employee illnesses and absences may vary from time to time. The number of employees who leave work permanently and must be replaced (called *employee turnover*) should be considered. Promotions, dismissals, deaths, or retirements can all create openings and are often difficult to plan for. Sometimes changes in procedures, equipment, or products that are on the drawing board create uncertainty about personnel needs. Normal growth will usually be reflected in production plans, but changing business conditions and unknown market factors can make actual growth considerably different.

*Action Brief*

**EQUAL OPPORTUNITY REPORT**

*Affirmative action programs encouraged by the Equal Employment Opportunity Commission (EEOC) ask that a company put its good intentions into practice. Sears—the nationwide retailer, banker, and insurance company—felt that it was particularly vulnerable. After establishing a good record in employing minorities, however, it wanted to tell its story, not only to the EEOC but also to its stockholders and its public. Accordingly, Sears published figures showing that during the early 1980s, it had reduced its work force by over 80,000 persons, or 20 percent. At the same time, the proportion of minorities in its work force rose from 19.9 to 23.5 percent. During the same period, it reduced the number of its officials and managers by 19,311 persons. In spite of this reduction, the proportion of women and minorities in this category rose to 42 percent.*

**TABLE 16-1**
**SAMPLE JOB DESCRIPTION**

*Position:* Shipping Clerk     *Department:* Shipping and Receiving     *Location:* "C" Building Warehouse

**JOB SUMMARY**

Under general supervision of warehouse manager, processes shipments to customers in accordance with shipment authorization forms forwarded by the sales department. Together with other clerks and packers, removes goods from shelves by hand or by powered equipment and packs them in containers for shipment by truck, rail, air, or parcel post. Prepares and processes appropriate paperwork and maintains related files.

**EDUCATION**

High school graduate.

**EXPERIENCE**

None required.

**DUTIES PERFORMED**

1. The following represent 70 percent of working time:
   a. Removing stock from shelves and racks and packing into proper shipping containers
   b. Weighing and labeling cartons for shipment by carrier designated on the shipping order.
   c. Assisting in loading carriers.
2. The following represent 15 percent of working time:
   a. Preparing and/or processing authorization forms (e.g., packing lists, shipping orders, and bills of lading).
   b. Maintaining shipment records by tally sheets or keypunch.
   c. Doing miscellaneous typing of forms and labels.
   d. Maintaining appropriate files.
3. The following represent the balance of working time:
   a. Driving company truck to post office or for an occasional local delivery.
   b. Assisting in taking inventory.
   c. Acting as checker for other shipping or receiving clerks.
   d. Keeping workplace clean and orderly.

**SUPERVISION RECEIVED**

Except for general instructions and special problems, works mostly on his or her own.

**RELATIONSHIPS**

Works in close contact with packers, material handlers, and other clerks. Has contact with truck drivers when loading. Has occasional contact with order department personnel.

**EQUIPMENT**

Operates mechanized stockpicker, powered conveyor belts, carton sealing machinery, keypunch recorder, and typewriter.

**WORKING CONDITIONS**

Clean, well-lit, and heated. Requires normal standing, walking, climbing, and lifting. Subject to drafts when shipping doors are open.

For an example of how an electronics firm forecasts its human resources needs, see Table 16-2. It begins with (column A) a list of existing position categories and the present number of staff incumbents. It adds to that list (column B) all the new jobs that will be created to fulfill growth plans as well as anticipated cutbacks to provide a picture (column C) of the future staff. An estimate is then made of how many of the present job

**TABLE 16-2**
**HUMAN RESOURCES PLANNING**

| Components Division | A | B | C | Forecast Period Jan.–Dec. | | | G |
|---|---|---|---|---|---|---|---|
| | | | | D | E | F | |
| POSITION CATEGORIES | PRESENT STAFF JAN. | PLANNED CHANGES, GROWTH AND CUTBACKS | FUTURE STAFF DEC. | ATTRITION* | | | NET OPENINGS |
| Managers | | | | | | | |
|   Operations | 30 | +10 | 40 | +3 | +1 | +2 | +16 |
|   Sales | 10 | 0 | 10 | +1 | 0 | +1 | +2 |
|   Other | 20 | +5 | 25 | +1 | +1 | +2 | +9 |
| Engineers | 20 | −5 | 15 | 0 | +3 | +2 | 0 |
| Technicians | 40 | +10 | 50 | 0 | +2 | +2 | +14 |
| Clerical | 80 | −10 | 70 | +5 | +5 | +3 | +3 |
| Hourly, skilled | 300 | +50 | 350 | +20 | +13 | +13 | +96 |
| Hourly, other | 500 | +90 | 590 | +20 | +40 | +25 | +175 |
| Total | 1,000 | +150 | 1,150 | +50 | +65 | +50 | +315 |

*Attrition = **Column D** (promotions and transfers) + **Column E** (unplanned outs) + **Column F** (planned retirements).
**Columns A + B = C** Future staff size in December.
**Columns B + D + E + F = G** Net openings to be filled between January and December.

incumbents will leave for one reason or another, including (column D) promotions and transfers from that location, plus (column E) unplanned quits and discharges, plus (column F) planned retirements. The total number of open positions predicted for the future (column G) will simply be the sum of those needed for growth plus those needed to replace employees who leave.

Work force estimating is made more difficult by the trend toward using part-time employees, as described in the opening section of this chapter. A U.S. Department of Labor study, for instance, showed that temporary workers are engaged in productive work 90 percent of the time, while permanent employees only 65 to 80 percent of the time. Part of this difference is caused by peaks and valleys in the work load of a business. Permanent employees report for work even in slack time; temporary employees are hired only during busy periods of the year. Another related factor involves flexitime schedules (described in Chapter 15) and the desire of many creative and professionally qualified people to vary their hours from a traditional fixed workweek.

## LEGAL INFLUENCES ON WORK FORCE PLANNING

*Equal employment opportunity is a major factor*————————

Numerous laws and federal executive orders may affect a business's work force planning. Most federal laws to eliminate discrimination are administered by the Equal Employment Opportunity Commission (EEOC). In general, the regulations bar employers from failing to hire or promote because of sex, age, race, religious beliefs, or other similar reasons. Job specifications regarding age, sex, and other characteristics, as well as questions asked during recruiting interviews, are restricted to those that can be demonstrated to be undeniably relevant to job performance. This legal requirement is called a **bona fide occupational qualification (BFOQ).**

Differences in salaries paid for equal work are also against the law. The regulations normally apply to companies with 15 or more employees, to most public institutions, such as local governments, to most labor unions, and to organizations with federal grants or contracts. Some organizations may be required to have **affirmative action plans** that not only rule out discrimination but also spell out positive steps to increase the hiring and promotion of minorities and other groups.

In an attempt to offset years of discrimination in employment that affected minorities, especially blacks and women, the EEOC occasionally seeks to have employers agree to **employment quotas.** These are usually based upon population makeup in the surrounding community. If, for example, 25 percent of the community is black, the quota target might be for a company to employ 25 percent blacks. Another aspect of the quota concept is that minorities should also be proportionately distributed throughout the range of jobs within a company. If, for example, 75 of the positions are at the management level and one-third of all employees are women, then the company is asked to try to see that 25 of the management jobs are filled by women. As companies try to conform to this concept, they often are subject to charges of "reverse discrimination." That is, white candidates may feel that they are being excluded in favor of blacks. Or men believe that they are unfairly passed over for promotions in order to place women in jobs where their representation is not proportional.

## 3 MANAGING THE EMPLOYMENT PROCESS
### Creating an effective work force

Businesses need systematic procedures for recruiting, selecting, hiring, and orienting new employees if personnel plans are to be met.

## RECRUITING
### Searching for the best candidates

When jobs are open, most organizations look first to their current employees to find possible candidates. Promoting someone from within to fill a vacancy has important advantages. A present employee will already be familiar with company operations and will usually need less orientation and training. The work habits, interests, and abilities of a current employee will also be well known to management. Promoting from within improves morale: workers will see that it is possible to progress in their work and will often remain more loyal to their employers. Moving a current employee into an opening also saves the time and expense of recruiting from outside the company.

## Action Brief
### RECRUITING BIRDS FROM THE SAME FLOCK

*"Birds of a feather flock together"* is a time-tested and ornithologically accurate adage. Many employers believe that the same principle should be applied when recruiting new employees. "Before placing a want ad or calling an employment agency," says human resources consultant Andrew Sherwood, "encourage your own employees to recruit for you." Employee referrals result in better candidates, he says. Good employees will generally know and refer well-qualified applicants, and employees usually have a better feel for the skills requirements of open positions than employment people. Such word-of-mouth recruiting is a time-tested technique. Its major drawback is that it tends to build a bias in favor of present employees and makes it difficult for true outsiders to enter a company and feel comfortable.

In many cases, however, no current employee is really suitable for a position that is open. Organizations then are compelled to go outside to find candidates with the combination of skills, training, and experience the position requires. A variety of recruitment practices are commonly used:

■ Private or state employment agencies maintain records of many people who are seeking work. These agencies can do preliminary screening and refer candidates to the hiring company. Private agencies charge a fee to be paid by the employer or the employee. State agencies normally do not charge for their services.

■ Recruiting at colleges, universities, vocational schools, or trade schools has been successful for many companies. It is often possible to pick a candidate with exactly the training desired.

■ Most employers at some time must advertise in newspapers or in trade or professional association publications. These advertisements often draw a number of well-qualified candidates.

■ Many labor unions keep registers of members seeking work. In some fields, such as the construction trades, this is a major recruiting method.

■ Present managers or other employees will often be able to suggest friends or acquaintances for unfilled positions.

■ Most companies receive numerous unsolicited applications for employment. Some of these candidates may also be qualified for an opening.

Recruitment to fill managerial and certain professional vacancies may get special treatment. ***Executive recruiters*** (sometimes called "head-hunters") actively search for qualified individuals who are already employed successfully in similar positions elsewhere. This costly practice, however, is used only when the positions are critical to a company's success and the qualified candidates are scarce.

## SELECTION
### *Picking the most suitable people* ━━━━━━━━━━━━━━

*Selection* is the process of picking the one candidate thought to best match the job specification and thought to be the most likely to succeed in the job. A thorough selection procedure will typically include application, testing, interviews, investigation, and physical examination:

■ A written *application* form is an effective selection tool. By asking all candidates to describe their job interests, training, work history, and other experience and to provide business or personal references, employers can eliminate applicants who are clearly unsuited for a particular opening.

■ *Testing* has a clear role in the selection process, but its use must be carefully controlled to avoid unfairness. Some employment tests are clearly relevant to a candidate's ability to perform on the job. Asking an applicant for an office clerk job to type a sample report or an auto mechanic to rebuild a carburetor is an example. Personality, motivation, or intelligence tests may also be useful to companies that have had wide experience with them. They have been particularly effective in selecting salespeople and managers. A frequent problem with these tests, however, is that they generally reflect the values and interests of white middle-class Americans and may unfairly penalize minorities who do not share that cultural background. For this reason, there is active pressure from many sources, including the EEOC, to validate the usefulness of tests before using them for selection purposes.

■ The face-to-face job *interview* remains a central part of the selection process for most employers. Careful interviewers can learn important information about a candidate's attitudes, experience, interests, and aspirations. A disadvantage of interviews is that irrelevant facts, such as a style of dress or personal bias, may interfere with objective evaluation. The potential for bias in a job interview (or in an application blank, for that matter) is so great that the EEOC either prevents or inhibits the asking of certain questions that might bring prejudice to bear on the applicant. Table 16-3 lists some of the questions that generally are avoided in order to ensure equal employment opportunities for all candidates.

---

**TABLE 16-3**
**WHAT ONE COMPANY TELLS ITS INTERVIEWERS**
**NOT TO ASK OF JOB APPLICANTS**

---

■ *Race or color.* Don't ask. Don't comment.

■ *Religion.* Don't ask. Don't say, "This is a (Catholic, Protestant, Jewish, or other) organization."

■ *National origin.* Don't ask. Don't comment.

■ *Sex.* Don't ask. Don't comment. Don't indicate prejudgment about physical capabilities.

■ *Age.* Don't ask age. Don't ask for a birth date. You *may* ask if the applicant is between the ages of 18 and 65.

■ *Marital status.* Don't ask for this, or for ages of children, or if (or where) a spouse works.

■ *Disability.* You may ask if the person has a present disability that will interfere with the job to be performed, but not about past disabilities or illnesses.

■ *Address.* You may ask for this and how long the person has lived there. You may ask if the applicant is an American citizen and, if not, whether the person has the legal right to remain permanently in the United States. It is generally unlawful to press for answers beyond this point.

■ *Criminal record.* You may ask if the person has ever been convicted of a crime and when and where it took place. You may *not* ask if the person has ever been arrested, nor can you deny employment on this basis unless it can be proved that this would damage the employer's business.

■ *Physical capabilities.* Don't ask how tall or strong an applicant is. This may imply a sexist prejudice. You may explain physical aspects of the job—such as lifting, pulling, and so forth—and show how it must be performed. You may also require a physical examination. The intent is that if the applicant has a clear opportunity to estimate the job's physical requirements, the application will be withdrawn if the job appears too demanding or beyond the person's capabilities. Legally, however, you may not make that decision during an interview.

Questions about *education* and *experience* are generally unrestricted. It is vitally important, however, that all questions asked bear an undeniable relevance to the job for which the applicant is a candidate.

■  Most companies carry out at least a brief *investigation* of the information given by the applicant. The investigator may contact past employers, former teachers, or other people who know the candidate. One goal of the investigation is to check the accuracy of the information given on the application and to uncover any facts that might point to future problems with the applicant, such as a poor attendance record or dishonesty. Great care is needed by investigators to treat the applicant fairly.

■  Many companies require a *physical examination* before hiring. One purpose of this is to eliminate candidates who may be disabled in the near future because of an existing health problem.

Selection of candidates for supervisory positions at the entry level of management is sometimes aided by an **assessment center** process. This method exposes a group of candidates to a number of exercises that enable them to demonstrate their skills (or lack of them) in getting along with others, communications, problem solving, and supervision. As the candidates engage in these activities, they are observed by other managers and behavioral scientists who make judgments about how the candidates approach their assignments. Applicants are rated according to ten or more characteristics of good supervision, and the selection is based on this rating.

## PLACEMENT AND ORIENTATION
*A supportive induction to the job*

The final step in the employment process is the assignment of the individual to an appropriate job and making sure that he or she starts off on the right foot. The personnel department must process the paperwork that puts the new employee on the payroll and introduce the newcomer to his or her supervisor and the employment procedures unique to the company. This is the time when rules and regulations must be made clear. The work required by the specific assignment must be detailed as well as the employee's limits of authority. An explanation of the procedures for reporting to work, calling in sick, eating lunch, getting paid, and other related matters helps to make the new employee more comfortable and feel more supported on the first day of the new job.

## 4  TRAINING AND DEVELOPING PERSONNEL
*Improvement of knowledge, skills, and attitudes*

One result of management's intensified interest in improving the effectiveness of employees is the emphasis on training. Many companies and other organizations, large and small, have formal programs to teach new employees specific job skills or to retrain present workers to use new technology. Oftentimes, managers are also aware of the skills needed in their own jobs and have established development programs to produce better managers, now and in the future.

## JOB TRAINING FOR EMPLOYEES
*From simulated to actual experience*

A number of approaches are used to teach specific job skills such as those used by production workers. Many kinds of work, such as machine operation and computer operation, can be effectively taught by the **vestibule method.** This training technique sets up a simulation of the work environment and allows trainees to perform the actual job activities in a classroom. To train a computer operator, for example, the actual console and equipment could be used for training. The student would receive simulated jobs to process and would be taught to use the equipment in the proper way. This method is useful when a large number of employees must be taught specific skills.

Actual **on-the-job training** is by far the most commonly used method for training employees in routine job competencies. This approach, widely used during World War II, was known as job instruction training (JIT). Hundreds of thousands of shop and office supervisors were shown how to use this method. They were given, as a reminder, a little card upon which the following four-step training procedure was listed (although with slightly different wording):

- Step 1: Prepare the worker to learn.
- Step 2: Demonstrate how the job should be done.
- Step 3: Try the worker out by letting him or her do the job.
- Step 4: Put the worker on his or her own gradually, and check back.

On-the-job training today follows much the same procedure. It takes advantage, of course, of modern technology such as audiocassette and videotape demonstrations. It still depends mainly, however, on the close attention of the employee's supervisor rather than on a professional trainer or instructor.

**Apprenticeship training** normally combines on-the-job training with classroom work, which covers the theoretical aspects of the job being taught. It is a very effective training method if adequate time and resources are committed to it. Straight classroom lecture and discussion training is useful when verbal information has considerable use on the job. All of these methods have been used successfully for retraining present employees as well as for training new workers.

**GOVERNMENT ASSISTANCE** Two areas of job training receive considerable attention from the federal and state governments. The first is the problem of providing job skills training for economically and/or culturally disadvantaged minorities. The second problem concerns the retraining of people whose jobs have been removed from their local communities or whose skills have become obsolete in the face of new technology. Many states provide skills training for both groups or make funds available to these individuals while undergoing training from private companies. The federal government makes funds available under the Job Training Partnership Act (JTPA). This program is administered by the Department of Labor and replaces the previous Comprehensive Employment and Training Act (CETA). Cooperating firms work with JTPA through private industry councils (PICs) in various states and local communities.

## SUPERVISOR AND MANAGEMENT DEVELOPMENT
*Insights and maturity are emphasized*_____

Many organizations have formal development programs that help managers perform their duties more effectively. **Management development** programs use a variety of techniques:

*Action Brief*

### McTRAINING TO MAKE McMONEY

The world's largest restaurant chain, McDonald's, also runs the world's largest chain of colleges. It operates 30 Hamburger Colleges around the United States, where thousands of eager candidates learn to become assistant managers at the local outlets. Emphasis is on company-specific training. "Just take care of that one hamburger," advises an instructor, for example, "and the rest will take care of itself." Or, consider pumpkin pie: it is cooked for 7 minutes, while cherry and apple pies require only 6 minutes. And how do you recognize that the fat in the fryer is going bad? It darkens in color, smokes excessively, and has slow, lazy bubbles. McDonald's makes no claim for the intellectual challenge of its Hamburger College courses. It does, however, say that its graduates will all know exactly where their next paychecks are coming from.

■  Formal classroom training is often used, either at workshops or training sessions given by the company or at colleges and universities. These courses usually aim at teaching specific information and management techniques.

■  New methods requiring managers to act out various management roles in a training situation are widely used. This role playing helps managers develop greater sensitivity to human expectations and interactions in organizations.

■  Coaching in actual work situations is still the most common management development technique. Managers with more experience and responsibility usually make a conscious effort to advise, guide, and train younger managers.

■  Many companies give managers special assignments that will broaden their experience and skill. Some companies use job rotation, placing a manager trainee in a number of different jobs in succession to widen his or her experience. This can give the employee a broad perspective on company operations and, at the same time, teach many different management skills.

No matter which techniques are used, the goals of development programs are usually similar. They attempt to give managers the insight and maturity they need. They teach specific techniques of administration and organization. They try to provide thorough technical skills and knowledge in a manager's particular area of concern.

## PERFORMANCE APPRAISALS

*In transition from subjective to objective judgments* ━━━━━━━

An important managerial and supervisory function is judging the quality of the work of others in order to maintain general productivity at as high a level as possible. ***Performance appraisals*** of subordinates are used in decisions about salary increases, training, promotions, assignment changes, and dismissals.

Most performance appraisals are guided by a form that lists several criteria against which the employee's performance will be judged. These criteria lend themselves to either objective or subjective judgments.

Objective judgments are those that can be readily counted or measured, like quantity of work output, work quality in terms of the number of errors made, and attendance in days absent or late. These judgments stress the results of an employee's efforts. When properly established, objective criteria also relate clearly to the company's goals and the extent to which an employee contributes toward their attainment.

Subjective criteria—no matter how important they may be—are difficult to describe and to measure. They suffer from distortions in human perceptions and from prejudice. As a consequence, the trend in business is toward appraisal criteria that are increasingly objective.

There are many variations of appraisal forms. Many of them include some sort of scoring system to simplify the summary of an employee's overall performance rating. Many such scoring systems also employ a *forced choice technique.* That is, the form lists a number of alternative gradings (such as unsatisfactory, acceptable, good, excellent, or superior). The appraiser is forced to choose the term or phrase that best describes the employee's performance in that category. Table 16-4 illustrates a

---

**TABLE 16-4**
**EXAMPLE OF A FORCED CHOICE PERFORMANCE APPRAISAL FORM**

Describe the employee's personal characteristics. Which is most (**M**) and least (**L**) characteristic of the employee?

*Group 1 Statements*

| | | | |
|---|---|---|---|
| a. | Always criticizes, never praises. | M | L |
| b. | Carries out orders by passing the buck. | M | L |
| c. | Knows the job and performs it well. | M | L |
| d. | Plays no favorites. | M | L |

*Group 2 Statements*

| | | | |
|---|---|---|---|
| a. | Commands respect by his or her actions. | M | L |
| b. | Cool-headed. | M | L |
| c. | Indifferent. | M | L |
| d. | Overbearing. | M | L |

---

forced choice technique for rating aspects of an employee's personality. This particular form forces the appraiser to choose not only the most descriptive but also the least descriptive phrase.

Still another appraisal technique is the use of **critical incidents**. This approach was devised to encourage superiors to identify and record incidents in an employee's performance that represent either exceptionally good or poor examples of behavior. It has the advantage of citing specific examples in support of an appraisal judgment rather than a general impression. It has the weakness, so common to most appraisals, of depending mainly upon the memory, impressions, and judgments of the superior.

The performance appraisal, in one form or another, is widely used in business and thought by many authorities to be an effective tool of personnel management. There are many critics of performance appraisals, however, who do not believe that the techniques can be used without bias or in a nonthreatening manner. For this reason, perhaps, the way in which performance appraisals are designed and conducted by a business is subject to challenge by the EEOC.

# 5  ADMINISTRATIVE AND CONTROL PROCEDURES
*From record keeping to accident prevention*

The task of record keeping in personnel departments is enormous. In small companies as well as large, there is a continual movement of employees onto or off of the payroll and within the organization structure. Changes normally result from transfers and promotions within the company or from those who leave for a variety of reasons. Additionally, the human resources function must regularly examine actual practices within the company to make certain that established personnel policies and practices are adhered to. Many of these concerns have to do with attendance and compensation. A particular concern is shown for health and safety.

## RECORDING JOB CHANGES
### Lateral, upward, or outward moves ━━━━━━

The three most common forms of job changes for people already on the payroll involve transfers, promotions, or separations.

A *transfer* is a lateral move from one job to another within the organization without a significant change in salary or in the amount of responsibility or authority. Transfers often result from changing company needs or to take better advantage of an employee's abilities or interests.

A change to a job at a higher level in an organization is a *promotion.* The employee who is promoted is given more responsibility and authority and usually receives a higher salary. Progressive companies try to tie promotions in closely with their performance appraisal system. Provision is often made in the appraisals to evaluate an employee's suitability for promotion. Evaluations based on merit are sometimes combined with, or replaced by, evaluations based on length of service with the firm or in a particular position. This basis for promotion or for salary increases is called **seniority.**

A **separation** occurs when a worker leaves a company. **Layoffs** are temporary separations. These occur when a certain number of employees are told not to report to work because the company wishes to reduce production because of declining demand. When sales increase, workers who have been laid off are given priority for rehiring.

*Terminations* are permanent separations from a firm. Voluntary termination has many causes. Workers may decide to leave a job expecting higher salaries, faster advancement, or greater benefits elsewhere. They may have lost interest in their present job or may have decided to change careers altogether. Each year, thousands of workers resign voluntarily. Involuntary terminations also have various causes. Workers may have to be permanently let go if part of a business fails or if new procedures or products eliminate certain jobs. Poor attendance, dishonesty, or poor work performance may cause workers to be dismissed.

## MONITORING ATTENDANCE AND APPRAISALS
### Indicators of performance and possible discipline ━━━━━

It is traditional that blue-collar employees punch time clocks when they report to work to record their attendance. The attendance of white-collar employees is often simply noted by their supervisors, or is maintained by the employee on a personal attendance sheet. These time cards and personal records become the basis for their pay. In addition, many personnel departments maintain copies of these records as a continuing indicator of an employee's absences and tardiness. When these exceed certain minimums, the personnel department alerts the employee's supervisor. The supervisor then discusses this problem with the employee and often issues a warning of the consequences if unsatisfactory attendance persists.

*Action Brief*

## WHO WORKS OVERTIME?

When employees work overtime, it reduces the total number of people needed to get the work done. Employees who are paid for working overtime sometimes look forward to it. Others, who do not receive additional pay for overtime, don't particularly like it. What kinds of workers put in the most overtime, that is, over 40 hours a week? Salespeople top the list: 46 percent work more than 40 hours. Many of them do not get paid extra. Professionals and managers come next with 41 percent working overtime. They usually don't get paid extra either. Some 33 percent of craft workers and group leaders work overtime, and most of them get paid for this. Only 17 percent of all clerical workers work more than 40 hours a week, but most of them get paid extra when they do.

Many companies also maintain in each employee's personal file a record of the employee's performance appraisal. These appraisal records may be used, if necessary, to support terminations as well as promotions. In the case of termination, the performance appraisal is one of several documents needed to substantiate legally the decision of the company to exercise the disciplinary action.

## ENSURING SAFETY AND HEALTH
*For economic as well as legal reasons*

The provision of safe working conditions and the protection of employees' health are prime concerns of human resources management. These are important legal considerations, but their value goes far beyond compliance with the law. Careful safety and health management also helps to reduce insurance costs, protect against liability losses, and attract better workers. Reducing injuries and damage to health usually requires a formal management effort. Collecting information and devising solutions cost money. The expenditure is justified by a genuine regard for the welfare of workers. Profits can actually increase by avoiding the interruption of work and reducing insurance costs and liability claims.

**ACCIDENT PREVENTION** At the beginning of this century, work accidents took a tremendous toll in American industry. Today, work-related accidents are relatively infrequent. This is a direct consequence of enlightened business action taken to (1) design safer machinery and workplaces and (2) provide safety education programs for managers and employees. Human resources management plays a major role in these actions.

Before accidents can be prevented, their causes and the causes of the resulting injuries must be determined. A careful, long-term record of accidents and their causes is essential to creating a safe working environment. Similar records for other companies and for whole industries can usually be obtained from the government or from industry trade associations. This information, combined with a thorough analysis of operations, will suggest changes for safer workplaces. Many companies institute safety training programs for their employees, redesign machines, place guards over dangerous machine parts, require hard hats in areas where tools or materials may fall from above, start new traffic patterns, or change the whole layout of their operations to make them safer.

**HEALTH PROTECTION** For over a century, businesses took little responsibility for health hazards caused by exposure to dangerous contaminants in the work atmosphere or in the materials of manufacture. Today, the law has clearly shifted this responsibility to the business and its managers. The most notorious recent case involved the Johns Manville Corporation, where for nearly 50 years employees were exposed to the crippling and often killing effects of asbestos. Employee lawsuits against that company eventually forced it to resort to bankruptcy to protect itself. Many industrial environments present less obvious, more subtle hazards to employees' health. Dust, dirt, unsanitary washrooms, biological compounds, chemical fumes—and even noise—endanger health. Management must now apply the same prevention techniques it uses with accidents. It must locate the sources of potential health hazards and find ways to eliminate them or protect employees against them.

*OSHA STANDARDS* Since 1970, employers have been required by law to provide safe and sanitary working conditions. The *Occupational Safety and Health Administration (OSHA)* administers a complex set of safety and health standards. OSHA regulations apply to all workers except government employees and those covered by other safety laws. They are especially aimed at industries with high injury rates, such as roofing, metalworking, construction, mining, and manufacturing of wood products. Portable toilets seen at construction sites and the plastic bag placed in public wastebaskets are examples of OSHA requirements. So, too, are the warnings placed on stepladders, power lawn mowers, and portable gasoline cans.

OSHA requires businesses to avoid many specified work hazards and to take positive steps to create a safe workplace. Failure to comply can result in fines. Many businesses, especially small ones, have objected, stating that compliance is expensive and complex. As experience with the regulations increases, however, companies are finding affordable ways to meet the intent of the law: to protect the health and lives of their workers.

# 6  COMPENSATION PROGRAMS
## *Wages and salaries form the basis of employee motivation*

Although for many people the rewards of working go beyond monetary values, salary and wages are extremely significant to most employees. They are especially important as a means of attracting and holding good workers. Only on this basis can other efforts to stimulate morale and motivate good performance be effective. Great care is therefore necessary in setting up and administering compensation programs. *Compensation* includes everything of monetary value that employees receive in return for work. It includes salary, wages, bonuses, and many other benefits.

## JOB EVALUATION
### *Measures difficulty and importance*

The basis of a rational compensation policy is often a formal *job evaluation.* By using existing job descriptions, personnel specialists are able to analyze every job to determine its responsibilities and its requirements for skills and training. These analyses are then used to rank jobs in order of their difficulty and their contribution to the objectives of the organization. The job levels thus established are then assigned a monetary pay range. Table 16-5 illustrates one approach to evaluating jobs using a scale of points for various job factors.

Like many human resources management techniques, job evaluation has its flaws, both technical and human. Because of the proliferation in some industries of jobs that were in the past evaluated as "men's" or "women's" or "black" or "white," job evaluation plan design and implementation are open to scrutiny by the EEOC.

An issue that continues to crop up regarding job evaluation and, ultimately, job pricing is the concept of *comparable worth.* This con-

**TABLE 16-5**
**POINTS ASSIGNED TO FACTORS IN A JOB EVALUATION PLAN\***

| Factor | First Degree | Second Degree | Third Degree | Fourth Degree | Fifth Degree |
|---|---|---|---|---|---|
| **Skill** | | | | | |
| Education | 14 | 28 | 42 | 56 | 70 |
| Experience | 22 | 44 | 66 | 88 | 110 |
| Initiative and ingenuity | 14 | 28 | 42 | 56 | 70 |
| **Effort** | | | | | |
| Physical demand | 10 | 20 | 30 | 40 | 50 |
| Mental or visual demand | 5 | 10 | 15 | 20 | 25 |
| **Responsibility** | | | | | |
| Equipment or process | 5 | 10 | 15 | 20 | 25 |
| Material or product | 5 | 10 | 15 | 20 | 25 |
| Safety of others | 5 | 10 | 15 | 20 | 25 |
| Work of others | 5 | . . . | 15 | . . . | 25 |
| **Job conditions** | | | | | |
| Working conditions | 10 | 20 | 30 | 40 | 50 |
| Unavoidable hazards | 5 | 10 | 15 | 20 | 25 |

\*Points vary for each factor according to the degree of job demand for that factor. For example, if the physical effort required on a job is low, it may rate only 10 points (first degree), but if it is a very physically demanding job, it may rate 50 points (fifth degree).

cept tries to find a way of equating the worth to a company of, say, a truck driver and a secretary. Or it may try to compare the value of the work performed by a cafeteria employee with the value of the work performed by a garbage handler. Underlying the issue is that many jobs (like the secretary and the cafeteria worker) have been held traditionally by women, while other higher-paying jobs have traditionally been held by men. Advocates of comparable worth believe that this approach would eliminate discrimination in pay. Women, collectively, earn only 60 cents for every dollar earned by men. Those who oppose comparable worth insist that the concept would try to "compare oranges with potatoes" and that it is the marketplace that determines pay rates rather than any intent to discriminate.

## JOB PRICING
*Determines how much a job is worth*

Setting the pay scale for each level and type of job is called *job pricing.* A number of factors combine to influence job pricing decisions. The general prices of goods and services have a double effect. A company that receives high prices for its goods and services is financially able to pay higher wages as long as sales remain good. High prices for consumer goods also cause workers to demand higher pay in order to maintain their standard of living.

Surveys of prevailing pay rates within an industry are almost always a strong influence on the salaries and wages paid by individual companies.

Variable production costs also affect a company's ability to pay wages. General economic conditions have the same kind of effect. Supply and demand in the labor market are important considerations. A skill that is in short supply will usually justify higher pay than one that is common among large numbers of workers. The existence of labor unions in a particular industry or company will influence pay rates. Collective bargaining by labor unions with management sets wage levels through negotiation. The effect of collective bargaining, in a particular company or in an entire industry, is thus a major consideration in setting pay scales.

## METHODS OF COMPENSATION
*From straight salary to incentives*

Compensation for work done by employees can be paid in one or more different ways:

- A straight *salary* pays a set amount at regular intervals. Salaried workers are usually paid weekly, semimonthly, or monthly. Their pay is not based directly on the number of hours worked or on the amount produced. Management, white-collar, and professional employees are usually paid salaries.
- Time *wages* are directly based on the amount of time worked within a pay period. Each wage position has a pay rate that is multiplied by the number of hours worked to calculate the amount to be paid. Time wages are usually paid blue-collar workers for production work and for direct labor jobs as in construction or mining.
- *Piece rates* base pay on the number of units produced by an employee without regard to the number of hours worked. Piece rates are common in certain skilled and semiskilled manufacturing jobs, such as garment making. They are also commonly paid in conjunction with, or as a supplement to, wages. When this method is used, piece rates are called *wage incentives.*
- *Bonuses* are often paid in addition to a regular wage or salary as compensation for outstanding performance or unusually high production. These extra payments are usually thought of as incentives for better performance.
- *Commissions* are paid to certain kinds of workers, especially sales personnel, as a variation on piecework rates. Salespeople often receive a percentage of their gross sales as their pay. Pay is thus based directly on productivity. As an incentive, commissions are sometimes paid in addition to a regular salary.

**TWO-TIER SYSTEMS** Triggered by the recession years of the late 1970s, many firms established *two-tier compensation systems.* These systems generally specify that employees hired after a certain date will be paid less for the same kind of work than those already on the payroll. In 1984, more than 10 percent of all labor union contracts had such a provision. On average, the pay scales for new employees are 15 percent below those for incumbents. Typically, starting wages are considerably lower but catch up with existing pay scales eventually. Proponents claim that the two-tier system is realistic and enables many companies to remain profitable and to create more employment. Critics of the system say that it is, at best, only a stopgap measure and that it alienates workers.

## LEGAL REGULATION OF COMPENSATION
### *Wages and Hours Law sets standards*

As with most other areas of management, legal restraints affect compensation programs. The most important is the requirement that no employee be paid less than a minimum wage established by state or federal law. The Federal Wages and Hours Law (Fair Labor Standards Act) requires most companies to adhere to established policies concerning overtime pay. According to this law, a higher wage rate (1 1/2 times the base hourly wage) must be paid for any hours over 40 worked in 1 week. The Walsh-Healy Public Contracts Act requires companies on government contracts to pay overtime for all work over 8 hours a day.

Additionally, the Equal Employment Opportunity Commission (EEOC) also watches over pay practices to ensure that they do not discriminate on the basis of age, sex, race, religion, or national origin. The Commission's board, when asked to rule on the issue of comparable worth in 1985, refused to accept this concept as a remedy for wage discrimination, however.

## 7 EMPLOYEE BENEFITS
### *Add up to major employment costs*

Hard cash is usually only a portion of the financial reward that employees receive for their work. **Employee benefits** (sometimes called "fringe benefits") make up the balance of this reward. These benefits are things of value given to employees in addition to their pay. Benefits are often not paid in money, but may have some present or future monetary value. Employee benefits are an important form of payment for workers and an important source of expense for employers. Benefits often cost 30 to 40 percent or more of the amount paid for basic compensation.

## LIFE AND HEALTH INSURANCE
### *Group insurance is an American way*

Among the most common benefits are life and health insurance. They are valuable because they protect workers from possible future losses. Employers normally are able to buy group policies and can provide high-quality insurance at a lower cost than is available to individual purchasers. Health insurance has the added benefit of encouraging employees to seek medical care early when they suspect illness. Without insurance, employees might put off checkups or treatment because of lack of money. This widespread practice contributes to better medical care for employees who are covered and may possibly result in a generally healthier population in the United States.

## PENSIONS AND PROFIT SHARING
### *Supplement social security*

A **pension** is a payment made at regular intervals to a retired employee or, in some cases, to his or her family after the worker's death.

*Action Brief*

**AN END TO MANDATORY RETIREMENT?**

In 1979 Congress made it illegal to force most employees to retire before age 70. The fear at that time was that companies would be saddled with unproductive, aging workers. Surprisingly, there have been few complaints in this regard, and relatively few older workers have opted to keep working anyway. Furthermore, 16 states have banned mandatory retirement in private businesses entirely. These laws state that workers over 70 can be terminated "only for just cause," like any other worker.

Payments are made from pension funds built up from regular contributions while the employee is working. Sometimes, the employer makes the entire contribution; sometimes it is shared by the employee.

*Profit sharing* is an increasingly popular benefit which distributes part of a company's profits to employees even when they do not share ownership in the company. Profit sharing is thought of as an incentive. If workers increase productivity, profits will usually rise and more will be available for sharing.

## OTHER BENEFITS
*From holidays to family picnics*

Supplementary unemployment benefits (SUBs) are important, especially in industries where layoffs are common. They pay a compensation in addition to unemployment insurance to help employees maintain their standard of living during a layoff.

A guaranteed annual wage (GAWs) is offered by some companies and is a popular union demand in contract negotiations. This offers almost complete protection for workers from layoffs as it provides a minimum salary or wage to be paid should a layoff occur.

Many other benefits are available in different combinations. These include sick-leave pay, recreation programs, company-paid doctors and nurses, credit unions, holidays, vacations, paid rest periods, severance pay, free meals, educational assistance to workers and their families, workers' compensation and unemployment insurance, parties and picnics, stock and bond purchase plans, discounts on purchases, and others.

Because the number of potential benefits seems inexhaustible, and their cost is so high, some companies offer a *cafeteria benefit plan*. Under such a system, the company establishes a maximum dollar figure for each employee. The employee can then choose from a number of available benefits until their cost matches the maximum.

# *Key Concepts*

**1.** Human resources are the most unique resource of most businesses. Accordingly, management must seek to obtain and maintain a workforce that is most appropriate to the firm's objectives. Human resources management is the concern of all managers, but it receives special attention from human resources managers who provide related services, advice, and controls in this area.

**2.** Human resources planning requires estimates of the number and kinds of employees that will be needed by a company in the future. Based on these estimates, plans are made for hiring and developing workers to meet those projected needs.

**3.** Managing the employment process requires procedures for recruiting and selecting employees and orienting them to their new work. A thorough selection process includes a written application, testing, one or more interviews, investigation, and a physical examination.

**4.** A variety of methods are used to train and develop workers and managers. Job instruction, on-the-job, and apprenticeship training are commonly used for rank-and-file employees. Most management development programs teach specific administration and organization techniques. Performance appraisals serve as guides for training and work improvement.

**5.** Personnel management provides record

keeping services and coordination procedures for:

    **(a)** job changes, including transfers, promotions, and separations,

    **(b)** attendance, and

    **(c)** performance appraisals.

It also monitors safety and health programs in conformance to federal law. This is an important social concern, but it also lowers insurance rates, reduces work interruptions, and helps to avoid liability claims.

**6.** Compensation programs form the basis of employee motivation. Administrators evaluate jobs in order to rank them, assign monetary ranges, and decide on compensation methods for each type and level of job.

**7.** Employee benefits—including life and health insurance, pensions and profit sharing, vacations, educational assistance to workers, and many others—are an important source of reward to employees and a significant expense to business.

# Review Questions

**1.** Define, explain, or identify each of the following key terms and phrases, found on the pages indicated:

*affirmative action plans (p. 363)*
*apprenticeship training (p. 367)*
*assessment center (p. 366)*
*bona fide occupational qualifications (BFOQ)
(p. 363)*
*bonus (p. 374)*
*cafeteria benefits plan (p. 376)*
*commission (p. 374)*
*comparable worth (p. 372)*
*compensation (p. 372)*
*critical incidents (p. 369)*
*employee benefits (p. 375)*
*employee turnover (p. 360)*
*employment quotas (p. 363)*
*executive recruiters (p. 364)*
*human resources management (p. 357)*
*human resources manager (p. 357)*
*job analysis (p. 360)*
*job description (p. 360)*
*job evaluation (p. 372)*
*job pricing (p. 373)*
*job specification (p. 360)*
*layoffs (p. 370)*
*management development (p. 367)*
*Occupational Safety and Health Administration
(OSHA) (p. 372)*
*on-the-job training (p. 367)*
*pension (p. 375)*

*performance appraisals (p. 368)*
*piece rates (p. 374)*
*profit sharing (p. 376)*
*promotion (p. 370)*
*salary (p. 374)*
*seniority (p. 370)*
*separation (p. 370)*
*termination (p. 370)*
*transfer (p. 370)*
*two-tier compensation system (p. 374)*
*vestibule method (p. 367)*
*wages (p. 374)*
*wage incentive (p. 374)*

**2.** Explain the role of human resources managers in relation to other managers.

**3.** Describe the basic steps in estimating future work force needs.

**4.** What are some of the resources for recruiting new employees when openings exist?

**5.** How might employment quotas affect a company's selection decisions?

**6.** Distinguish between objective and subjective criteria for performance appraisal.

**7.** Define the three major kinds of job changes personnel departments must record.

**8.** Differentiate between job evaluation and job pricing.

**9.** In what ways would a two-tier compensation system affect wages paid by a company?

**10.** Name some of the benefits that workers may receive in addition to their wages or salaries.

# INDEX